This engaging book i[s] ... people whose encounters with the living God transformed not only their lives but also their worship. These experiences of meeting God head-on stand at the core of a genuine spiritual revival—an awakening to the presence of God, who directs from the inside out the formation of our character and our mission in the world. Shaped by the deep maturity of an anointed leader who has witnessed God at work in his life and in the lives of many others, this inspiring book is a pastor's well-timed call for the church's spiritual renewal.

ROBERT W. WALL, THD
The Paul T. Walls Professor of Scripture and Wesleyan Studies, Seattle Pacific University and Seminary

Just as Moses refused to leave for the Promised Land without God's presence, I never want to enter the operating room without first welcoming God's presence by praying with my patient, and by filling the room with the sounds of worship music. In the same way that the many facets of a diamond draw attention visually, Pastor Alec's *The Presence* has encouraged me to focus my attention wholeheartedly on seeking more of God's presence in my life.

MICHAEL M. HAGLUND, MD, PHD
Endowed Professor of Neurosurgery, Neurobiology, and Global Health, Duke University Medical Center

I've had the privilege of sitting under the teaching of Pastor Alec Rowlands many times over the years, and his insight always cuts straight to the heart. I had the same experience while reading this book. It's life-changing, empowering wisdom on how to live in the daily pursuit of God's presence. This book is a beautiful and powerful reminder that we serve a God who loves to be close to us. Alec gives practical advice on how to truly experience God and be aware of His life-altering presence on a daily basis.

NATALIE GRANT
Five-time GMA Dove Award–winning singer/songwriter

With a solid biblical foundation, historical wisdom, and contemporary pastoral insight, Dr. Alec Rowlands reflects on his life in light of the broader Christian story—in a way that honors and depends on the sovereign presence of the holy God whose joy is fresh every morning. Here is truth on fire. Here is Christian humility that invites us all to share in the longing of Christ for the deep renewal of His church and sustained outreach to the lost sheep of our day.

DR. STEVEN J. LAND
President and professor of Pentecostal theology, Pentecostal Theological Seminary, a Church of God ministry

The Presence identifies the key to the transformation of individuals, families, churches, and nations—spiritual revival. Pastor Alec combines Scripture with powerful anecdotes from his own pursuit of God's presence, his family and church life, and history's great awakenings that God used to draw nations back to Himself to show how prayer, deep repentance, and obedience characterize every true revival. He shows readers how to pray and see their head knowledge of the Almighty become heart knowledge—in God's presence.

TONY PERKINS
President, Family Research Council

The reality of the presence of God is a theological fact but also a spiritual mystery. Pastor Alec Rowlands deals with the most important issue in every person's life, the reality of both knowing God and experiencing His presence. Weaving the biblical text with historical accounts, personal experiences, scholarship, and a rich personal walk with God, Pastor Rowlands shows how God reveals Himself in the Bible and in personal encounter, and how revivals have erupted from time to time to move people from head knowledge to heart experience. This is a wonderful and much needed book.

GORDON ANDERSON, PHD
President, North Central University, Minneapolis, Minnesota

THE PRESENCE

Experiencing More of God

ALEC ROWLANDS

with Marcus Brotherton

TYNDALE
MOMENTUM

An Imprint of
Tyndale House Publishers, Inc.

Library of Congress Cataloging-in-Publication Data

Rowlands, Alec.
   The presence : experiencing more of God / Alec Rowlands, with Marcus Brotherton.
      pages cm
   Includes bibliographical references.
   ISBN 978-1-4143-8724-6 (sc)
   1. Spirituality—Christianity. I. Title.
   BV4501.3.R687 2014
   248.4—dc23   2014013145

Printed in the United States of America

20	19	18	17	16	15	14
7	6	5	4	3	2	1

To my wife, Rita, a true and faithful partner
in the pursuit of God's presence

CONTENTS

FOREWORD

FROM THE BEGINNING, the Holy Spirit has played a vital part in bringing about God's purposes on earth. We see him first hovering over the waters in Genesis as God prepares to bring beauty out of dark chaos. Later, he comes upon men and women, enabling them to accomplish incredible victories against great odds. The Spirit inspires prophets to deliver God's word with power and conviction; he helps kings rule with justice and compassion; he even anoints craftsmen to work with unusual skill and vigor.

But it's only with the coming to earth of the Savior, Jesus Christ, that we see the enlarged ministry of the Holy Spirit. Coequal with the Father and the Son, he settles upon the Messiah at baptism in the Jordan River and thus initiates three years of powerful public ministry. And after being crucified for the sins of the world, Jesus is raised to life by the power of this same Spirit.

But now comes the best part for believers in Jesus. The risen Christ promises that this same Holy Spirit will be given in a new way to all who put their trust in him. Christians will be indwelt by the same Spirit who raised the Savior from the dead! His activity in and through our lives, then and now, is frequently identified as *the presence of God*. No longer must we live in defeat and despair, for now the Holy Spirit, God's very presence, will be our source of strength. This is one reason why Christ, before he went back to heaven, chose lowly fishermen and tax collectors to represent him on earth. Conscious of their own inadequacy, they would feel the need to depend on his presence to work in and through them as Jesus had promised. And that promise was fulfilled as the Christian church began to deeply impact the world two millennia ago.

Alec Rowlands is a friend, a fellow pastor, and a careful student of both the Scriptures and church history. *The Presence* is especially timely, because without God's presence—welcomed and treasured—Christianity's impact as a force in the world would prove weak. The history of spiritual renewal and revival is nothing more than Christians coveting the presence of God more than anything else, so that they can be a people pleasing to the Lord. *The Presence* will do more than inform you. It will stir within you a burning desire for the one thing that will satisfy—the presence of the Lord.

Jim Cymbala
MARCH 2014

CHAPTER I

UNTAMED LION

Revival is the overwhelming sense of God's presence that falls powerfully on a Christian people who have become dead or lethargic in their spiritual lives, reviving those elements of the Christian life that God intends to be normal for his church.

I RECENTLY RETURNED to my homeland of South Africa, with a camera crew. I wanted to interview people from my father's church who had witnessed a dramatic display of God's presence during a season of spiritual awakening back when I was a boy. After days of recording interviews, the crew asked if they could see some of Africa's wildlife in its natural habitat before we left for home. We drove them several hours out into the bush, west of Johannesburg, to Pilanesberg National Park. The officials at the main gate informed us that visitors had seen no lions or elephants for several days, but that other game would be easy to find. Cameras poised, we proceeded in our rented van on one of the many dirt roads that crisscross the park.

While my brother drove the van, I sat in the back with the camera crew and pulled the sliding door open so we would have an unrestricted view of whatever animals we could find.

We hadn't traveled more than a mile from the gate when my brother spotted a huge male lion off to the left of the van, no more than a hundred feet from the road, lying in the dirt with his face resting on his paws, facing us. The rest of the pride was behind him, camouflaged by the tall, brown savannah grass. They were so well concealed that the cars ahead of us had completely missed them.

The sliding door of the van was already open, and the cameras were rolling as my brother gently applied the brakes. It was a magnificent sight, except for one tiny detail. In the midday heat, none of the lions were moving. They were so still, in fact, that the video was going to look like a snapshot.

We have all seen lazy lions at the zoo, and we had traveled too far to simply replicate that experience. So I decided to shout at them. No response. Then, despite my brother's protests, I quietly slid out of the van, and with my eyes trained on the lion, picked up a stone from the side of the road. (I don't recommend that anyone try this.) I threw the stone in the direction of the lion, but on my windup, my throwing hand hit the roof of the van behind me and the stone didn't make it more than fifteen feet in front of me. The lion was watching me but seemed fairly disinterested in my antics.

By now, my brother was reciting how quickly a lion could cover the distance between us. But I was determined. Still watching the pride very carefully, I bent down for a second stone. Stepping far enough away from the van so my hand wouldn't hit it again, I was able to bounce the stone a few feet from the nose of the male lion. He jumped straight up and roared. Perfect footage for the camera!

Not knowing if he was going to charge me, I stumbled backward onto the floor of the van and tried, in the same motion, to close the door. To my horror, the door had latched in the open position.

This all happened in a matter of seconds, but it felt like it took an eternity to close the door. As it turned out, the lion didn't charge, but to this day I still think about how quickly he could have covered the distance between us and had me for lunch before I ever got the door shut. *What was I thinking!*

Most of us have seen the ferocity of a lion catching and devouring its prey in a *National Geographic* special, but all from the safety of the family room couch. I can testify that it is an entirely different matter to be eye-to-eye with the real thing only a hundred feet away. Your heart beats a little faster. Your palms get sweaty. Your brain races to calculate escape routes. Every nerve and muscle in your body is alert and ready to respond. It is not for the faint of heart. No wonder C. S. Lewis uses Aslan the lion to represent God in his famous Chronicles of Narnia.

"Is he—quite safe?" asks Susan. "I shall feel rather nervous about meeting a lion."

"Who said anything about safe?" replies Mr. Beaver. "'Course he isn't safe. But he's good."[1]

Lewis was right. There's nothing safe about pursuing and being near to God, if by *safe* you mean being left as you are, to follow your own agenda and depend solely on your own wisdom and resources for living. Those are the things that Aslan will devour.

The Christian life is not a game or a quiet pastime.

But if you are willing to have your life turned upside down, your values reshaped and your energies redirected by God, who is always loving and good; if you are willing to be used by him for the extension of his Kingdom here on earth, then drawing near to him is the only way to live life fully. The only things at risk are things not worth living for. And living in the daily pursuit of God's presence is the best way I know to get to the quality of life and unmatched sense of adventure with God that we desire. It is the Christian life lived the way God intended.

The amazing good news is that we serve a God who loves to be close to us and to make himself known. Given what we know about our lives and our brokenness, that's often hard for us to really believe. But that is God's loving nature and his design for us. He has been drawing near to reveal his love to broken, imperfect people from the times when he walked with Adam and Eve in the cool of the Garden to my quiet time with him just a few days ago in my study, when his presence flooded my heart through a single verse of Scripture and brought me to worship with tears of joy.

The reason Jesus came was to open the door to this kind of intimacy with God for all humanity. It is part of the inheritance of our salvation. And after Jesus ascended to the Father, he sent us the Holy Spirit expressly to facilitate our intimacy with God—in revelation, in worship, in prayer. God invites us to seek his presence.[2] He welcomes our pursuit of him. He rewards it. And his presence will be revealed to us in limitless ways as he makes himself known. But there is risk involved. Proximity to God involves not just having a good feeling. We have to be willing to be wholly consumed by his love and to have our lives rearranged by his grace.

So let me ask you: How satisfied are you with your Christian life, with the way you experience God? Be honest. How often do you enjoy his presence? Do you live too much of your life feeling empty, weary, abandoned? Do you wonder about a God who promises to love and provide for you, but who too often seems distant and silent? Maybe, like many Christians, you live somewhere between those two extremes, occasionally sensing God's presence, but at other times feeling as if he's a million miles away.

What about the church you attend? How frequently do you sense *awe* and *wonder* in Sunday worship when you gather together? Is the presence of God producing a humble and ready willingness within the congregation to repent of sin and receive the grace to change? Are lives being transformed? Are people there to serve rather than be served? Are they passionate to bring the gospel to those who don't yet know Christ? Or does church seem rather rote and predictable—even dull? Are people just going through the motions, singing the same songs and participating in the same programs year after year? Do they attend only when it's convenient—and even then, with an eye on the clock to see how quickly they can get out the door and on to lunch or to watch the football game on TV?

Too many of us have settled for far less of God than he wants to reveal. Yes, we've been saved. Yes, we've been forgiven and justified. But there is so much *more* to living the Christian life. God wants to be intimately *known* and *experienced* in the life of every believer. God is alive and on the move. He is, very literally, "God with us."³ He's not distant, unapproachable, or uninvolved in our lives. He's here. He's now. He's around us and in us and through us, ready to communicate, guide, empower, challenge, bless, and fill us with the full measure of his joy and wisdom and strength.

He wants us to experience him, to be aware of his presence.

Before the first word of Scripture was ever written, Abraham, Jacob, and Moses experienced God's presence—in person—and those encounters changed absolutely everything about their lives. It was dangerous and wonderful at the same time. The question is, have *we* resigned ourselves to living our lives of faith vicariously through the experiences of these biblical heroes, or can we in any way expect to experience God's presence for ourselves as they did?

Salvation is by faith in Jesus Christ alone. We understand that. But if we're honest, there are times when, like Moses, we long to experience something more of God, to *see* the glory of God. God never rebuked Moses for his request. On the contrary, he rewarded Moses with a glimpse of his glory.⁴ Remember, God loves to make himself known. I don't believe this kind of "seeing" is a substitute for faith, nor are our encounters with God ever to be elevated above Scripture. But I believe we were created to *experience* God's presence, and that he "rewards those who earnestly seek him."⁵

I am convinced that God has not changed since his intimate encounters with Abraham, Jacob, and Moses. In the beginning, he created us with the capacity to experience him intimately. It's a capacity that Adam and Eve forfeited in their foolish desire for independence, but it is restored in you and me when we are reborn in Christ. Our highest purpose is to *know*, *experience*, *enjoy*, and *glorify* God.

It is time to recapture our spiritual birthright and God's design and purpose for the Christian life!

That's why this subject is so vital for us today. There is a growing hunger for God, as well as increasing dissatisfaction with the Christian life as it is typically defined, especially in the Western church. Church attendance is in decline. Young adults are abandoning the faith in unprecedented numbers. Far too many Christians have come to view church as lifeless and irrelevant, and as a result, are not connected to any community of faith. An alarming number of Christians are experimenting with nontraditional spirituality to fill the void. Many are being misled by a manufactured spiritual vitality promised by alternative church ministry models, alternative worship styles, and in some tragic cases, spurious theological innovations presented as the solution to their deep dissatisfaction. Electronic media today provide instant access to these spiritual alternatives for a global audience, negatively affecting the body of Christ in many nations of the world.

Many "solutions" to spiritual discontentment today are being presented as "new wineskin" alternatives for discarded church traditions. I understand new wineskins, but filled with *what*? New wineskins are for new wine. Where is the new wine of God's presence and power in the church? The apostle Paul told the Corinthians that he didn't come to them with carefully crafted and persuasive rhetoric, but with a "demonstration of the Spirit's power."[6] Contemporary Western Christianity offers innovations in style, clever marketing, therapeutic self-concern, and well-rehearsed worship sets. The Western Christian experience is simply and desperately in need of *the presence of God*. So in a sense, the new wine is old wine rediscovered.

We need a fresh and dynamic experience with God that warms our hearts and transforms our lives. That's why I write with a sense of urgency today. To those who pursue the presence of God, this book doesn't merely offer a new wineskin—it offers *new wine*! It is only in God's presence that hearts will be stirred and filled and our struggles will find resolution.

My prayer is that this book will change us, that it will dislodge our faulty understanding of a distant and aloof God—our notion that he somehow isn't alive and moving *actively* in the world today. At the same time, I pray that this book will increase your faith and open your heart to a deeper experience of God's abiding presence.

I'll admit that it's an intimidating task to write about the presence of God, one that reminds me of the time when a friend's first-grade daughter was asked about her father's work. Because she didn't have the words to tell her classmates that he was a seminary president, she simply explained that he studied God. At a subsequent parent-faculty gathering, the teacher retold the story and then turned to my friend and asked, "Just how does one study God anyway?"

"Very carefully, ma'am!" he replied.

That note of caution describes the attitude of my own heart as I invite you to join me on a quest to discover what it means to experience the awesome yet very tangible presence of God.

Prayers for Revival

The current spiritual climate in North America, with its declining church membership, especially among the younger generations, is reminiscent of the situation in much of Europe after World War II.

As the war drew to a close in 1945, the effects of those years of horror took a terrible toll on many cities around the world, including Stornoway, a town on the Isle of Lewis in the Outer Hebrides, a chain of islands off the west coast of Scotland. Originally a Viking settlement, the town is the largest in the area, though it has only a few thousand residents.

A disproportionate number of young men from the islands had died in battle, and the postwar years were bitter for many families there. Young people were disillusioned, and many had abandoned even a pretense of faith in God. In fact, by 1949, there wasn't a single young person to be found in any of the churches on the Isle of Lewis.

Not one.

Alarmed by this state of affairs, two elderly sisters from the Church of Scotland in the town of Barvas spoke to their pastor and the elders of the church, sharing a surprising vision. While deep in prayer, they had seen the sanctuary packed to the doors with young people. But for this to happen, the women said, the church absolutely needed to dedicate itself to prayer. They challenged the church's leaders to join them in their barn every Tuesday and Friday evening for prayer.

For six weeks they prayed, and nothing happened.

They kept on praying.

And they prayed.

And they prayed.

Still nothing.

One night, one of the elders opened the evening prayer meeting with a reading from Psalm 24: "Who shall ascend the hill of the LORD? And who shall stand in his holy place? He who has clean hands and a pure heart . . ."

Suddenly, the man could read no further. Dropping the Bible, he fell to his knees on the barn floor and cried out, "God, are my hands clean? Is my heart pure? It is not the young people of this island who need reviving. It's me!"

Gripped by a deep conviction of sin, everyone else dropped to their knees alongside the elder and began praying prayers of repentance. That prayer meeting continued late into the night. Years later, the pastor of that church recalled the scene, describing how "the power of God swept into the parish" that evening. According to one account, "The following day, the looms were silent, little work was done on the farms as men and women gave themselves to thinking on eternal things gripped by eternal realities."[7] One man I spoke to concluded that the prayers for revival and that single act of repentance had released something from heaven over the islands.

But what exactly did it release?

God's presence.

God's overwhelming presence was poured out over the islands for the next four years.

God's Presence and Glory

In the Old Testament, many people encountered a special sense of God's presence in a pillar of fire, a cloud, a wind, an earthquake, a burning bush, and a still, small voice.[8] Moses encountered the presence of God on the top of Mount Sinai for forty days, and his face glowed for days afterward as a result.[9] *Glory* is a noun used to describe God. It is the effect of God's revealed presence. It is not just a theological description of God. Glory is *real stuff*. As used in the Old Testament, glory means *weightiness, heaviness*—a substantial manifestation of God that we experience when he makes his presence known to us.

In the New Testament, the same word, *glory*, describes the majesty, the shining splendor, and the power of God, which is visible and accessible to all of us in Jesus, as revealed by the Holy Spirit. Paul says we are drawn to salvation by "the light of the gospel that displays the glory of Christ."[10] He adds that an even greater glory than what Moses experienced will transform our lives, revealing "ever-increasing glory, which comes from the Lord, who is the Spirit."[11] Has that been your experience?

There is nothing lackluster, boring, or run-of-the-mill here! Glory is far more compelling than a market-driven set of truth statements. Glory commands our attention and demands our response. It is a far cry from encountering a domesticated God made in our own image. No, this is a powerful display of the untamed Lion of Judah.

Is God's presence truly available for us today? And if so, how? What might our experience of God's presence look like? Can I expect to experience the presence of God every time I read the Bible or worship or go to church? Is every true encounter with God dramatic, like Saul's experience on the road to Damascus? What are some of the ways God will make his presence known in my life? What do I need to do to prepare for God's presence? When I do sense his presence, is it just to make me feel good, or is there a greater purpose? What should I be looking for?

These questions have captivated me all of my life, ever since I had my own first experience of God's supernatural presence and power in Durban, South Africa, when I was a boy (a story I'll tell a bit later). These questions motivated my study of church history, and they have taken me around the world in pursuit of Christians who have experienced the presence of God in ways not unlike those we see in the New Testament.

One of the places my search took me was to the Isle of Lewis, the site of the remarkable revival mentioned previously, one that lasted from 1949 to 1953. More than sixty years later I met with two of the island's residents, Colin and Mary Peckham, who, along with hundreds of others, had witnessed that extraordinary occasion of God's presence. It changed their lives, propelling them and many of their friends to missions around the world, and it turned life in the Hebrides upside down.

The Peckhams agreed to meet me in Stornoway and tell their story in full. They also promised to introduce me to more people around the island I could interview. As soon as they stepped off the ferry from the mainland, we headed to a local tearoom. As we sat around a small table, Colin and Mary began to tell me stories I will never forget. Mary said that the presence of God in those years was like a "canopy of God-consciousness that covered the whole island."

Blown Away in Stornoway

In the days that followed, I was able to interview many of Colin and Mary's friends, people who had come to Christ in dramatic ways during that 1949–1953 revival. Some lived in Stornoway. Others lived in the island villages of Barvas, Shader, Carloway, and Port of Ness. Some of the homes we visited were where the famous "after-meetings" had happened, where every square inch of floor space was jammed with worshipers until the early hours of the morning.

In every interview, one name kept surfacing: *Duncan Campbell.* He was an evangelist from Edinburgh who had been called in to help the local pastors respond to the spiritual awakening on the island. Campbell was a person of great integrity, a man of prayer who was led by the Holy Spirit. Forceful in the pulpit, he was also sensitive to God's presence and gentle in dealing with new converts.

After the two elderly women, their pastor, and church elders had experienced the breakthrough from God in the barn, the sisters encouraged their pastor to invite Duncan Campbell to come and help the churches on the island during the time of God's visitation. Ten days later, Campbell stepped onto the pier in Stornoway. Meanwhile, the church in Barvas had been meeting every night since that prayer meeting in the barn. Members of the parish couldn't get enough of God.

On the night that Duncan Campbell arrived, the pastor in Stornoway had arranged for the congregation to gather at 9:00 p.m., which would allow him time to drive Campbell to the church, twelve miles from the ferry at Stornoway. When they arrived, three hundred people were already in the sanctuary, singing psalms and hymns. Campbell preached, but by his own account, "nothing really happened during the service." By 10:45 p.m., the meeting was dismissed.

Then, as Campbell and the pastor were walking down the aisle to leave, something surprising began to unfold. The elder who had read from Psalm 24 in the barn fell to his knees and cried out, "God, you cannot fail us! You promised to pour water on the thirsty and floods upon dry ground. God, you cannot fail us!"

At that moment, the door of the church burst open, and one of the parishioners came running in, crying, "Mr. Campbell, something wonderful has happened!"

Outside the church, a crowd had gathered, including many young people, and most of them visibly under conviction of sin. They arrived just as the service was being dismissed and the church doors were opened.

Remember—there had not been a single youth at church in the whole island before this.

Years later, Campbell described this scene to a jammed auditorium at a college in Alberta, Canada.

Over 100 young people were at the dance in the parish hall and they weren't thinking of God or eternity. God was not in all of their thoughts. They were there to have a good night, when suddenly the power of God fell upon the dance. The music ceased and in a matter of minutes, the hall was empty. They fled from the hall as a man fleeing from a plague. And they made for the church.[12]

When the doors of the church were opened, the young people flooded in past those who were leaving. Some came in singing. Many came in weeping. By the time the pastor asked Campbell to address the congregation, there wasn't a seat left. Many young people were kneeling or lying facedown in the aisles or in the area around the platform. All were praying. As Campbell made his way to the pulpit for the second time that night, he overheard a young woman lying on the floor near the platform. She was crying out over and over, "Oh, God, is there mercy for me?" Campbell preached on God's grace and forgiveness. The meeting did not dismiss until 4:00 a.m. By then, most of those present had received Christ as their Savior.

Mary Peckham said of those days on the Isle of Lewis that the *presence* of God engaged with the *knowledge* of God she had learned as a child in catechism. It moved that knowledge from her head to her heart. Before the revival, when she had on rare occasion attended Communion services, she had felt unmoved. She had listened dully as the minister read from the prophet Isaiah at every Communion: "'Who is this that comes from Edom, from Bozrah in garments stained crimson? Who is this so splendidly robed, marching in his great might?' 'It is I, announcing vindication, mighty to save.'"[13]

After Mary came to Christ as a teenager in the Barvas church, Isaiah's words gripped her heart so powerfully, she said, that at the next Communion, when the minister read those same words, she was surprised her trembling hands could hold on to the Communion chalice when it was passed to her.

The impact of God's presence was felt in all of the communities on the island over the next three years. Casual conversations turned quickly to the things of God. Places of entertainment no longer held attraction for the people, and many went out of business. When there were no church meetings, people met in homes to pray and study the Bible. And they sang with joy wherever they went. One man told us that the singing was so powerful that it "went through you like fire." Some said it could be heard from a mile away. Even the unconverted began cleaning up their language, their humor, and their relationships as they experienced God's presence.

I have spent the better portion of my life collecting stories like this one from Colin and Mary Peckham, many of which I'll share with you in the pages ahead. In the process of collecting these stories, I have come to believe that encounters with the presence of God are more frequent than most of us realize. Not every encounter results in an area-wide revival, of course; but they are nonetheless powerful and transformative in the lives of those touched by the presence of God.

If your experience of God until now has felt more like his *absence* than his *presence*, or if you simply long to deepen your understanding of God's presence in your life, there's good news ahead. Undoubtedly, God is already at work in your heart, stirring a desire within you for greater intimacy with him. It doesn't matter whether you're a brand-new Christian or you've been a Christian all your life. You may be a congregant or a pastor. You may attend a small church or a large one. You may live in Topeka, Kansas; Brisbane, Australia; or Mumbai, India. It doesn't matter. The common denominator is that you're hungry for more of Christ. The good news is that hunger comes from him. It is God's Spirit already at work in you. The even better news is that he is not playing games with your life. If you act on the hunger he has given you and pursue him, he has promised to draw near to you. You may not know when, where, or how, but he will make himself known to you.

I pray that the journey we embark on together in the pages of this book will answer many of your questions and will be used of the Spirit to generate a deep hunger in your heart for more of God. And may his presence in you touch and encourage others to seek him until there is a ripple effect in churches, towns, and cities across the nation.

But first, there's a common misconception we need to resolve: namely, that experiencing God's presence is *our* responsibility, something we can bring about through our own efforts. As we'll see in the chapters ahead, God reveals his presence in surprising ways at surprising times.

He is in charge.

Are you ready?

SIGNS OF REVIVAL
The fear of the Lord among believers brings a deep conviction of sin and results in repentance.

CHAPTER 2

DRIVEN TO WORSHIP

My wife, Rita, and I have two daughters, both now grown and living nearby with wonderful families of their own. Growing up, our elder daughter, Vanessa, was the more compliant of the two, and she was always sensitive to spiritual matters. Our younger daughter, Kathryn, had a lively temperament that pushed the limits on everything. She was always moving so fast from one interest to the next that there were times in her life when Rita and I were not sure she thought very much about her relationship with the Lord.

We knew Kathryn had made a decision when she was young to follow Jesus. But the teenage years can be rocky for any family, and as Kathryn matured, Rita and I wondered whether she had personalized her faith in Christ. She was active in youth group, youth choir, summer camps, and at the church, but how much of that was because we insisted she go or because she was naturally social and enjoyed being with her friends? With her dad being the pastor, was she just doing what was expected of her?

Our concern peaked when Kathryn entered her college years. She chose a university in Tennessee, a long way across the country from where we live in Seattle. It was a strong, faith-based school, my alma mater in fact, so we weren't concerned about the school. But through my years in pastoral ministry, I had seen a number of students attend Christian universities and make poor choices nevertheless. Rita and I were concerned that Kathryn's foundation wasn't yet solid enough for her to stand on her own so far from home.

The plan was for me to help Kathryn drive out to Tennessee at the start of the school year, get her settled, and fly home. We loaded up her little red Acura Integra with all her belongings and hit I-90 eastbound for the four- or five-day road trip. Have you ever longed to have a deep conversation with someone you love dearly, but you're just not sure how to ask the hard questions so they'll be well received? *Hey, Kathryn, do you love Jesus with all your heart? Are you going to toss your faith once you get out on your own?* For the first two days of the trip, I wrestled with that tension. I knew I didn't want to squander this opportunity, but I'd made mistakes before being too heavy-handed. This drive was going to be one of my last chances to see how she was doing before she moved away, but I desperately didn't want to *push* her away.

Funny, I never got to ask those questions because on the third day of the trip, something happened that can only be described as otherworldly.

That morning, we got up before dawn, ate a quick breakfast, and hit the road before the sun rose. We headed east again on I-90 out of Sheridan, Wyoming. The early August grass was still a glorious green in this part of the country, and we followed the winding highway along a gradual right turn to where it dropped down into a wide, expansive valley. Far off to the west we could see the spectacular, ice-capped Bighorn Mountains reaching into the sky. As we drove, a song filled the car. It was on a CD we started out with every day:

Hear the morning start the day,
Hear the sunrise streaming rays,

Hear the mountains point the way
  To their Creator's glory.[1]

Right at that moment, the sun broke over the eastern horizon. Sunlight slammed against the facing slopes of the Bighorns, and the last lines of the song—*hear the mountains point the way to their Creator's glory*—burst into our hearts as the valley filled with an extraordinary golden glow. Instantly, I was reminded of Isaiah 6:3: "The whole earth is full of his glory!"

Something happened at that moment. Something words can never fully describe. The presence of God filled that little car and overflowed in our hearts. Love drew near!

I looked over at my daughter and saw huge tears in her eyes. There were tears in my eyes as well. Neither of us said a word. The moment was too sacred. Right then—and it's hard to fully articulate—as a dad, I felt a deep and abiding sense that my job in leading my daughter to Jesus was done. I knew Kathryn owned her faith without me. I knew she loved and worshiped Jesus with all her heart. She knew the presence of God in her own life. She was going to be just fine out on her own.

Sometime later, I spoke to Kathryn about our experience, just to compare notes. She described identically everything I had felt: an immediate sense of God's majesty and awesome power visible in creation, a specific sense of being humbled by God's love to reveal himself to us in that way and at that moment, and a sense of abandoned and extravagant worship from us in loving response to his self-revelation. We had both witnessed beautiful scenes of nature before, yet this was something different—something transformational. Our hearts had been deeply stirred by an unexpected encounter with the God who wants to be known by us—and I use the word *known* to describe not a purely rational comprehension of facts, but rather an intimate experience.

Both of us are convinced to this day that what we experienced on that road in Wyoming was none other than God's holy presence. I am equally convinced that it is precisely the kind of thing that God loves to do. He loves to surprise us in our pursuit of him with a tangible sense of his presence.

> Behold, I am doing a new thing;
>> now it springs forth, do you not perceive it?
> I will make a way in the wilderness
>> and rivers in the desert.
>
> ISAIAH 43:19

Not Every Circumstance Comes with Pomp

Here's the catch! My daughter and I could drive that same stretch of Wyoming highway for the rest of our lives with no guarantee that God would show up again like he did on our road trip east. In fact, I can almost guarantee that he won't. We love those dramatic moments with God. We hope for them and long for them, and undertake any number of well-intentioned spiritual journeys in an effort to discover God's presence. But our untamed God will not be drawn into a predictable, cause-and-effect relationship with us that essentially leaves us in the driver's seat. Encounters with God simply cannot be manufactured by our own efforts.

Certainly we need to seek the Lord with all our hearts, to draw near to him. But there is no guarantee that the faith practices we engage in will automatically and immediately bring God near to us with the kind of dramatic demonstration of his presence we experienced in the car that day in Wyoming.

Personally, I set aside a specific time every day to read the Bible and pray. Each day, I read five chapters of the Bible—one chapter from each main section of Scripture: history books, Wisdom Literature, Prophets, Gospels, and Epistles. I also draw near to God through faith practices such as study, prayer, worship, fasting, giving, and serving others.

But do I experience the overwhelming presence of God every day?

No.

Certainly not in such a dramatic fashion. I practice spiritual disciplines in order to learn and grow, and to hear God's voice through his Word, but primarily to put myself in a place where I am accessible to God when he chooses to reveal himself to me.

Is it beneficial for every believer to consistently embrace the faith practices? Yes. But we cannot expect a one-for-one causality in our faith-based relationship with God. Just because we walk in the spiritual disciplines doesn't mean that we'll encounter God's tangible presence every time.

God is sovereign, and he moves according to his own wisdom and purpose.

Stood Up by God?

The prophet Elijah was running from the murderous threats of Queen Jezebel. Elijah had ticked her off by executing the prophets of Baal at Mount Carmel. But I believe he was also trying to put some distance between himself and the fickle people of God, running from his prophetic calling. We find him depressed and hiding deep in a mountain cave, far south of the capital city, on Mount Sinai. This was the lowest point of his life. If he ever needed a dramatic encounter with God, it was now. He'd had his share before. A miraculous supply of flour and oil in the midst of a famine.[2] A widow's son raised from the dead when Elijah prayed.[3] Fire from heaven on a waterlogged altar and sacrifice.[4]

But this time it was different. This time, Elijah was not on a ministry high. He was tired, discouraged by the hard-heartedness of God's people, hidden away in a cave, and wanting to die. Then God drew near.

He called Elijah out of the cave, saying, "Go out and stand before me on the mountain."[5] But Elijah was too despondent to move. A dramatic windstorm ripped through the mountain, dislodging rocks and boulders. "But the LORD was not in the wind"[6] and the prophet stayed in the cave. Then an earthquake shook the mountain. Then fire. But the Lord was not in those dramatic demonstrations either. In fact, in this instance, the transforming presence of God came in "the sound of a gentle whisper."[7] Elijah knew it was God. "He wrapped his face in his cloak and went out and stood at the entrance of the cave."[8]

It's interesting that this encounter came at a time when Elijah was running—running, he thought, in the opposite direction of God's calling on his life. Even more interesting is that God used this encounter to *reassign* Elijah to his intended mission.

We all love the Bible stories of dramatic encounters with God. They make some of the most exciting faith builders. The problem is that they can generate an unhealthy alternative to living by faith if we seek them as an end in themselves. Hebrews 11:6 says, "It is impossible to please God without faith."[9] But living by faith is not the opposite of experiencing God. It wasn't for Abraham or Paul. The love of God draws us into a pursuit of his presence—not for the experience itself, but for relationship, for who God is. He is the journey *and* the destination. We can pursue him, confident that he wants to, and will, reveal his presence to us in ways, and at times, that he knows will be best for us and will advance his purpose in our lives. Sometimes he's in the fire that doesn't consume the bush, sometimes in the thunder that shakes the mountain, and sometimes in the gentlest whisper.

God is forever outside the box. He is in charge. And as we seek him, he draws near to us in love.

God's Presence: On/Off Switch Not Included

Sometimes, God is not easily found. How's that for a cold, stark truth? Yet we're to pursue him—and it's a pursuit with surprising benefits. Do you believe it?

The benefit comes to us when we embrace the truth that God is a person of remarkable mystery and wonder. His invitation to us is to be caught up in his divine unpredictability. If he popped up every time we searched for him, like a figure in an arcade game, we would be left with the inevitable conclusion that God is our servant—like a genie in a bottle, available to us any time we rub the lamp. But he offers so much more than three wishes.

When I think of searching for God's presence, I find some important lessons in an unlikely account from Scripture—in Song of Solomon.

The Song can be interpreted a number of different ways. On the one hand, its most literal interpretation shows the book as a steamy, ancient-Eastern love poem. On the other hand, it's a book of profound metaphor. It pictures the complex and amazingly beautiful relationship between a lover and his beloved, representations of God and his people, of Jesus and the church. In my interpretation of the book, I fall somewhere in between the two perspectives. I don't deny the literal understanding of Solomon's song, yet I acknowledge the *greater story* it represents. God is love. Costly love. Extreme love. God intensely loves his people. And our relationship with him is primarily a love response to his love initiatives. The Song of Solomon is a picture of that love.

One dark night, the lover shows up at the beloved's door. She is already asleep, though her heart is awake, a picture of a deep and abiding desire for her suitor stirred within her by his advances. Her first inclination when he knocks at the door is to roll over and go back to sleep.

> I have taken off my robe—
>   must I put it on again?
> I have washed my feet—
>   must I soil them again?
> SONG OF SONGS 5:3, NIV

But love wins out. Her lover thrusts his hand through the latch opening, and her heart begins to pound. She quickly dresses and runs to open the door to him. Her hand comes away from the latch with the lingering fragrance of the myrrh that was on his hand. But when she opens the door, to her great surprise, he has already gone. She rushes out into the street, distressed, and begins searching for him, even to the point of getting roughed up by the city watchmen. "If you find my beloved," she appeals to the daughters of the city, "tell him I am faint with love."[10]

This story illustrates some timeless truths. God is love, but love, by definition, must have an object—that's you and me! By its nature, love is compelled to draw near. From our own experience we know that true love wants to be as close to the beloved as possible. So why does it seem as if God sometimes makes overtures of love toward us and then is not easily found when we wake up and search for him?

Yes, "everyone who calls on the name of the Lord will be saved,"[11] which means that salvation is offered freely to all and is received as a gift from God through faith alone. But God's *presence* can sometimes be much more elusive. Seldom are we able to find him directly, and never will we find him by our own efforts alone.

That's something we must always keep clearly in mind. It's an apparent contradiction, but we must understand it. It's not up to us, ultimately, to find the presence of God. *He* finds *us*. But it *is* up to us to wake up, get up, and follow our hearts in pursuit of him, hearts that have first been touched by his amazing love for us.

So yes, we are in pursuit of a God who is not always easily found, but who loves to be found!

Is there a tension there? Yes. But it is a tension that acknowledges that God is God, and we are not, and that is a good thing.

Is a Good God Hard to Find?

Whenever I teach on the impossibility of finding God's presence through our own efforts alone, I always encounter a few Christian friends who are deeply bothered by this. They say, "Oh, that's not my God," and point to verses such as Jeremiah 29:13: "If you look for me wholeheartedly, you will find me."[12] And, yes, I see the genuine concern that motivates their understanding of God. They don't want to serve a God who is seen as playing a cruel game with us. But if we look more closely at the context of the Jeremiah passage, we see that it's about God's promise always to return to us, to save us from our exile and bring us back into right relationship with him. It's much more about encouraging a deep heart longing for God than it is about pinpointing his exact location or instant accessibility.

Think of it this way: If I get up in the morning and go looking for my car keys because I need to drive to the office, and if I know they're exactly where I left them the night before—on the table at the front entry—there is not much searching required to find them, right? But my goodness, if I'm late for an important appointment and those keys aren't on the table by the front entry, and if I can't find them anywhere, then watch out, world! I'm going to search for those keys with all my heart. Just like the woman searching for the lost coin in Luke 15, I'm going to turn my house upside down until I find them. And in similar fashion, just like the beloved bride awakened from sleep by her lover's voice at the door, I am going to head out into the streets and search for God until I find him. That's what Jeremiah 29:13 points us to—a level of deep hunger for God that he wants to cultivate in us.

Our search for God's presence is more like that of a little kid playing hide-and-seek with a parent. The parent's involvement in the game actually comes from a desire to love and be with the child. That is why, as parents, we would never want to hide so as never to be found. No! In fact, we cannot wait to be found. We get behind the couch and purposefully leave a foot sticking out into the room. The joy is all in the play, as squeals of delight reverberate from different places in the house as the child looks for us with great excitement and anticipation. When at last we are found, shouts of delight ring out—and any parent reading this can accurately predict what comes next: "Let's do it again!"

In the same way, God's presence is not always easily found by us, but his purpose is to evoke in us a God-given hunger in the pursuit, and then the mutual delight when that pursuit bears fruit—on a mountain pass in Wyoming, in the mouth of a cave on Mount Sinai, or in the everyday ebb and flow of life.

My friend, take heart: If you have been searching diligently for God's presence but haven't encountered him yet, don't be discouraged. It can feel as if there's something wrong with your spiritual life, but that may not be the case at all. Rather, it may just be that God is inviting you to wake up, get up, and pursue him with a deeper sense of his love for you. Be patient, be faithful, keep seeking him with all your heart, and someday you'll round a mountain pass and God will completely surprise you—even overwhelm you—with his presence. He will reveal himself to you exactly when and where and how he wants to. Never before. Never because you're in the driver's seat. And always just in time.

We must receive and accept this truth: *God is not beholden to us.* I know that's not easy to hear, particularly in the immediacy of our modern culture. If it's dinnertime and we're hungry, we can zip down to the corner and pick up a bucket of chicken. Five minutes later, we're home again with the meal plunked on the table, ready to eat. That's often how we mistakenly approach the Christian life. We want God, we want him now, and we want him on our terms!

But experiencing God's presence is much less like fast food and much more like an old-fashioned meal. I think back to when I was growing up in South Africa. Each day, when I got home from school, one of my chores was to help my mom prepare the evening dinner. There were no microwaves in those days. No frozen-food-stocked grocery stores near where we lived. Each day, my mom started the evening meal preparation around three in the afternoon. I'd have to help her string and cut the green beans, shell the peas, and slice and scrape out the seeds in the squash. Then my mom would put it all with the meat in the different compartments of the pressure cooker. Hours later, after we were good and hungry, our dinner was ready and we sat down as a family for the feast.

The pursuit of God is like that. There's preparation involved, simmering and stirring. God is not on our timetable. And that's actually a very good thing.

Durban Renewal

When I was seven, my father accepted a pastorate in the city of Durban, South Africa, where I grew up. He arrived at the church and discovered, unfortunately, that circumstances were not as they had seemed when he candidated. One of the church leaders was paying older girls in the Sunday school for sexual favors. The church treasurer no longer attended services, but arrived only at the end of services to collect the offering. Bills were not being paid. The church was deeply in debt. And certain members of the congregation had been feuding for years.

My father was short, a five-foot-six-inch Englishman with Winston Churchill's bulldog type of personality. His approach to dealing with the problems was simply to try to preach things straight. He was a self-taught expository preacher. His preaching was forceful and very direct. He felt confident that a few months of preaching would get things straightened out in the congregation.

Unfortunately, year followed year, and nothing changed. After three years in the church, ministry was still very difficult. There was little responsiveness in the hearts and lives of the congregation. My father became extremely disheartened and ended up in the hospital with bleeding ulcers so severe that doctors actually feared for his life. For more than a month, my father received blood transfusions as the doctors worked to keep him from bleeding out.

The ulcers were just symptoms of a deeper issue. My father had reached the end of himself in a seemingly incurable ministry situation. A sense of desperation ultimately drove him to his knees. When he was finally released from the hospital and returned home, he and my mom called a family meeting with my brother and sisters and me to discuss the future. My dad was so disheartened by his experience in the church that he and Mom informed us that they were going to take a month off to seek the Lord in prayer and fasting and try to receive some direction from him.

When they came back after that month off, they felt more at peace, but nothing much had changed in the life of the congregation, and Dad didn't feel released yet to quit. Three more months went by. Still nothing changed. Dad preached and prayed and called on the name of the Lord, and came home discouraged every night.

Each Friday night, there was a regularly scheduled prayer meeting at the church. I was eleven by this time and not particularly interested in the proceedings, although I always went. It was at one of these prayer meetings that I remember a lady praying aloud for half an hour. She droned on and on, covering everything she could think of—every missionary, every family in the church, every scraped knee and bruised big toe. By the end of her filibuster, Dad told us later, his words to himself were, *This prayer meeting is dead. Let's just gather together and give it a decent burial. Then we can at least go home.*

As he gathered the fifteen or so people around the front of the church to close the prayer meeting, he felt even more discouraged than before. But just before he dismissed everyone, the Holy Spirit spoke to him. It wasn't an audible voice, but making a clear impression on my dad's heart, God said, "You've been here for an hour and a half, and you—Pastor—have done little except complain. Why don't you have these people worship me for a moment?"

Without any sense of expectation, without any huge rush of faith rising up in him, but just out of sheer obedience, Dad said to the handful of people, "All right, before we go home, let's just worship the Lord for a moment," and he led out in a hymn.

What happened next is hard to put into words.

As the people began to worship God, the presence of the Lord descended on us. I remember the scene well. Some of the people began weeping. Two or three began spontaneously confessing sins. A couple of people from the feuding factions fell into each other's arms in confession and mutual forgiveness. A spontaneity and freshness in worship and prayer was instantly evident. People prayed aloud and sang from their hearts with great joy. That little prayer meeting went on until midnight.

The sense of wonder and awe in the car that night as we drove home was intense. *What was that? What just happened?* we asked ourselves. For the next day or so, it was the only thing anyone in our family could talk about.

Two days later, the next Sunday morning, as our family rounded the corner a block away from the church in our old 1949 Ford, the first words out of my father's mouth were, "Look, there must have been an accident."

When we caught sight of the church building, we saw more than two hundred people standing outside on the sidewalk. So many, in fact, that they spilled out onto the street. All were waiting for the church building to open for that Sunday's service.

Apparently, between the Friday night prayer meeting and Sunday morning, word that God's presence had come among us had spread throughout the community. What had been a congregation of thirty-five people instantly multiplied more than fivefold.

But as we soon discovered, it was about much more than the number of people. Over the next few weeks—and then the next few years—that little church was completely transformed. Remarkable spiritual growth took place in the congregation. Hearts were changed. People were reconciled to God. Families stopped fighting and bickering. People talked about what a pleasure it was to come to church. The spirit of revival touched many, many lives for *years* following that weekend when God drew near.

After that Friday night prayer meeting, a new and fresh sense of God's presence was felt in every service. It was not uncommon to see people come to Christ every week. Water baptisms became regular occurrences in the life of the church. Sincere and enthusiastic worship filled the people's hearts and voices. There were even some occasions when the miraculous occurred, although not on a regular basis. One Sunday, a woman who had been wheelchair bound for a few years stood up and began to walk. I remember one Sunday when a young man with a withered arm came forward to receive prayer. He'd had polio as a child and favored his withered arm by keeping his hand in his suit pocket. As my father prayed for him one morning for some other, minor illness, the man's hand came out of his suit pocket and the muscle tone instantly became normal. His previously afflicted arm became healthy literally in front of our eyes, and he could now use it the same as the other one. Along with me, several hundred other people witnessed the miracle with their own eyes. You can imagine the impact on the church for months afterward. There was a divine electricity, as if the Lord were right there with us in the room.

Eighteen months after that momentous Friday night prayer meeting, the old church building could no longer accommodate all the people who were coming as a result of the amazing things God was doing in people's lives. The church moved to a new, seven-hundred-seat sanctuary we called Elim Tabernacle. The new building was immediately filled to capacity with people joyfully worshiping the Lord. It was an amazing experience—when God drew near to one congregation. In me as a teenager, it set a marker for God's presence.

What can we make of this story from my father's church in Durban? Was this one of those rare, historical seasons of revival that we read about but rarely, if ever, experience for ourselves? Or is it possible that the story you've just read is God's intention for his people and his church in *every* season and lifetime?

God is love, and love always wants to draw close. It is the nature of love to be close. And it is God's love for us that calls us and enables us to live in an intimate love relationship with him—a love that can be experienced whenever he draws near. Draw near to God and he has promised to draw near to you with refreshing glimpses of remarkable love and grace.[13]

That's what we're talking about in this book. Call it revival, spiritual awakening, or even simply spiritual refreshing. I have two words for you as you start this journey: *persevere* and *expect*. Persevere in your pursuit of God and expect that he will make his presence known in your life and in the life of your church. You will be marked by him, and you will be transformed.

Yes, God is always with us—he's omnipresent. But there is so much more that we're invited to discover. That's what we'll talk about in the chapters to come.

SIGNS OF REVIVAL
Worship becomes spontaneous, joyous, and authentic.

CHAPTER 3

A CANDLESTICK IN
THE DARKNESS

HAVE YOU SEEN the movie *Les Misérables*? Maybe you've read the book by the nineteenth-century French novelist Victor Hugo. Near the beginning of the story, a hardened ex-convict named Jean Valjean steals costly candlesticks and silverware from the kindly bishop, Monseigneur Bienvenu, who had fed him and given him a bed for the night. Valjean runs away with treasure in hand but is immediately caught by three fierce French policemen. They are convinced that no one in Valjean's condition or station in life could have come by the silver legitimately. Suspecting where he has acquired the loot, they haul him back to the bishop, expecting to secure an indictment, prosecute justice, and exact the appropriate punishment. This crime will likely mean the guillotine for the repeat offender, Jean Valjean.

But the bishop does the unexpected. Instead of condemning the thief, the bishop hands him back the bag of stolen goods, explaining to the policemen that it was a gift. The policemen are sent on their way. No arrest is made. Jean Valjean is a free man. Stunned by the bishop's gracious actions, the trembling ex-convict whispers that no person has ever before demonstrated that kind of love to him.

"Jean Valjean, my brother," the bishop says, "you no longer belong to evil. With this silver, I have bought your soul. I have ransomed you from fear and hatred. And now I give you back to God."[1]

Whenever I think of that scene, my eyes fill with tears. Surely that is a picture of God's unconditional love and grace in our lives. Our sin condemns us to eternal separation from the holiness and wonder of a sinless, perfect God. Yet the undeserved free gift of God's grace in Christ's death and resurrection provides us with new identities and new hope for the future. In Christ, we are purchased (redeemed) from a life of fear and hatred by the love of God.

That pivotal scene also brings to mind the differences between two prominent nineteenth-century European philosophers, Søren Kierkegaard and Georg Hegel—differences that relate to how we understand and participate in the grace of God's presence in our lives today.

The two men disagreed about how we know that things are true, particularly as they relate to experiencing God.[2] We base everything we know about God on Scripture, yes, but it is Scripture that teaches us that there are ways to know and experience God in addition to a purely academic investigation of the facts about him.

God invites us to enter into the drama of his love and saving grace, which unfolds in our lives every day. We are darkened, bitter prisoners of sin, with absolutely no hope for the future, and yet Christ hands the silverware and candlesticks back to us, delivering us from certain death or bondage to our sin. It is far more than we deserve.

What do we do with such love? How do we respond? We're trembling. We're stunned. And yet we realize that something great and wondrous and *free* is being offered to us, and it will change our lives forever.

Even more than the gift, the experience of this amazing grace leaves us eager to know the Giver himself. And that is where our experience of God's presence comes in.

It's Not "Just the Facts, Ma'am"

Back to the differences between Kierkegaard and Hegel for a moment. Hegel's premise was that people can know things for certain only by processing facts (that's a bit of an oversimplification, but it will do). In Hegel's view, we arrive at an understanding of God by accepting a *thesis* about him, and considering the *antithesis* from the evidence at hand. After we've analyzed the subject for a while and reasoned things through, we are able to arrive at a *synthesis*. It is a purely intellectual, or analytical, way of arriving at knowledge. In a nutshell, the only way to know something for sure, according to Hegel, is by carefully thinking about it from all angles. It puts humanity and human reason at the center of our understanding of God. "For a Hegelian, philosophy is essentially superior to theology; . . . 'God' is [merely] the Absolute Idea, the process of truth being realized through the rationality of the human mind."[3]

Kierkegaard, by contrast, identified more of an *experiential* approach to knowing God. He envisioned the Christian life as a drama on a stage, with actors who have entered into the story. Each actor plays a character, engages with the story through the lines of the script, follows the commands of the director, and interacts with other cast members as the story unfolds. From this perspective, Hegel's way of knowing truth is like watching the play from the seats, as members of the audience, where the cast members, the lines, and the plot can be dispassionately analyzed and critiqued with a measure of academic detachment and even intellectual superiority.

But Kierkegaard encouraged people to break out of the audience, jump onto the stage, and take their places in the unfolding story. For Kierkegaard, we receive our lines from the director, watch for cues from the other actors, and learn the story by living it out, experiencing God firsthand, not just by sitting back, disconnected and aloof.

I think that's why so many people today, especially young people, are abandoning the church—and even their faith. They've been led to believe that the only way to experience God is the way Hegel described it: by intellect and analysis alone. Read the Bible and identify moral lessons for application and principles for Christian living. Analyze the teachings or lives of people in the Bible who actually experienced God, and then come to know God purely by reason. What an unsatisfying and unbiblical approach to faith!

Yes, Scripture will always be the foundation for our faith. Always. But the Bible itself is a collection of stories of real-life people just like us, and it describes a way of experiencing God that is much like Kierkegaard's drama.

Life is not merely a set of principles to be applied to our lives. It is an invitation, through Christ, into God's unfolding drama. We hear his lines as we read Scripture; we receive cues from the Holy Spirit at work in the people around us (who are also cast members of this drama); and we learn the story as we live it out. The Bible includes *living letters* "from Christ . . . written not with pen and ink, but with the Spirit of the living God, . . . carved not on tablets of stone, but on human hearts."[4] God calls us to be right in the middle of his drama, alive in Christ by the power of the Holy Spirit and attentive to him moment by moment, fully convinced that God is active and moving every day, in *our* world, for *his* glory.

Surely we can see that we have been forgiven a greater debt than we could possibly repay in a thousand lifetimes. In a sense, we who have received the gift of life in Jesus Christ are all like Jean Valjean. We step out into the world humbled and trembling, yet with our shoulders back and our heads held high. No longer are we convicts condemned to death. We are *forgiven*. We are free! We have been transformed into members of God's own family. We're sons and daughters of the King! The silverware and candlesticks are ours to keep! We have encountered the Giver himself—not merely the kindly bishop, but God, the dispenser of all goodness, the possessor of all glory.

That's what a living encounter with the presence of God is like. No wonder John Wesley, the famous eighteenth-century British evangelist, described the moment of his salvation at Aldersgate as having his heart "strangely warmed."[5] Concerning Wesley's dramatic encounter with God that night, church historian Clifford Towlson writes, "It could hardly be a new idea, a new intellectual attitude, which effected such a mighty change so much as a new *experience*."[6] Although we indeed encounter God through our minds, our experience of his presence cannot be the cold or dispassionate result of intellectual pursuit alone. God is the *living* Word, immanent and engaged with us. He is as living and active in our lives today as he is depicted on the pages of Scripture. When we encounter him, our hearts can—and must—be "strangely warmed."

This all matters greatly because many Christians are openly skeptical of our ability to experience God's presence. Some deny even the necessity for an examination of the subject because, they insist, God is already omnipresent. It's a plain fact in Scripture that God is already everywhere, so why would we ever strive to seek *more* of him than already exists? Why would we long for a greater sense of his presence if he is already always everywhere?

To help answer this important question, I invite you to jump into the drama—to put yourself into God's story and not merely study it on the page. In what ways could you expect to encounter God's clear presence? How has he made his presence known to others?

Richard Owen Roberts, a student of historical revivals, has identified three distinct ways in which God's presence can be known. He calls these *essential presence, manifest presence*, and *cultivated presence*. Recently, I had the unique privilege of spending a day with Mr. Roberts in the basement of his antique bookstore in Wheaton, Illinois. Here I have adapted his teaching on the three ways we might describe our experience of God's presence.

Essential Presence ✗

God is omnipresent. That simply means he is everywhere, filling all of his creation, without any limitation of space or time. The material universe and time exist only because of God, and for his good pleasure. Through Jesus, God created "everything in the heavenly realms and on earth."[7] Not only did God fashion all of creation, Scripture also teaches that God's presence *continues* to fill the universe.

"Can anyone hide from me in a secret place?
    Am I not everywhere in all the heavens and earth?"
    says the LORD.

JEREMIAH 23:24, NLT

Tremble, O earth, at the presence of the Lord. .

PSALM 114:7, NLT

If I ascend to heaven, you are there!
    If I make my bed in Sheol, you are there!
If I take the wings of the morning
    and dwell in the uttermost parts of the sea,
even there your hand shall lead me,
    and your right hand shall hold me.

PSALM 139:8-10, NLT

In other words, God is everywhere! He fills the universe, everything in it, and everything beyond it.

In his letter to the Colossians, the apostle Paul further describes the effects of God's omnipresence: "He is before all things, and in him all things hold together."[8] In this verse, Paul recognizes God's eternal preexistence, and that God's presence holds the universe together. The writer of Hebrews explains that through Jesus, God "created the universe . . . and he sustains everything by the mighty power of his command."[9] So God is present everywhere at the same time, and his presence is essential to the continued existence and order of the universe.

It is God's *essential presence* that is revealed to all humanity, saved or unsaved, through the work of creation. Paul writes that God's "invisible attributes, namely, his eternal power and divine nature, have been clearly perceived, ever since the creation of the world, in the things that have been made."[10]

Every summer, when I ride my motorcycle on westbound Highway 12 over White Pass in the Cascade Mountains in Washington, I look forward to rounding one particular corner. For miles, heading out of Yakima, the highway is hemmed in on both sides by the Snoqualmie National Forest. Then, at one particular bend in the road, Mount Rainier appears out of nowhere and suddenly fills your field of vision—fourteen thousand feet of snowcapped grandeur. It takes my breath away every time. Fortunately, the Washington State Department of Transportation has provided a turnout right at that spot, because whether you recognize God or not, you need to pull over and take a moment to experience his majestic presence in that view. Travelers who know God are compelled to worship him right there, seeing his eternal power and divine nature on magnificent display.

God is omnipresent—yes! But this is not a cold, dry doctrine. It is a wondrous truth, meant to be plunged into like a vast ocean. Wherever we swim, wherever we sail or ride a motorcycle, as far as we can look to any horizon, there is our great and awesome God. Leap off the page with me! See the wonder of God's omnipresence for all that it means for us. By holding God at arm's length, we have missed so much of the excitement that he has for us. We have misunderstood the vibrant life he has for us in Christ by focusing on *facts* about him and neglecting the *reality* of his presence. Far too many people in our day associate God in their minds with a televangelist's appeals for money, a politician's lip service to win votes, a bumper-sticker slogan, a message on a T-shirt, or curse words uttered in anger. But God—the truly omnipresent God—has nothing to do with shallowness, fakery, or the argumentative social crusades associated with so much of the Christian religion. His presence invites all of our reverence, all of our respect, all of our worship, and all of our love.

Manifest Presence

Merely knowing about the doctrine of God's *essential* presence does not guarantee that we are aware of his *actual* presence—surrounding us, touching us every moment of every day. It is too easy to get caught up in life—in taking care of the kids, weeding the yard, balancing the checkbook, and planning next year's vacation. Too easy to forget. We don't intend for it to happen this way, but God gets choked out of our lives by the cares of this world. We simply ignore him, forgetting that he is near.

God warned Israel that this would happen to them as soon as they got into the Promised Land and started enjoying the wealth of "milk and honey." This same forgetfulness happened to the church in Ephesus, and Jesus needed to tell them they had lost their first love for him.[11] They had been very busy doing God's work, going through all the motions, but they had lost their heart for his presence. It was even worse for the Christians in Laodicea.[12] There, Jesus was so forgotten that he describes himself as being on the outside of the church. He was knocking on the door, waiting to be invited in for fellowship by the very people who professed to be Christians. It can happen to a person, a family, a church, even a nation. When we forget that God is near, it isn't long before our actions start to reflect the coldness of our hearts.

This is where God's *manifest presence* enters in and he shows up in special, forceful, tangible ways. It is his way of getting our attention when we have wandered off on our own and forgotten him. The word *manifest* simply means tangible or evident—something that is overt or noticeable. We can feel it.

Or think of the word *revealed*—something that has been lost or hidden but is now right in front of our eyes and can't be ignored any longer. We might even think of it as *experienced*—something that is not merely studied but is encountered in flesh and blood, a real-life story or drama.

The effect of God's manifest presence is usually pretty dramatic.

On the night when Jesus was betrayed in the garden of Gethsemane, a motley band of thugs was recruited to arrest him. Matthew describes it as a "great multitude with swords and clubs."[13] John notes that the mob included "soldiers and some officers from the chief priests and the Pharisees" who came to the garden with "lanterns and torches and weapons."[14] John's account also includes an interesting twist—the manifest presence of God.

Jesus fully realized all that was going to happen to him, so he stepped forward to meet them. "Who are you looking for?" he asked.

"Jesus the Nazarene," they replied.

"I Am he," Jesus said. (Judas, who betrayed him, was standing with them.) As Jesus said "I Am he," they all drew back and fell to the ground! Once more he asked them, "Who are you looking for?"

And again they replied, "Jesus the Nazarene."

"I told you that I Am he," Jesus said. "And since I am the one you want, let these others go." He did this to fulfill his own statement: "I did not lose a single one of those you have given me."

Then Simon Peter drew a sword and slashed off the right ear of Malchus, the high priest's slave. But Jesus said to Peter, "Put your sword back into its sheath. Shall I not drink from the cup of suffering the Father has given me?"

So the soldiers, their commanding officer, and the Temple guards arrested Jesus and tied him up.

JOHN 18:4-12, NLT

As soon as Jesus says, "I Am he," the whole group of soldiers, thugs, and officers takes an involuntary step backward and falls to the ground! These were rough-and-tumble men, mind you—thick-necked, burly guards familiar with the ways of fighting. Yet, when Jesus makes himself known, they all topple over. Why?

The manifest presence of God.

Now watch closely. After they get up from the ground and dust themselves off, Jesus asks them the very same question a second time: "Who are you looking for?"

Again they say, "Jesus the Nazarene."

Even then, the band of brutes doesn't spring into action. Jesus has enough time to finish his sentence, requesting that his disciples be allowed to leave, Peter draws his sword and cuts off the ear of the high priest's servant, Jesus heals the ear and rebukes Peter, and then—and only then—do the soldiers, their commanding officer, and the Temple guards actually step forward to arrest and bind Jesus.

Why did it take two attempts for a gang of tough soldiers to arrest Jesus—and even then, only with great caution?

God's manifest presence.

"I Am" is a clear formulation from the Old and New Testaments of divine self-revelation. For that mob of men, it was the difference between *knowing about* God and *encountering* God.

God's *essential presence* means that he had been there in the garden all along. He was present, but he wasn't known or experienced by those who had come to arrest him.

God's *manifest presence* is what caused the soldiers to lose physical strength and fall backward to the ground. The same thing happened to the prophets Ezekiel and Daniel and the apostle John when they encountered the glory of God's manifest presence.[15] That night, in the garden of Gethsemane, God made himself known in Jesus Christ, even though the soldiers probably had no idea why they suddenly found themselves on the ground. Jesus pulled back the veil of his glory ever so slightly—and the gang had a hard time getting back on their feet.

Here's another important example of God's manifest presence. In 1 Kings 8, King Solomon and the congregation of Israel assemble to dedicate the new Temple to the Lord. The priests bring the Ark of the Covenant, where God's presence rests, into the inner sanctuary of the Temple, to the Most Holy Place. "When the priests came out of the Holy Place, a cloud filled the house of the Lord, so that the priests could not stand to minister because of the cloud, for the glory of the Lord filled the house of the Lord."[16]

Yes, God had been there all along. Because of his omnipresence, there was never a time when he was absent. Yet, that day in Israel, God chose to make himself known in a way that arrested the attention of everyone present in worship. He pulled back the veil and allowed Solomon and the people of Israel to experience his glory, draining their physical strength and making it impossible to stand up.

This picture of God's manifest presence in the Old Testament Temple is important for Christians today because Paul tells us that we are now God's temple. "Do you not know that you are God's temple and that God's Spirit dwells in you? . . . For God's temple is holy, and you are that temple."[17] As the temple of the Holy Spirit, we can fully expect that God is present and active in us, and that when he decides it is needed, he will make himself known to us in powerful ways, just like he did at the dedication of Solomon's Temple.

A study of historical spiritual awakenings reveals that God often responds to the prayers of a remnant of believers and sends his manifest presence when days are the darkest for a church, a people, or even a nation. God's intention in making himself known in such extraordinary ways is to regain the affections and attention of his people. When the church's love for God is revived, it becomes an attractive witness to the world, and sinners are dramatically saved. Every historical account of spiritual revival, at its core, includes amazing stories of God's manifest presence and its effect on individuals, families, towns, and nations.

The Second Great Awakening, a revival that arose rapidly among Baptist and Methodist congregations in the early 1800s, happened at a time when the spiritual temperature in the United States was very low. Americans had, for the most part, forgotten God, and life in the towns and villages of New England reflected it. Meanwhile, a holy dissatisfaction was growing in the lives of many Christians across the country, and much prayer was focused on the national need for renewal.

One of God's answers to prayer at this time was through the life and ministry of evangelist Charles Finney.

In his memoirs, Finney describes countless experiences with the manifest presence of God in towns throughout New England. He was careful not to encourage the natural emotional responses that people had to God's manifest presence. He shunned emotionalism and used no other method to inspire revival other than extended periods of prayer followed by spiritual conversations with seekers and the preaching of the Word.

In one house prayer meeting, prior to the revival that broke out in Rome, New York, Finney arrived to find the sitting room crowded beyond capacity. The bulk of those in attendance, mostly men, were described as "the most intelligent and influential members" of the town. Though Finney tried to keep a tight lid on emotional outbursts, everyone present was already stricken with what Finney described as a most uncommon "agitation." God had obviously preceded Finney to Rome with his manifest presence.

> We spent a little while in attempting to converse with them; and I soon saw that the feeling was so deep that there was danger of an outburst of feeling that would be almost uncontrollable. . . .
>
> Nothing had been said or done to create any excitement in the meeting. The feeling was all spontaneous. The work was with such power that only a few words of conversation would make the stoutest men writhe on their seats as if a sword had been thrust into their hearts.[18]

So Finney stopped his remarks, invited the group to kneel, and led in prayer, purposely using a "low, unimpassioned voice," praying that the Savior would lead all present to accept salvation, and that those in attendance would accept the work of Christ on the cross.

> They all arose, and I said: "Now please go home without speaking a word to each other. Say nothing—try to keep silent, and do not break out into any boisterous manifestation of feeling; and as you cannot talk or speak to each other and still control your feelings, please to go without saying a word, to your rooms. . . ."
>
> They went out sobbing and sighing, and their sobs and sighs could be heard till they got out into the street. . . . [Mr.

Wright] afterward told me that he was obliged to hold his mouth with the full strength of his arms till he got home, his distress was so great.[19]

The next morning, when a "meeting of inquiry" was to begin, the townspeople came running to the meeting room, so eager were they to hear the Word of God.

This meeting was very much like the one we had had the night before. The feeling was overwhelming. The Word of God was truly the sword of the Spirit; and some men of the strongest nerves were so cut down . . . that they were unable to help themselves and had to be taken home by their friends. This meeting . . . resulted in a great number of . . . conversions.[20]

Story after story like this can be found in Finney's memoirs. The point is not that God always manifests his presence in our lives like he did with the groups Charles Finney encountered. It's simply that God shows up in *tangible, experiential* ways. He seems to manifest his presence especially where and when his people have fallen asleep and need to be awakened. History shows it, and it's confirmed scripturally. This is God's manifest presence on display. And we can and should live in expectation that when things look the darkest, God seems predisposed to make himself known when a remnant of his people commit themselves to a protracted season of prayer.

Cultivated Presence

We know that God is present everywhere and always. We know that at certain times, he manifests his presence (makes himself known) in tangible, experiential ways in order to wake up a spiritually sleepy people. And we know that God is the *initiator* of every good thing.

So here's an obvious question: Must we simply *wait* for these big, historic breakthroughs, such as were seen on the Isle of Lewis; in Durban, South Africa; and through the ministry of Charles Finney? Is there anything we can do to *invite* a revival or prepare ourselves for an awakening? Or are we left to sit around with our hands tied, hoping against hope that God will somehow manifest his presence?

Richard Owen Roberts says that it's possible to *cultivate* God's presence. He suggests that the *cultivated presence* of God is an experience that any of us can have when our hearts are rightly prepared. The Holy Spirit empowers the Word, and our faith practices, for this very purpose, for any who want to draw near to God.[21] When our hearts are cultivated and shaped by the Spirit through our intentional pursuit of God, we position ourselves for much more frequent experiences of God's tangible presence.

I can almost hear the objections. Who are we to think that we can approach God in our own wisdom? Aren't we in danger of trying to manipulate or control the sovereign God by our actions? God is not a genie in a bottle, compelled to respond to our advances.

I agree with each one of these concerns—*but!*

But . . . the good news is that God is always moving toward you and me. Regardless of our present spiritual condition, he has not abandoned us. "God is working in you, giving you the desire and the power to do what pleases him."[22]

The desire and power to do what pleases God is not in any of us naturally. Adam and Eve had it before they sinned, but that's part of what was spoiled by the Fall. We were created for face-to-face fellowship with God, made in his image and likeness so that we would have the capacity for intimacy with him. But that capacity—and even the *desire* for intimacy with God—was damaged, though not destroyed, in the rebellion in Eden. When we are born again, we experience a transformation that restores our capacity for intimacy with God. And this same God is at work in you and me right now, giving us the desire for him and the power to draw near to him. He is definitely the initiator of this great love story.

But that doesn't mean we're puppets on the end of a string that God is manipulating.

The result of God's initiatives of love and grace creates in us what theologian Randy Maddox calls "responsible grace."[23] Maddox is concerned that most of us think of God's grace primarily as pardoning our sin and guilt through Christ. According to Maddox, that is too limited a view of God's love-motivated initiatives in our lives. He believes that God's grace is primarily the power to heal our broken lives as we participate with God in his presence.[24]

The Holy Spirit living within us gives us the ability to respond to this grace of God. The *doing* is from God; the response (response-ability) is on us. And it is our grace-enabled response to God that he in turn responds to when, in his mercy and goodness, he reveals himself to us in special ways. This is what we call God's *cultivated presence*. He provides the desire and the power for us to respond to him. When we do, he draws near to us.

To be clear, this is not a one-for-one, cause-and-effect relationship. If it were, it might tempt us to think we're in the driver's seat. Just because our hearts are right and we're engaged in regular faith practices does not guarantee a deeper experience of God's presence in every circumstance, nor does it mean we're capable of pushing buttons that force God to respond in any particular way. His presence is always revealed within the context of his sovereignty—that is, in his time and his way. God reveals himself when he chooses, according to his own wisdom and purpose. Yet, cultivating our hearts for God's presence puts us in the proper position and condition for God to make himself known. Keep in mind that God loves to make himself known. It's part of the reason for creation, the reason for his relationships with Bible characters, the reason for the Bible, the reason behind his relationship with us, and the reason he has sent the Holy Spirit to live within us.

This experience of God's cultivated presence can be seen throughout Scripture. For instance, in 2 Chronicles 34, the story of King Josiah's discovery of and response to God's Word, God identifies the pattern we've just described. Josiah was distressed about the spiritual condition of God's people. As a result, he took steps to cultivate God's presence in his life. And God spoke to Josiah through a prophet, saying, "Because your heart was tender and you humbled yourself before God when you heard his words against this place and its inhabitants, and you have humbled yourself before me and have torn your clothes and wept before me, I also have heard you, declares the LORD."[25]

God initiated the process by rescuing the Scriptures from a place of obscurity and bringing them into the king's hearing and heart.[26] But Josiah's heartfelt response to God's Word put him in a spiritual position where he was able to experience God to an even greater degree.[27] So was it God's initiative or Josiah's heart response that resulted in God's presence in the king's life? The answer is both.

Again, cultivating our lives for God's presence is not so much about our own *effort* as it is about responding to God's initiatives of love and grace in such a way that we are in the right place at the right time and in the right heart condition when God shows up. It is about *faith* and *expectancy*.

God promises that if we draw near to him, he will draw near to us.[28] So I pursue him—drawn by his love for me and inspired by the Holy Spirit—with a confidence that, at any time and in any place, I can round a corner on my motorcycle, as it were, and run smack into his majestic presence.

The same is true for you, whether you ride a motorcycle or not.

SIGNS OF REVIVAL
The Word of God comes alive among believers, resulting in renewed obedience to God.

CHAPTER 4

START EXPECTING

REALLY QUICK NOW . . . list three words that describe your faith.

What did you come up with? Did you choose words like *passionate*, *intimate*, and *genuine*? Or was it more like *routine*, *dry*, or *average*?

Howell Harris was someone whose faith most certainly fell into the first category—passionate, intimate, and genuine. An itinerant Methodist preacher who ministered throughout Wales and England in the mid-eighteenth century, Harris was one of the leaders of the Welsh revival, and thousands of people were saved as a result of his ministry. Biographer Edward Morgan writes of many remarkable events that occurred during the revival—one of which was at an all-night prayer meeting in London, where Howell Harris was praying with some sixty people.

> About three in the morning, as we were continuing in prayer, the power of God came mightily upon us, in so much that many cried out for exceeding joy and fell to

the ground. As soon as we were recovered a little from our awe and amazement at the presence of the divine Majesty, we broke out with one voice, "We praise thee, O God; we acknowledge thee to be the Lord."[1]

First of all, it's fairly remarkable that five dozen people were participating in an all-night prayer service. I wonder how many people would show up in the average North American church today? What's also remarkable—and here's where I'm going to put a little twist on the story—is *not* that the people encountered God, but that such occurrences are not uncommon, even today.

Do you believe that? Have you ever experienced anything like it?

Mrs. Fulmer's Nighttime Waking

As Christians, we are meant to regularly experience a deep and vital connection with the living God. In fact, we were created for it! But many believers seem to think the opposite—that stories of revival happened only in the distant past. But nothing could be further from the truth. The same God who spoke and was active in the lives of the Christians in the first century, and in England and Wales in the eighteenth century, is living and active today—in your life as well as in mine.

Let me give you an example from my own experience.

Early in our pastoral ministry, Rita and I were happily serving at a church in Cedar Rapids, Iowa. I'd been the pastor there for seven years. It was my first senior pastorate, and God had done remarkable things. The church had grown so rapidly that we'd built and dedicated a new fifteen-hundred-seat sanctuary, with additional classrooms and office space. Our new building was wonderful, but not as amazing as the work God was doing in the hearts and lives of the congregation and community. Rita and I loved our church and envisioned ourselves ministering in that location for years to come.

One day, in the summer of 1987, we received a phone call

from representatives of Westgate Chapel, a church in Edmonds, Washington, a small town just north of Seattle. They were looking for a new senior pastor and had heard about us from three independent sources. Was I interested in being a candidate?

My response was immediate and firm: *no.*

Why would I ever leave the church in Iowa? To my natural mind, it made no sense. The church in Edmonds was considerably smaller at the time, and it was struggling with a variety of internal crises: The last two senior pastors had suffered moral failures, attendance was down, the church was deeply in debt, and staff layoffs were imminent. From a sheer career perspective, traveling across the country to take the pastorate of a struggling church was the last thing I wanted to do.

I respectfully declined the offer and thought I'd heard the last of it. But a month later, they called again with a similar invitation. Again I said no. Two months after that, I received a third call—and unbeknownst to us, the Edmonds church had sent a delegation to Iowa to scout us more closely.

"We feel we've heard from the Lord," the caller said. "We'd really like you to consider becoming our pastor. We need what you are experiencing in Cedar Rapids. Would you take time to pray about this again?"

Oh, sure.

After mumbling a weak "yes," I hung up the phone. Truthfully, I hadn't prayed much about the decision since responding to the first call. It just seemed so obviously a *no.* But I phoned Rita anyway from my office and said, "The church in Edmonds has called again. Why don't we take a week and pray and fast about this more seriously."

That evening, when I drove home, the first cracks began to appear in my wall of resolve. I found Rita sitting on our bed, crying. This was very unusual for her, so we began talking. What came out was that, right after my phone call home, the Lord had begun the process of separating Rita's heart from the church in Cedar Rapids. She loved the people and the work, but she could feel a strange sense of being torn away from her friends and ministry in that location.

At the end of our week of prayer and fasting, Rita and I felt free to enter into a formal dialogue with the church in Edmonds. We agreed to go out to Washington and spend a week with them in January, making no promises concerning the future.

In the meantime, we started looking for people to pray with us about this potentially life-changing decision, asking the Lord to clearly show us the way to go. But whom would we ask? We didn't think it would be prudent to ask anyone from the leadership in Cedar Rapids. They didn't even know about the offer yet. What if the Lord didn't move us to Seattle? We didn't want anybody in Iowa feeling antsy, thinking we were looking for other positions—which we truly weren't. A few weeks passed, and Rita and I continued to pray, but without receiving any particular answer or direction from the Lord. We really needed to enlist other prayer warriors to help us in this decision.

Right before Christmas that year, it was our responsibility to host a holiday dinner in our home for regional pastors from our denomination. Eighteen pastoral couples attended. Among those who came that evening were Johnny and Meredith Fulmer, an elderly missionary couple who had just retired from a lifetime of service in the Philippines. They had family in the area and had been attending our church for about a month following their return to the States.

When the dinner was over, I stood by the front door with Rita, shaking hands with the different pastoral couples as they left. The Fulmers were the last to leave, and it suddenly dawned on me to ask them to pray with us. They were new to the area and new to our church, and had no vested interest in our staying or going. As I shook hands with the Fulmers, I said, "There's something I'd like you to pray with us about."

(Here's where the story turns astounding.)

Before I could even tell them what the prayer request was, Meredith Fulmer said, "Oh, I already know. The Lord is moving you. Three weeks ago, he woke me up in the middle of the night to pray for you. He told me he was getting ready to relocate you."

Our mouths hung open.

Now, we didn't base our entire decision to relocate to Edmonds solely on Mrs. Fulmer's encounter with the Lord. Rita and I continued to pray and fast, and the visit to Seattle a few weeks later helped confirm that the move to Westgate was indeed something God wanted us to do—as crazy as it looked on paper. But the experience with the Fulmers assured us that the decision had nothing to do with climbing a career ladder or getting a better ministry opportunity. It was a decision being worked out in supernatural realms. We said yes to Westgate out of obedience to the Lord, and in response to a sense of his presence in our lives during our visit there. We said yes to Westgate because we believe in a living and active God who still draws near to his people, still wakes us up to pray in the middle of the night, and still speaks.

Maybe you've had similar experiences where you've sensed that God was at work in direct and supernatural ways. These encounters are not supposed to be uncommon for Christians today. If fact, we are to *expect* them. But first we must overcome a mind-set that says the only way to know God is to know things *about* him intellectually. We've been convinced that we should not even expect to experience God in supernatural ways. That's not biblical—as we'll discover shortly—but it's a common perspective in the church today.

We were created in God's likeness and image so that we would have the ability to know him and experience his presence intimately. It is the promised blessing of every believer to have a close, growing relationship with God. God is not static, and neither is our relationship with him. He is living, acting, and speaking today.

That's marvelous news! The capacity that God has given us to experience him puts every one of us squarely in the middle of the story that God is still writing today. No, he's not adding chapters to the Bible—that's not what I mean. By *story*, I mean he's still actively working in the hearts and lives of people today to make himself known to us and to those around us. You and I are part of God's ongoing story, which will continue into eternity. As humans, we were created with the capacity to experience God's presence and to live out an adventure of hearing him, experiencing him, responding to him, and following him every day.

Let's take a closer look at this remarkable fact.

The Westgate Swings Wide

The Bible is always God's primary means of communication with us. I will continue to emphasize this point because I want us never to forget it. At the same time, why didn't God use his written Word to reveal to Rita and me his will about the decision to move to Westgate?

Well, he did—at least, in part. As Rita and I read the Bible and prayed and fasted about the decision, God revealed many scriptural truths to our hearts—concerning the priority of God's Kingdom in our lives (rather than our own goals), concerning God's faithfulness to complete the work he had begun in us, concerning our complete dependence on him for guidance, and concerning our need for him to monitor and shape our motives in the whole process. Yet even if we had read the Bible from cover to cover, we never would have found a specific verse that said, "Alec and Rita Rowlands, move to Edmonds, Washington—thus saith the Lord."

From Scripture, we gained insight into God's purpose, plans, and priorities, and God used these insights to test our hearts and our willingness to submit our plans and desires to him. But that didn't lead us to a definite decision about making the move. So God provided supernatural supplemental guidance that came to us in the form of Meredith Fulmer's middle-of-the-night encounter with God. Why?

I think it's because Rita and I were fainthearted, even fearful of the outcome of a bad decision.

Oh sure, we had confidence in the Lord, but God knew that when the going got tough in Edmonds (and the going *always* gets tough at some point in every calling), it would be incredibly helpful for us to be able to look back on a supernatural encounter with him that helped confirm that he wanted us there in the first place.

And that's precisely what happened. When the battle eventually became so intense at the new church that I wanted to run away, Rita and I had an additional degree of certainty that God had called us there from the beginning.

It came to a head in 1997—the hardest year of my life. It started with someone driving a truck through the front doors of the church in the early hours of a Sunday morning, vandalizing the lobby, and leaving broken glass and furnishings to be cleaned up before services. Then, within weeks, the custodians put out an attempted arsonist's fire that was started in the sound booth just before they left the building late one Saturday night. A few months later, our landscaper was stabbed to death while mowing the church lawn. Then, if you can believe it, bomb threats canceled services in late summer. Then we had a painful and divisive staff departure. Finally, in the early hours of time-change Sunday, I received a call from someone who lived close to the church, informing me that the entire church building was on fire, and there were four fire trucks in the parking lot, fighting to keep the church from being totally destroyed.

I remember standing in the parking lot that morning, looking at more than half of our campus in charred ruins. I was cold, afraid, tired, and deeply discouraged. We spent the next few weeks finding temporary facilities for the church's various ministries, using a nearby school auditorium for Sunday services, and trying to reassure a shaken congregation that we would make it through. But deep down in my soul, the year had taken its toll. I was convinced I was finished in pastoral ministry. If not for my concern to try to hold together our frightened congregation, I would have resigned right then and there. I would have been happy doing just about anything else, as long as it was as far removed from pastoral ministry as possible.

What I really needed to know at that moment was that God still wanted us at Westgate Chapel, difficulties and all. And that's when he brought to mind Meredith Fulmer's prophetic prayer and confirmed in my heart that he was the one who had moved us to Edmonds in the first place. Rita and I were able to draw courage not only from verses of Scripture that God gave us throughout the ordeal but also from what Meredith Fulmer had said that December night at our front door. We didn't equate Meredith's word to us on the same level as Scripture—no. But her words were nevertheless confirming. The experience was far too uncanny to have been merely a coincidence, and it was a further indication that, yes, this church in Edmonds was exactly where God wanted us—despite everything that had happened.

Now let me ask you a question: How does this story sit with your heart? Maybe you've had a similar experience and are already in agreement with this line of teaching. Maybe you have no problem drawing near to God because you're already convinced that he wants to be intimately and actively involved in your life.

On the other hand, it wouldn't surprise me if Meredith Fulmer's experience with God makes you squirm a little bit. Maybe the story seems a bit weird or far-fetched. If that's what's going through your mind, I understand. There are days when my heart wrestles with it too. I'm naturally skeptical. I'm often satisfied with keeping my relationship with God at an intellectual level. Even though I'm a pastor of a nontraditional church, there are times when I'm uncomfortable with anything that appears "out of the ordinary" spiritually.

But that's precisely why I wrote this book.

You see, supernatural encounters with God aren't as out of the ordinary as we might think. Nor should they be. In fact, we should find the tangible experience of God's presence to be quite normal and natural—even *joyful*.

The Westminster Shorter Catechism says, "Man's chief end is to glorify God, and to enjoy him forever." Think about that wording a minute. What does it mean to *enjoy God*?

The most straightforward answer is that we were designed to take as much pleasure in God as is humanly possible. That's what the word *enjoy* means. But for many Christians, *pleasure* and *joy* are not words they would typically associate with their Christian faith. Their sense of "glorifying God" is something solemn, sedate, and reverent. And while I would agree that we must always approach God with proper reverence, that doesn't rule out joy and pleasure. In fact, joy is part of the *fruit*—the very evidence—of the Holy Spirit's indwelling and activity in our lives.[2] Joy originates from God. The apostle Paul says that "the kingdom of God is . . . a matter of . . . righteousness and peace and joy in the Holy Spirit."[3] So if God is the *source* of all joy, and we were created to be in God's presence, should we not *experience* his joy in the process? That's our chief aim. It's what we were created for. It's why we exist.

Unfortunately, there's a tension between the Westminster Shorter Catechism and what we're often taught about God's transcendence—namely, that he is so completely "other" and we are too far removed from him to even consider having a personal experience of his presence. Or we're taught that as sinful, fallen human beings, we're so depraved that we can't expect to have any direct contact with a holy God. Even a desire to draw near or to approach him is viewed as presumptuous. Or we're taught that we draw near to God by learning propositional truths about him found in Scripture and applying those truths to our lives; but any encounter outside the pages of Scripture is seen as too subjective and therefore suspect.

Add it all up, and it's easy to stay trapped in a skeptical mindset about having an actual firsthand encounter with the presence of God. Surely Meredith Fulmer's experience is uncommon at best; we shouldn't expect to hear God's voice or experience his presence very often, if at all. Such encounters are something reserved for ancient mystics.

Or are they?

Strangers in the Night

A young couple who had just finished seminary training on the East Coast were heading back across North America to Vancouver, British Columbia, where the husband had grown up. They were driving an old truck and pulling the rickety old travel trailer they had lived in for the past several years as they both worked and studied. They felt a general call from the Lord to be involved somehow in ministry in Vancouver, but other than a vague sense of direction and purpose, they didn't know what type of church, organization, or ministry they should pursue.

After all their years of schooling, they were dirt poor, and without a job or secure income waiting for them at the end of the road, they were worried about the future. As the trip progressed, the tension increased. They knew they would need to find jobs quickly. Surely the Lord would guide them as they continued to pray for his direction. But day after day as they drove across the country, no answers came.

One night, their anxiousness was running at an all-time high. Exhausted after a long day on the road, they parked their trailer and both quickly fell asleep.

In the middle of the night, the husband awakened with a strange and beautiful song running through his mind. He was fully conscious, not dreaming, and he had never heard the song before. Never on the radio. Never in church. The melody and words fit together perfectly, and the words of the song offered an answer to the couple's circumstances. Not a specific answer, but it was a worship song of reassurance, hope, and encouragement. The Lord would provide. God would meet their need. They didn't need to worry.

After grabbing some paper and writing down the words, the husband woke up his wife and told her about the song. He taught her the melody and the lyrics, and they sang together in worship to the Lord before falling back into a deep and peaceful sleep, the first restful night of their journey.

In the morning, they awakened refreshed and renewed. They spoke to each other about the song, but strangely neither one could recall a single word or a single thing about the melody. These were both musically minded people who regularly sang and played piano and guitar—and they both remembered singing the song the night before—but now it was simply gone. Confounding matters, they couldn't find the paper on which they'd written the lyrics.

They searched the entire trailer from top to bottom—the trailer wasn't very big in the first place—but the song had vanished without a trace. Before long, the couple called off their search. They realized that something supernatural had taken place, that the presence of God had visited them. They continued on their way, at peace, rejoicing and worshiping.

Okay, skeptics, let's go to work. From a theological perspective, what might have happened that night in the trailer? Did the husband eat some bad pizza before he went to sleep? Or did God truly show up and give this couple the gift of that miraculous song?

Why wouldn't we believe the more spectacular explanation? Why wouldn't we assume that our relationship with a supernatural God would include some supernatural communication?

The problem is our lack of *expectation*.

For so many in the church today, salvation has come to be viewed as a one-time event anchored in something Jesus accomplished on the cross two thousand years ago. Under the conviction of the Holy Spirit, we pray a prayer, or we walk forward at a meeting and kneel at the altar to receive this free gift of salvation, which we see as primarily about forgiveness. We mark our "salvation day" on the calendar, and now we have our ticket to heaven. From there, we set about working to "live the Christian life," which typically consists of going to church, reading the Bible, and trying to conform to some combination of dos and don'ts that will keep us in right standing with God. We give lip service to our "relationship with God" and "how much we love Jesus," but what we really mean is that we believe God is out there somewhere; we believe he sent Jesus to die for our sins; and someday (when our life on earth ends), we believe we'll see both of them in heaven and it will all make sense. Isn't that what it's all about?

Not quite!

Salvation is about far more than forgiveness in our lifetimes and heaven when we die. Salvation is primarily about *reconciliation* with God for the purpose of an *ongoing, intimate* relationship with him.[4] Yes, our salvation is rooted in Christ's past sacrifice for us, which we have received as a gift. But that gift is our entry point into *life*. Salvation, therefore, is not a static moment in time; it is something that happens to us *every day* as we participate in an active and immediate relationship with God.[5]

Think of it this way: How real and vital would your family relationships be if your only interactions came through reading a written family history and through one-way "conversations" spoken into the air?

That would be crazy, right?

The age-old dilemma in our Christian faith is how to have a meaningful relationship with someone we can't see or touch. That's where the element of faith comes in. And that's why we need to learn how to *listen*. God is eager to make himself known to us. But we have to draw close to him. When we do, we find he is present and involved in our lives every step of the way, waiting to speak, to guide, and to encourage. It's what he loves to do. But the mind-set we must continually challenge is that we don't expect God to show up tangibly, remarkably, or powerfully in our lives.

It Ain't Brain Surgery

Dr. Michael Haglund, a graduate of the University of Washington Medical Scientist Training Program, completed his neurosurgery residency training at Harborview Medical Center in Seattle, one of the leading trauma centers on the West Coast. His wife had visited Westgate Chapel and invited him to a Sunday service. He came to church reluctantly, with a significant amount of scientific skepticism toward anything spiritual. He was trained in one of most demanding of the medical sciences and tended to think about the world in very pragmatic, rational, and scientific ways. He'd been raised in a mainline church, but very nominally, so he had no background by which to have an expectation of God or to experience God's presence (or really, to know anything about God at all).

As it happened, on the first Sunday he visited, there was an incredible sense of God's presence in worship. At the end of the service, I made an altar call, and Dr. Haglund was one of the first ones down to the altar to pray to receive Jesus as his Savior. He later told me, "I sensed God's presence and knew in that instant that there was a God, and he was there in that service, and it humbled me and overwhelmed me." For the rest of his time in Seattle, he didn't miss a service or prayer meeting, sometimes changing out of his scrubs in the car before coming to church after surgery. He traded Saturday nights off for on-call duty so he could be in church on Sunday morning.

Because his initial encounter with the Lord was so dramatic, it affected how he viewed God and his Christian walk. His expectation was that dramatic encounters with God's presence should be normative and regular—and I agreed with him, even though it caused some complications in our relationship.

A few months into his newfound faith, he phoned me one Monday morning. He was irritated because we'd had a guest speaker the day before and I had shortened the worship time in the service. He explained how he had lost three patients on Saturday night and had to tell three separate families that their loved one would not survive the night. With a deep sigh, he told me that what got him through the traumatic night in the ER was his expectation that if he could just get to Sunday morning service, he would be able to have an extended time of worship and feel God's presence and peace.

I like that. I like the passion and expectancy of it. In fact, I wish all believers hungered for the presence of God the way this man does. But his story doesn't end there. He finished his training and was courted by Brigham and Women's Hospital, a teaching affiliate of Harvard Medical School. They flew him to Boston and offered him a great position on their staff. The offer looked fantastic, and conventional wisdom said he'd be a fool not to take it. But he told the university chairman he wanted to take an evening to pray about it.

Having missed his early-morning devotions that day due to the busy interview schedule, he turned to his devotional reading that evening. While reading Psalm 16, he was very excited when he got to verse 6: "The boundary lines have fallen for me in pleasant places."[6]

Just as he was thinking about how pleasant it would be to work for this most prestigious university and how perfectly this verse fit his heart's desire, he heard the Lord say, "But this is not it."

That couldn't have been God! he thought.

The institution and job offer meant everything in the eyes of the medical community. Dr. Haglund read Psalm 16 again, still in prayer, and when he got to verse 6, the Lord again said, "But this is not it."

Flabbergasted by this turn of events, he called the chairman of the department and declined the offer. He then flew back to Seattle, not understanding why he had just turned down his dream job, other than that he believed he had heard from the Lord.

Within days of returning to Seattle, Dr. Haglund received a different job offer, this one from another very prestigious school. It was an even better offer, with more lab resources and more staff. He and his wife prayed and felt peace about accepting this job offer, and so he did. Here is the amazing twist to the story: Within days of his accepting the second offer, he heard about a major shakeup in the department at Harvard, the job he had turned down. The person who would have hired him might not have been in charge when he arrived a year later. If he had taken the first job, he might have been involved in the reorganization, a potential career killer for a young faculty member.

Today he excels in his field and is respected by colleagues around the country. He's just been put in charge of his hospital's outreach to physicians and hospitals around the world and has recently built and equipped a new neurosurgical wing at a hospital in Uganda. He's doing amazing work helping people all over the world. God specifically led him to that place—I don't doubt it for a moment.

In the years I've spent in pastoral ministry, I've seen firsthand how this man's story is not that unusual. And why should we expect it to be? In Ephesians 1:17, Paul prays that God "may give you the Spirit of wisdom and of revelation in the knowledge of him." The word *knowledge* here is key. It's an experiential word, not divorced from head knowledge, but going far beyond that. The Greek word translated "knowledge" is closely tied to the Hebrew word for "knowing" that describes the deepest intimacy between a husband and wife. Paul is praying, therefore, that the Ephesian believers would have an enlarged capacity to know God, to experience him closely. God has given us the means to know him in far deeper and richer ways than we have been led to believe. The longer I'm married to Rita, the more I'm going to know her—through daily communication and regular engagement in our lives together. So *knowledge*, in the context of relationship, is not just an accumulation of facts; rather, it's directly tied to *intimacy*.

You have an incredible capacity to experience God. You were made this way—to be led by God and nurtured by him. If you haven't already begun, it's time to start *listening* and *expecting*.

SIGNS OF REVIVAL
A new love for one another results in restored relationships among believers.

CHAPTER 5

REMEMBERING THE WAY WE WERE

LET ME TELL you a love story.

It's a love story about two people who believe the best about each other, who are patient and kind and not easily angered with each other, and who are trusting, hoping, and persevering together until the end of their days.[1]

But it hasn't all been without a ripple.

Some years back, Rita and I needed to navigate an extremely busy season in our lives. She taught at a parochial school in San Diego, had developed their graded-choir program, and was heavily involved in the school's chapel services. I was a new associate pastor at a church downtown, responsible for administration and operations during a massive building program. Rita and I also taught an adult Sunday school class. Each day, from dawn until dusk, our individual lives were immersed in our respective ministries and careers. Evenings, Rita graded papers and I worked on planning projects for the church. We were both going flat out—in opposite directions. Though we were physically living in the same house, our schedules and preoc-cupations were preventing us from experiencing each other to the fullest degree possible—or really even much at all.

Have you ever been in a similar spot with someone you love?

You are committed to each other, but you're on different tracks. You don't spend enough time together to nurture the relationship and let it grow.

What do you think will inevitably happen in a relationship like that?

Love on the Rocks . . . And in the Woods

Rita and I quickly learned—the hard way—that an overly busy life-style like ours was unsustainable and not conducive to a healthy mar-riage. The only place we could afford a house at that time was in Encinitas, a thirty-minute commute from our jobs. We had only one car, so the only time we were together without any work between us was during our commute. Now, that might sound like a solid block of time to spend with each other, but I confess we often squandered the opportunity. Instead of developing our relationship, we listened to the radio, groused about the traffic (at least I did), or decompressed in silence from our day's duties.

One morning on the way to work, we started arguing about something. It was usually about finances, but this was no ordinary disagreement. I honestly don't remember the specifics, but what I do remember is that it felt like a matter of life and death at the time. We argued all the way to San Diego, with our communication eventually deteriorating to harsh jabs. I was so angry at Rita I could have kicked her out of the car by the time we arrived at the schoolyard, and she was equally disgusted with me. When I dropped her off, she slammed the car door and never looked back. I squealed the tires as I pulled out and drove past Balboa Park to my job at the church.

The senior pastor spotted me coming in the office door, and he could tell immediately that something was wrong. He called me into his study and pulled the whole ugly story out of me.

"There is nothing more important in your life right now than your relationship with your wife." His voice was deadly serious. "I don't want to see you for the next four days. A member of the church has a cabin up in the mountains. Call the principal of Rita's school and get a substitute teacher for Rita—right now, not tomorrow. You go pick her up from school, get alone with your wife, go for walks in the woods, and work this out. I don't want to see you until next Monday."

I am so thankful for that pastor's wisdom. We followed his advice to the letter. In fact, even as we started on the drive up to Idyllwild, we realized what had gone wrong. In all of our busyness, we had neglected *us*. We asked each other for forgiveness and broke down the barriers that had developed between us. We used that time away in the woods to reestablish and recommit to a regular pattern of connecting deeply with each other. It helped reset the path our marriage was taking, and we've had a solid and loving relationship ever since—occasionally needing to remind ourselves of the critical lessons learned in Encinitas.

Here's the heart of the matter: Unless we regularly invest time in our relationships with the people we love, there will be no depth or strength to navigate the hard times. Without time and energy invested in really being with each other, the relationship may exist on paper, but it will not be meaningful. In fact, unless we allow the passion and commitment of our first love to guide us, our love will eventually wither and die. Love does not thrive on its own. A relationship of love must be continually nurtured.

Love *must* be continually nurtured. There is a parallel between a marriage relationship and our Christian faith—our love for God must be continually nurtured as well. I believe one of the ways our love for God is nurtured is through time spent in his presence, just like Rita's and my love for each other was nurtured during our time in Idyllwild. If our love for God isn't cultivated, it will wither and die, just like any other relationship. We'll start to allow busy schedules and difficult circumstances to create distance between ourselves and God. We'll get angry with him, shouting at him because we believe he has let us down. We'll stop communicating with him or listening for his voice from the pages of his Word. Our relationship will grow distant and cold. We might be Christians in name, but our relationship with God will be missing a vital passion, fervor, warmth, and depth.

Besides neglect, another reason for distance from God is that we tend to become convinced that we are completely passive in our salvation—that there is nothing for us to work on. We pray a prayer or go forward at a meeting, receive God's gift of salvation, and feel excited about Jesus for a while. But then, as in the parable of the soils, the vitality of our faith gets choked out by the cares of life or withers in the sun on shallow, rocky ground.[2] Has anyone ever explained to you that the Christian life is a relationship that requires your participation?

Paul's words of encouragement to the Christians in Philippi hold the key for us: "Work hard to show the results of your salvation, obeying God with deep reverence and fear."[3]

To many of us, those words are like fingernails on a chalkboard. *Work? I thought the Christian life was a free gift!* So we hurriedly skip over to the next verse with a sigh of relief: "For God is working in you, giving you the desire and the power to do what pleases him."[4]

Did you catch the paradox in those two verses? Yes, it is God who works in us. And he works *first*. It's called *grace*! We are utterly dependent on him to draw us to himself and save us.[5] So God does the real work of drawing us and dispensing his grace and saving us for all eternity. It's all true!

Then what is this work that Paul says we are to do? It is the work of participating with God in a growing, increasingly intimate relationship with him. We are not passive spectators in our relationship with God. It is not a one-sided friendship, and we are not just along for the ride. Just like the effort it took for me to get Rita out of town for a few days of intentional communication and intimacy, so the work of our salvation is drawing near to God in faith, assured that he will draw near to us.[6] The good news from Philippians 2:13 is that God goes before us and is continually working in us to draw us and empower us for our relationship with him.

I think Paul intentionally starts with the imperative command for us to *work out our salvation* just to get our attention and to let us know that there is something for us to do. Yes, God is the *initiator* of this love relationship, but this love requires our grace-fueled *response* and our *effort* to help fan the flame into a living passion within us.

We must continually *respond* to God's love in order to develop an even deeper level of intimacy with him. It may involve coming into his presence through regular times of worship. It may include humbling ourselves to serve others and watching God work out his love in their lives. Overall, it means embracing faith practices such as the ones we'll discuss in a later chapter. The spiritual activity involved in drawing near to God is never for the sake of the activity alone. It is always God-initiated as he draws us toward himself.

Have You Lost That Lovin' Feeling?

With my interest and background in studying historic revivals, I am frequently asked why the word *revival* never appears in the New Testament. Some wonder whether it is even a biblical concept for our faith today. Maybe we shouldn't be seeking or praying for revival in our lives or in our faith communities.

In response to this criticism, I point out that most of the New Testament was written between AD 45 and AD 70 and it mostly addresses first-generation believers. These were people who, for the most part, either knew Jesus personally because they had interacted with him while he was on earth or were being instructed and led in their faith by people who knew Jesus personally.[7] These were all first-generation believers, and they hadn't had much of a chance to have their love for God grow cold. It was all too new and fresh.

It's not until we get to the apostle John's epistles or the book of

Revelation that we find books written primarily to second-generation believers. Although the dating of these books is debated, most scholars agree that Revelation was written several decades after the rest of the New Testament, around AD 95, when John was an elderly man. It's no surprise, then, that when Jesus writes a letter through John in Revelation 2 to the church in Ephesus, he addresses the lack of intensity of their passion and love for God. In fact, he says they have left or abandoned their first love.[8]

There is a striking parallel between the condition of the church in Ephesus and Christianity in North America today. Jesus begins the letter by saying, "I know your works [and] your toil."[9] Just look at the average North American church bulletin today. Nobody is working harder. It wasn't very long ago that church-growth experts coined the phrase "the seven-day-a-week church" as a desired goal. We have a profusion of church ministries, strategies, methodologies, workbooks, goals, vision statements, marketing plans, programs, and more. When it comes to sheer activity, today's church is as busy as it gets.

Jesus commends the believers in Ephesus for their resilience against the onslaught of evil, for their careful testing of false teachers, and for their patient endurance in doing the work of the Lord.[10] The same can be said for North American churches today. We've certainly tested our share of false teachers and called out heresies in books and on radio broadcasts, and we are hunkered down, enduring in our faith while we wait for the Lord's return.

But then Jesus changes his tone and begins to rebuke the Ephesian church. "But I have this against you," he says, "that you have left your first love."[11] The Greek verb for *left* (sometimes translated *forsaken*) connotes a letting go, abandoning, or a sending away. The Ephesians had abandoned their passion for God. Despite their orthodox *beliefs* and tireless *activity*, their hearts had grown cold. The situation in Ephesus is a snapshot of many, many churches in North America today. We are so busy with everything else that we don't even realize that time, neglect, and indifference have taken their toll. The love for God we once enjoyed is gone. We didn't intend to lose it, but the passion we once had for the Lord has grown cold.

So is the word *revival* found in the New Testament?

No.

But did the Christians in Ephesus need revival?

Yes—according to Jesus.

Is there any doubt that we need revival in our day and age?

That's why, when people ask me if we should even be talking about revival today, I point to Revelation 2. The word *revival* may not appear in the New Testament, but the concept is deeply rooted in Jesus' letter to Ephesus.

Look at the church you attend today—or better yet, look at your own life—and ask: What will motivate me to actively share with others the story of my relationship with Jesus? What will make me want to pray? What will motivate me to dig into the Bible and truly study the Word of God with an eye toward having my life changed? What will infuse my worship with a deep and authentic hunger for God's presence? The only answer is a restored (revived) love for God.

This is serious business. Having a deep and fervent love for God is not *optional* for Christians. Jesus told the Ephesian Christians that he would personally remove their lampstand from its place unless they repented.[12] A lampstand is a source of light. The light is the gospel of Jesus—that which shines through us and sets us "above reproach in the midst of a crooked and perverse generation."[13]

What a strong warning for us today! Unless our love for God is fervent, we have nothing to say (or do) that will have any saving effect in our world. Without love for God, there is no real worship, no real fellowship, no real service, no real study of God's Word, no real life transformation, no community or global impact. Our faith, without love, is *powerless*. We may be Christians in name, we may even be saved; but we are missing out on the richness of God, on a life-transforming *communion* with God.

What's the solution? Jesus was very clear about it to the Ephesians: "Remember . . . from where you have fallen; repent, and do the works you did at first."[14] If your love for God is not in evidence, your first task is to *turn back*, to *remember*, to *reimagine* what life was like when you first encountered the passionate love of God. Think for a moment about your early experience as a Christian. *First love* is often characterized by an uncommon hunger for God. New believers devour the Word, reading it at every opportunity. They can't get enough of worship. They love being with God's people. They're at church every time the doors open. And when it comes to telling others about Jesus, they can't stop talking about him. They tell everyone who will listen what has happened to them, and they tell all their friends the reason for the sudden change in their lives.

If you received the Lord as a young child, this might be harder for you to remember; but don't let that stop you. Remember what it was like to "receive the kingdom of God like a child,"[15] reconnect with past times of sustained passion and devotion for God, and then turn back to your first love and ask God to rekindle your love for him in your heart. *Remember . . . repent . . . return.* That is the pathway to passionate revival in your heart and your life.

I'm not suggesting that the goal is to live our lives on a spiritual mountaintop; that is not sustainable. But by remembering, repenting, and returning, we position ourselves for ongoing *refreshment* and *renewal* in our relationship with God.

Try to Remember

Let me take you back in time to the beginning of my love story.

After I graduated from high school in South Africa, where I grew up, I had an opportunity to come to the United States to attend a college in Tennessee. I spent two years there before I discovered that the college was unaccredited (it has long since remedied this situation), which meant that if I continued with my degree, it would be worthless back in South Africa, where I intended to return. I didn't know what to do. I was convinced that I had just wasted two years of my life. The only thing I could think to do was get a job for the summer to earn enough money to fly home and figure out a new direction for my life.

A college friend from Dayton, Ohio, invited me home with him for the summer, and we quickly landed jobs in a church in Middletown, Ohio, as interns on the pastoral staff. I was scheduled to preach the first Sunday evening service after we arrived. All the ministers sat on the platform in those days. As we took our seats, I looked out across the congregation of some three hundred people. To my surprise (and embarrassment), my eyes met those of a young lady seated in the pews with her family. It's hard to explain, but there was an immediate connection between us across the crowded sanctuary. Maybe even *electricity*. It wasn't like I was sitting there checking out girls. In fact, my father had taught me that a young, single man involved in church ministry was never to get romantically involved with a parishioner. The relationship would inevitably become too complicated.

After the service, a mutual friend introduced me to the young lady and her family. I could tell from our brief conversation that she was intelligent and gracious, in addition to being beautiful. I was smitten. She seemed to take a genuine interest in who I was and what I was doing at the church for the summer. There was only one problem—a *big* problem—which became evident when I was introduced to the young man seated next to her. Her fiancé!

I took note, but for some reason was not deterred.

A week later, her grandmother invited me over to their home for dinner with the family. They did this with all the church staff, she explained. The young woman and I got more of a chance to chat then, and my attraction to her only grew. She was a vocalist and had just completed a year touring with The Spurrlows, a traveling Christian music group. The fiancé was a trumpet player in the same group. He was heading back home to Detroit to work for his father, and the young lady was going to work locally at a Christian youth camp for the rest of the summer.

Again, I took note.

Weeks passed. With every Sunday and Wednesday night service, the young lady and I talked more, but always in the safety of a large group. I tried to keep a respectable distance, but when her fiancé left town, I knew I needed to act fast. After service one Sunday evening about a month later, I summoned the courage to ask her if she would like to get something to eat and play miniature golf with me. Much to my surprise—and delight—she accepted.

The evening went well, so I started calling more frequently and finding excuses to stop by the house. After she went to work at the camp, her brother and I put together a Smothers Brothers routine to perform at the camp skit night. I started calling her during her off hours. I sent a bouquet of flowers. And then another. And another. I wrote poems and attached them to the flowers. Days turned into weeks, and soon the summer was nearly gone. All I could think about was her looming wedding and my approaching departure for South Africa. Frankly, I had a hard time believing she could be interested in me. She was so beautiful. So talented. So gifted academically. She'd even won a full-ride scholarship to university. But I was madly in love.

Toward the end of August, she came back to the church for a weekend. After the morning service, she and I went out to eat. There hadn't been any physical contact between us at all—not even hand-holding. The lunch went well, and after I took her home, as we stood out under a big oak tree in front of her family home, I summoned the courage to look into her beautiful blue eyes and say, "I think I'm falling in love with you."

She pulled away from me and said, "Oh, I'm not ready to say anything like that at all."

Rebuffed!

What a fool I'd been to show my hand like that! I got into my car and drove away. I was so angry with myself that I actually pulled off the road, jumped out of the car, and kicked myself for being so stupid. She went back to camp the next morning, and I went back to another dozen red roses. Another poem. Another phone call . . .

Given her reaction to me under the oak tree, I was surprised that these overtures were not similarly rebuffed. Some nights we would talk on the phone for two hours. We talked about nothing and everything, and I didn't wonder anymore if she was the one. I knew it! If love was a tall cliff, I'd fallen over the edge with nothing to break my fall.

Unknown to me, toward the end of the summer, her fiancé visited the camp. His friends at the camp had informed him of my visits, flowers, and poems, and he had come to confront her. She told him that she was indeed having second thoughts about their relationship, and yes, there was someone else in her life.

That would be me! And that wasn't what the fiancé wanted to hear!

Once he was officially out of the way, the young woman and I became more and more involved emotionally. I canceled my flight back to South Africa and went through the painful task of calling my parents to give them the news that I wasn't coming back. I applied to the university she was attending and was accepted on academic probation, since none of my credits initially transferred. I secured a permanent job at her uncle's church and was given a little place to stay in back of the church.

By the end of that summer, we were officially boyfriend and girlfriend. I sold whatever I could for cash and sent the money to South Africa, where my parents bought a flawless half-carat diamond ring for me to give to her.

Rita and I were engaged in December 1968 and married the following summer.

Why do I tell that story? To *remember* it—in the fullest sense of the word. To even *relive* it a little bit. Jesus tells the church at Ephesus that the way to regain their first love for him is to remember the height of love from which they have fallen. The Greek word that John uses for "remember," in Revelation 2:5, is in a present active tense, which implies a continuous action. So according to Jesus, the first step in returning to our first love is to "remember and *keep* remembering" what it was like when we first fell in love with him. It's an *ongoing* love, not something we do just once. The verb is also an imperative, containing all the force of a command: *You must make yourself continually remember your first love.*

"Continually remembering our first love" is clearly what was missing on that horrible day, years later, when Rita and I argued so intensely in the car on our way to work. It is what our pastor, in his wisdom, knew we needed most when he sent us out of town for a few days. We needed to remember the height from which we'd fallen. When I first met Rita during the summer of 1968, I was head over heels in love with her. I pursued her with everything I had. I needed to remember those dizzying heights!

The same is true of our love relationship with God.

Love Means *Always* Having to Say You're Sorry

If your faith has become lifeless, Jesus calls you to repent of your neglect and passivity, and to remember your first love. In fact, if your salvation experience lacks a degree of passion or a significant measure of transformation in your life, you may even need to examine the authenticity of your initial salvation experience. As Paul told the church in Corinth, "Examine yourselves to see if your faith is genuine. Test yourselves. Surely you know that Jesus Christ is among you; if not, you have failed the test of genuine faith."[16] If you don't love God deeply and you can't remember ever loving him deeply, then you might not be a true Christian. You might be only going through the motions—a Christian in name only, not in actions or in truth.

Jesus calls all passive hearts to change direction—that is, to *repent* and *return*.

Repentance begins with the work of the Holy Spirit, who brings conviction to our hearts. Our part in repentance is to agree with what the Word of God says about our condition and to turn away from those things that got us into this predicament in the first place. Repentance includes a godly sorrow for our present, passionless condition and for the neglect of our relationship with the Lord. But repentance is not simply turning *away* from bad things. It also means turning *toward*—or returning to—those things that are good, the things we did when we first fell in love with the Lord.

It's interesting that Jesus doesn't tell us to go back to the *feelings* we had. He calls us back to the *deeds*. Why? Because feelings *follow* actions. So even if you're not "feelin' the love," you can begin, by faith, to do the things you did back when you were first in love—and the feelings will follow. When I was so angry with Rita in the car that day, I didn't *feel* in love with her. But I took steps in that direction. We took a trip and made our relationship a priority. We spent time away alone, just the two of us. We talked. We asked each other's forgiveness. When we *did* what we needed to *do*, sure enough, the feelings were (and are) still there!

Experiencing the presence of God is not optional in the Christian life; it's not something reserved for the spiritual elite or for mystics on the mountaintop. It is, and should be, an ongoing reality for all believers because it's only in God's presence that our love for him is revived and nurtured. Detached, coldhearted passivity is our enemy. That's why, if we have lost the passion and fervor and zeal and enthusiasm of our first love, we must seek to restore it.

The Bible says that God *is* love.[17] Love is the preeminent and predominant activity and atmosphere of God's existence and the relationship between Father, Son, and Holy Spirit. How could we possibly live detached from intimacy with him? Passivity is not an option in the Christian life. To be a Christian, we must be dedicated to loving God.

What that means for us is that the Christian life is never just an intellectual agreement with a set of propositional truths. Becoming a Christian is much more organic than that. It's a change of address from the hopeless isolation of living unto ourselves. It's a new home, where we live in the marvelous fellowship of being "in Christ." We are joined supernaturally to him and thereby to each other as the body of Christ.

After we become a Christian, we're still ourselves, but we are more truly ourselves because Christ lives in us. It's not that we become Christ—no, there's a separation there. But we are *in* Christ, and Christ is *in* us. Author Stephen Seamands offers an important clarification:

> Paul is not saying he has lost his personal identity. Though Christ lives in Paul, there is still a life that Paul lives. He is still Paul, and more truly Paul when Christ lives in him. . . .
>
> Sadhu Sundar Singh of India often used the example of the iron a blacksmith places in a red-hot coal fire. Soon the iron turns red and begins to glow like the coals, so you can truly say that the iron is in the fire and the fire is in the iron. Yet we know that the iron is not the fire and the fire is not the iron. When the iron is glowing, the blacksmith can bend it into any shape he desires, but it still remains iron.[18]

He Keeps the Light On for You

Christianity is a *heart* religion. It is lived as a heart response to the experience of God's love for us. The apostle John captures this relationship when he writes, "We love because he first loved us."[19] Love, by its very nature, is *relational*. And thus God's presence is essentially relational.

> A relationship necessarily involves the *presence* of an other who has a distinctive *identity*. . . . [But] the presence of an other is not sufficient in itself for there to be a relationship, for the other must be perceived, sensed, or experienced as present. Our lack of perception cannot alter the presence of an other, but it can prevent a mutual relationship between us and the other.[20]

We need an "other" for any meaningful relationship. Otherwise our Christian lives devolve into lifeless rules and routine activities. Moses encountered God on Mount Sinai and came away from the meeting with his face shining like the sun. This same radiance is promised to us today (though perhaps not literally) in greater measure than that which Moses experienced, as the result of our being in the presence of God. Does *radiant* describe your Christian life? The Holy Spirit is resident in every believer, and one of the Spirit's activities in our lives is to transform us with ever-increasing glory, always drawing us into greater intimacy with God, as Paul explains in 2 Corinthians 3:16-18:

> But when one turns to the Lord, the veil is removed. Now the Lord is the Spirit, and where the Spirit of the Lord is, there is freedom. And we all, with unveiled face, beholding the glory of the Lord, are being transformed into the same image from one degree of glory to another. For this comes from the Lord who is the Spirit.

These verses describe anything but lifeless formality.

When I interviewed people in the Outer Hebrides who had come to Christ in the 1949 revival, they all told a similar story of life on the islands before the awakening. Though the people were strong Calvinists, diligent in their doctrine and very defensive of Reformed theology, there was a general apathy toward the preaching of the Word. Though every child on the island was properly catechized and they knew the Scriptures inside out, no young people attended any of the churches, and their faith, by and large, meant nothing to them. Everyone was indifferent to spiritual things except for a very small remnant who committed themselves to praying for the spiritual temperature of the island.

When I asked Mary Peckham what had made the difference, she pointed from her head to her heart and said, "We had all that Scripture up here, but the Holy Spirit took the truth and transferred it to here."

At the first Communion after the revival, she said, everything in her heart was completely different. "When the cup was passed to me, I could barely hold on to it. I'm surprised I didn't drop it, I was trembling so deeply."

That, my friends, is the immediacy and impact of experiencing God's presence. That's *remembering* and *returning* to our first love. That's what happens when our hearts and our heads are *both* engaged in this marvelous mystery called the Christian life.

SIGNS OF REVIVAL
All revived believers exercise their ministry gifts inside and outside of the church.

CHAPTER 6

CAN YOU HEAR ME NOW?

ONE FATEFUL AFTERNOON when I was fifteen, I came home from school, put my bicycle in the garage, and headed into the house. I spotted my mom in the kitchen, and as I passed by I casually announced to her that I had been invited to a birthday party at Leonard's, a friend from school, and I would be going to the party later that afternoon.

My mother, however, saw things differently. She informed me that she and Dad did not know Leonard's family, and therefore I would *not* be going to the party. Subject closed.

I was six feet tall and starting to feel my oats as a teenager, so I answered back to my mother that I was old enough now to make these decisions on my own, and I *was* going to Leonard's party, thank you very much. To drive home my point, I walked upstairs to my bedroom and slammed the door behind me as an exclamation point to our conversation.

No one intentionally slammed doors in our household, so I wondered what might come next. But I felt pretty smug about my burst of independence. I knew my father wasn't home at that time of day. His church, Elim Tabernacle, had about seven hundred congregants in those days, and there were no associate pastors. Dad had a very strong commitment to the principle that you couldn't pastor people unless you were engaged in their lives and in their homes, so every afternoon until dinnertime he was out on visitation. I was surely on safe ground with my outburst.

A few moments later, I heard footsteps coming down the hallway. They sounded too heavy to be my mother's, and horror instantly filled my heart. Then the bedroom door opened and my dad walked in. He summarily informed me in no uncertain terms that he didn't care if I was fifteen or fifty-five, I was never to speak to my mother like that again. And though this may not sound politically correct in our day, he proceeded to give me the first spanking I'd had in a very long while—and as it turned out, the last spanking I ever received from him. Next, he informed me that I was to proceed downstairs immediately and offer appropriate apologies to my mother. Which I did.

For some people, unfortunately, this story illustrates their only view of God—that he's the "man upstairs" whose primary role is to discipline us when we're bad. I've even seen bumper stickers to that effect. Many people live their entire lives with the idea that God is so powerful and holy that he has removed himself from our day-to-day activities. They are convinced that God becomes involved with us only when huge world events are at stake, or to put us in our place.

In this chapter, I want to refute this erroneous perception of God as a distant, disengaged disciplinarian. God is not removed from our lives—he's very close and involved. Still, when we hear his footsteps in the hall, it should generate a healthy and appropriate fear in our hearts.

I realize that associating the word *fear* with God is cause for alarm among certain segments of the Christian community. In our generation, *fear* has mostly negative connotations, along the lines of abject *terror*. But the Bible uses the word *fear* to describe an appropriate response to God's holiness that is more akin to reverence, awe, and loving respect. We have far too little of this in our churches these days, and we would be wise to change course.

Discovering My Father in My Dad

Fast-forward to when I was forty-four years old and the senior pastor of Westgate Chapel in Edmonds. We were in the middle of hosting a conference on revival for several hundred pastors from around the country when I received a phone call from South Africa. My father had just been diagnosed with terminal esophageal cancer at the age of eighty, and had only a few months left to live. Having not seen him for several years, I made arrangements to fly home immediately.

My brother picked me up at the airport outside Johannesburg and drove me to my parents' house. Dad had been sick for some time, but he hadn't told anyone about it. He was in denial about his deteriorating health and had initially refused to see the doctor. By the time I arrived, he was very frail, already down to a hundred pounds.

When I walked in the back door and put down my suitcases, Dad heard my arrival. Tying his bathrobe around him, he shuffled out of his bedroom, wrapped his thin arms around me, and said, "Oh Son, I'm so glad you're here! The devil told me I was going to die without getting to see you again." He kissed me on the cheek, just as he had done all the years I was growing up. Even when I was in high school, if he dropped me off before school, he'd lean over and kiss me on the cheek. It embarrassed me then as a teenager. As an adult, it only warmed my heart.

Over the next three weeks, we spent every moment together as his strength would allow. In the mornings, we sat in the front room after breakfast and talked about revival and the need for God's presence in the church. In the evenings, I'd read to him from Scripture and from Charles Finney's memoirs. Then we'd pray together. That trip was the last time I saw my father alive.

Love and warmth truly characterized my father at his core. One of my earliest memories of him was when he taught me to fish. I was maybe five or six years old. At the time, he was the minister of a Baptist church in Port Shepstone, South Africa, and living on such a meager salary that he fished to put food on the table, not just for sport. Fortunately, the fish were plentiful in those days. We had a favorite spot on the South Coast called Splash Rock, where an outcrop of rocks lay at the mouth of a large cove. It was named Splash Rock because every twenty minutes or so, a rogue wave from the Indian Ocean would hit the rock with such force that it could easily knock over a small child. Dad would tie a piece of rope around his belt with the other end around my belt to keep me from being washed off the rock while we fished. We used to catch two- to three-pound ocean shad from Splash Rock, some days up to twenty at a time.

Fond memories characterize my growing-up years. My father and I were always close. He had a study off the porch of our home with a threadbare Persian carpet on the painted concrete floor. While he did his sermon preparation, I'd sneak into the study just to be near him. His library included atlases, handbooks, and books of biblical archaeology with wonderful pictures. I wasn't allowed to interrupt him, but I was allowed to thumb through his books for hours while sitting on the floor. I just liked being close to him while he studied.

These stories about my father—showing both distance and closeness—are not self-canceling or contradictory. That was who he was. We had a very loving family, and he and I enjoyed a loving father-son relationship. At the same time, my father required absolute respect, quick obedience, and appropriate deference.

I learned a lot about my relationship with God through the lens of my relationship with my dad. If our view of God is that he is completely inaccessible, our approach to him will risk being distant, overly formal, and dry. If our view of God is that he is no different from our buddy next door, our approach to him will risk being flippant, casual, and eventually irrelevant to our lives. There is a healthy tension that we cannot, and must not, avoid in our pursuit of God's presence.

Fire and Love

Consider passages of Scripture that describe God's transcendence. When Paul challenged young Timothy to live a holy life without spot or blame, he reminded Timothy that he served a God who "dwells in unapproachable light."[1] It is not unlike the time when Moses encountered God in the burning bush, and God told him not to come any closer and to take off his shoes.[2]

I love the phrase "unapproachable light." Think of what that must mean. Why would light be unapproachable? Is it too bright? Too glorious? Too blinding? Too radiant? Too white hot? In Leviticus 10:1-2, Aaron's sons Nadab and Abihu approach God with an arrogant disregard for his holiness, and it costs them their lives. In Acts 5:1-11, Ananias and Sapphira make a similar mistake, disregarding God's holiness by lying to him and holding back on what they had pledged—and it costs them their lives. In both the Old and New Testaments, the message is clear about God's presence: *Approach with great care.*

As we consider what it means to enter into and live in the presence of God, there will always be a point of tension in our understanding of God's nature. For instance, even though God "dwells in unapproachable light," he is also described as *love*.[3] Love is *relational*, and in God's infinite mercy and by his grace, he has chosen to include us in an intimate love relationship with him, that he provided at great cost to himself through his Son. So "unapproachable light" does not mean that God is distant, unfriendly, or aloof. It means there is a majesty, a holiness, a magnificence about him that must be recognized if we are going to draw near to him. He cannot, and should not, be approached casually or flippantly. After all, both the Old and New Testaments describe him as a *consuming fire*.[4]

As Christians, we are embedded in Christ and in the love that characterizes the Father, Son, and Holy Spirit. Because we are *in* Christ, the offense of sin that kept us from approaching God's presence has been removed. By Christ's blood we are made completely acceptable in God's sight. We are encouraged to approach him with confidence. The blood of Jesus gives us access into the most holy place of God's presence, formerly reserved exclusively for the high priest (and even then only once a year). Now, in Christ, we have continual access.[5] God's presence is the essence and expression of a love relationship in which God invites us all to draw near. At the same time, the closer we draw to God, the closer we come to his all-consuming holiness. And that's when things can get a little hot for us if our lives are filled with combustible "chaff."[6]

All-encompassing love and *unapproachable light*.

Complete acceptance and *all-consuming fire*.

God is both transcendent and immanent at the same time. It's not an either-or situation; it's both-and.

These paradoxes can be difficult for us to navigate. We prefer to live in neatly bordered boxes of meaning. We struggle with the tension between what seem to be opposite truths, and problems occur if the pendulum ever swings too far toward either extreme in how we understand and approach God.

You'll sometimes hear people talk about "the God of the Old Testament" versus "the God of the New Testament," but there is no difference between the two. God is one, and he remains the same yesterday, today, and forever.[7] The main difference between the two Testaments is that now, through the sacrificial death and triumphant resurrection of Jesus Christ, everyone is invited and welcomed into God's holy presence. This is what God's love does for us; it allows us to live our lives in his presence and to know him, not just at an intellectual level but also in our hearts. To say, as John Wesley did, that Christianity is a "heart religion"[8] is not to base our faith on feelings or physical effects, though these sometimes accompany a heart warmed by God's presence. But the intimate experience of God's presence is the fountainhead from which his life and mission overflow in us and through us on a daily basis.

After the revival that took hold in my father's church in the early 1960s, an overwhelming sense of God's presence continued in the life of the church for years. Wednesday prayer meetings were as well attended as Sunday services, and young and old alike would pack out the building.

On Wednesdays, we would sing hymns and worship choruses for about twenty minutes, Dad might bring a ten-minute devotional, and then he'd invite as many as possible to come to the altar area for prayer. He always insisted that our intercession be verbal and out loud. If we were going to sit and pray silently, he said, we could do that at home. We'd spend the next forty minutes or so praying. Sometimes individuals would lead out in prayer and others would punctuate with their amens. Just as often, Dad would provide a focal point for the evening and the several hundred people present would pray aloud at a conversational level, all at the same time. Frequently, an unusual sense of awe would move over a prayer meeting, and spontaneous and exuberant worship and prayer would result. Nothing "weird" would happen, but we would experience an energy in our intercession and worship that couldn't be explained by natural means.

On one of those nights, when I was about twelve years old, an unusual sense of God's presence covered the people gathered at the meeting. I remember being so moved by the presence of God that I felt compelled to pray out loud, just like the adults were doing. I felt fearful and exhilarated at the same time. I remember at one point having to stop midsentence in my prayer because I was so moved by the love of God.

After the prayer meeting concluded and the people went home, Dad locked up his office and our family headed out to our car in the parking lot. I remember chattering with Dad about what had happened to me that night. These meetings were so remarkable, so hard to put into words. I began to rattle on about what we had just experienced in the prayer meeting. Without a hint of displeasure or judgment in his voice, my father put his arm around me and wisely said, "You know, Son, sometimes it's better not to talk too much about these kinds of experiences with God. Rather, let it soak into your heart where God wants to do his work of making you more like him."

Nothing else was said. In his wisdom, Dad knew the importance of always remembering God's transcendence. He didn't want me to become overly familiar with the things of God to the point where they became commonplace. He wasn't telling me to never speak about God;[9] but he was inviting me to experience a greater sense of reverence for God in my heart. Habakkuk 2:20 says, "The LORD is in his holy temple; let all the earth keep silence before him."

Though we had just experienced a remarkable closeness to God in that prayer meeting, my father wanted me to understand—and never forget—the respect for God's transcendence that we are to live by.

Standing on Holy Ground

The problem with pendulum swings is that they can obscure God's true character.

Swings that focus too heavily on God's transcendence can produce a rigid formalism that lacks spiritually sustaining life. We can have all the vestments of formal worship, the beauty of stained glass windows, the poetry of the liturgy, and the sanctity of the sacraments, and miss out on God. He is certainly treated with respect, but he may not manifest his presence because the hearts of the worshipers are focused on the trappings of worship and not on the one whom we propose to worship. We've all seen or heard of churches that fall into this quicksand. In whatever way it is articulated, God is considered too lofty to approach, and all we are left with is doctrinal orthodoxy and pious rituals. God is, for all practical purposes, too far off to concern himself with our daily lives. He is holy and awesome, yet also distant, cold, and aloof.

Conversely, when the pendulum swings too far the other way, we treat God as if he is our fishing buddy. At this extreme, we discuss our experiences with God as if they exist for our entertainment. God is a cure for boredom. The name of the Lord is used for punctuation in our sentences or as a way to communicate surprise. In particular, I've noticed a type of slang in Christian media that betrays a far too casual view of God. As a pastor, I am committed to leading people into life-producing intimacy with God. But that can never be at the expense of our reverence for him.

Therein lies the tension in which we must live. On the one hand, Hebrews 4:16 encourages us to "draw near to the throne of grace, that we may receive mercy." On the other hand, when the prophet Isaiah draws near to God, he is so completely overwhelmed by the contrast between his own sinfulness and God's surpassing holiness that he cries out, "Woe is me, for I am ruined!"[10]

So which is it? Can we come near to God with confidence? Or are we to be in holy awe of him who dwells in realms we cannot fathom?

The simplest answer is *yes*. Draw near with confidence because in Christ you have been "raised up . . . and seated . . . with him in the heavenly places,"[11] but never forget, or make light of, whose presence you are in.

Gambling on God's Good Graces

As much as it may sound as if I lean toward God's immanence by advocating time in his presence, I urge you with utmost caution never to become flippant in approaching God.

One danger of thinking too lightly of God's surpassing holiness is that it creates a propensity toward self-justification and open sin. A man in one of our churches had been active in the church's music ministry for years as a choir member and soloist. He was well known and well liked by all. He came to my office one afternoon to inform me that he was secretly having an affair. It had been going on for years, and he had come to tell me that he had decided to divorce his wife and marry his longtime girlfriend, who also attended the church. Rather brazenly he said, "I know what I'm doing is wrong and that what I'm about to do is also wrong, but can you tell me that God won't forgive me on the other side of my divorce? I know I'm going to be happiest if I proceed with this."

The sheer audacity of this man astounded me. It took me a few moments before I was able to answer. Finally I said, "Fortunately for all of us, he's a merciful and forgiving God. I cannot tell you that God won't forgive you on the other side of a divorce. However, I want to ask you a question: Are you a gambling man?"

He wrinkled up his face, unsure of where I was going with this question, and would not answer me. I continued, "Because what you're getting ready to do is gamble on the mercy of God and the work of the Holy Spirit."

I took him to John 16:8 and read it out loud. "When he [the Holy Spirit] comes, he will convict the world concerning sin and righteousness and judgment." Then I pointed out how he was presuming on God that, after going ahead with the divorce, he would even be in a place spiritually to hear the convicting call of the Holy Spirit. I asked him if he was willing to gamble his future on that.

I concluded our time together by referring him to Romans 6:1-2: "What shall we say then? Are we to continue in sin that grace may abound? By no means! How can we who died to sin still live in it?"

I'm happy to say that the man ended up not divorcing his wife. By God's grace, he repented of his sin and was restored to his family. We might read that story with incredulity. Yet when we take an honest look at our own lives, are we ever guilty of doing something similar? We know a certain sin is wrong, yet we chose to do it anyway, gambling on the wonderful mercy and grace of God. Are we presuming on the presence of a God who is loving and near?

Thirty Minutes to a Better You?

Not long ago, I received a bulk mail flier from a church in our area that was well meaning but missed the mark. The flier said, "Give us thirty minutes and we'll give you God." The subtext of the flyer said, "For busy people with important things to do on the weekend."

Seriously?

First of all, can anyone presume to say that we can "give God" to anyone, as if the Lord of the universe were merely a commodity? At best, we can, like John the Baptist, point the way. But no one can *deliver* God—much less in half an hour.

It reminded me of the story of Simon the magician, which has always been a curiosity to me.[12] Simon was a Samaritan sorcerer who earned a living by amazing the crowds with his magical powers. When he heard Philip the evangelist preach about Jesus, Simon believed and was baptized, along with many others from the city, "and seeing signs and great miracles performed, he was amazed."[13]

Upon seeing the gift of the Holy Spirit given to people by the laying on of the apostles' hands, Simon wanted to be able to do what they did. He undoubtedly saw the power and presence of God as a money-making opportunity and a way for him to regain his status in the city. Offering money to the apostles, he said, "Give me this power also, so that anyone on whom I lay my hands may receive the Holy Spirit."[14]

Peter answered Simon, "May your money perish with you, because you thought you could buy the gift of God with money! You have no part or share in this ministry, because your heart is not right before God. Repent of this wickedness and pray to the Lord in the hope that he may forgive you for having such a thought in your heart. For I see that you are full of bitterness and captive to sin."[15]

Simon realized his mistake and answered, "Pray to the Lord for me so that nothing you have said may happen to me."[16]

Our approach to the God who is near must be with open, honest, and humble hearts. God always deserves our respect. In contemporary church life, one of our goals is to do whatever we can to help people realize that God is understandable and accessible. But there's a risk that we've removed the concept of holiness and God's all-consuming fire from much of what we do. In our necessary, and sometimes overdue, attempts to be relevant, we must never trivialize the presence of God in our corporate gatherings. He must always be recognized as holy.

If we're looking to "get God" in thirty minutes, we may get only Simon the magician's version of God. And if we go to the foot of the cross and look up into the eyes of the one who gave his life for us and say, "You know what, Jesus, I'm a busy person, with important things to do on the weekends," I'd say you're treading on very dangerous ground indeed.

Finding God in the Strangest Places

The solution to the risk of taking God too lightly is not to insert more formalism into our faith for the sake of creating appropriate distance between ourselves and God. Indeed, some practices and traditions that have been handed down in the church have become meaningless and devoid of authenticity. Again, there's that tension. We want to enjoy the biblical confidence we've been given to approach God boldly, to seek his presence, and to enjoy him forever. Yet we can never forget that we're talking about the Great King who dwells in unapproachable light. When we enter into God's presence, we must "take off the shoes of our hearts," for we are standing on holy ground.

This holy ground will look different to different people in different situations. We may encounter the presence of God in a church service. We might encounter him while driving on I-90 in Wyoming. We may find him in the quietness of a cave or in the thundering of a storm. But wherever, whenever, and however God chooses to reveal himself, he is still God.

During World War II, a young Marine sergeant named Clinton Watters was fighting with the Third Raider Battalion in the South Pacific. Before the invasion of the enemy-held island of Bougainville, Watters was made a section leader and put in charge of leading twelve men. Their orders were to come ashore and take a strategic area of land to build an airstrip. This was Watters's first time ever in combat, and he said, "We were very unprepared."[17]

As the battalion landed, the enemy unleashed a torrent of artillery blasts and bullets. Men were mowed down in cold blood. Shell after shell landed and exploded. Watters hit the beach with his twelve men behind him, and then found to his horror that he suddenly couldn't move. A wave of fear swept over him and his body froze, rendering him completely immobile. Soldiers in that situation know they need to keep moving. Their lives and the lives of the men they lead depend on it. But Watters ended up stopping his advance right in the middle of the invasion. He records the story in his own words.

> In the middle of that battle, I did the only thing I could think of. I dropped to my knees and asked God for help. There was nobody around me, but I'd swear somebody touched me. There was an actual physical presence, just like somebody put his hand on my shoulder. He told me to get up, stand up, go forward, and that he was going to take care of me.
>
> Well, that was all I needed. I stood up and led my men in. We went into Bougainville and cleaned up there and went on with the battle. That incident I had with God at Bougainville changed my life. I committed myself to serving God for the rest of my days, and I never felt fear in battle ever again.[18]

I hope you and I will never find ourselves in such horrifying conditions. Yet the God who met Clinton Watters on that sandy beach of terror in 1943 is the same God we serve today. God is close, and God is always holy. He cares about every aspect of our lives, whether we need to lead twelve men to safety or lead our family in a time of prayer. God is never removed from our lives—he's close and involved. Still, whenever we hear his footsteps coming down the hallway, a holy fear must fill our hearts, a fear born of reverence and respect, and yet a longing just to be near him.

SIGNS OF REVIVAL
Authentic personal and corporate prayer ministry is revived.

†

CHAPTER 7

SPEED BUMPS ON THE ROAD TO GOD'S PRESENCE

WHAT IS ONE thing that often hinders a person from experiencing the presence of God?

Becoming a Christian.

If that answer is hard to swallow, hang on and let me explain.

In the mid-1970s, Rita and I worked for Youth Development, Inc. (YDI), a ministry headquartered in San Diego that operated residential ranches and mountaineering programs for emotionally unstable teens, most of whom were involved with the court system and were wards of the state. We took the teens to live at one of two ranches we operated, one outside of El Cajon and the other not far from the town of Ramona, in the foothills of the Vallecito Mountains. During the summer months, some of the teens took part in a ten-day Christian mountaineering program run by Summit Expedition (now called Summit Adventure). The ministry saw great spiritual harvest and success, and it was a joy to be a part of it all.

But there were big challenges with the job too. Part of my responsibility as vice president of the organization was to visit churches in

California, Arizona, and Nevada to help raise funds and increase awareness of the ministry, which meant a lot of travel for me on weekends. Monday through Friday, Rita and I had administrative duties at the YDI office, including the production of *Reality*, a Christian rock outreach radio show for teens. Syndicated on more than two hundred secular stations around the country, the show enjoyed widespread popularity, and we received so much mail from needy teens that we had to hire a Christian counselor to take care of all the responses. The travel to churches in various states each weekend, coupled with my involvement at the office during the week, meant we were continually scrambling to get to where we needed to be. The schedule proved impossible to do by car, but the commercial airlines didn't fly to the small towns we visited on the weekends.

To solve this issue, the YDI board gave me the opportunity to become a pilot. A dream come true! The organization bought a small private plane, a Cessna 182, and paid for my flight instruction. I was happy to do this and excited at the new adventure, although becoming a pilot took some work.

Because of my already tight schedule, I needed to take the ground school instruction for my private pilot's license in a compressed weekend class. For three days straight, I learned the rudiments of aeronautics, flight controls, weather, navigation, radio operation, and FAA flight rules. On the Monday morning after the course was finished, I went to the local FAA office, took my exam for my private pilot's license, and passed with a 98 percent. Certificate in hand, I was now a pilot. A real pilot with a license.

There was only one problem: I hadn't left the ground yet.

Scanned but Not Converted

I tell that story about getting my pilot's license because it is a metaphor for the way too many Christians operate. Yes, they have the "license" that says they're believers, based on a profession of faith, but that's all they have. Somewhere along the line, they prayed a prayer and received Jesus as their Savior, but their spiritual "airplane" is still in the hangar. Technically, they might be *certified* to fly, but when it comes to truly soaring in their journey with the Lord, they've never actually flown at all.

Something important is missing among many North American Christians today, although I don't believe the exclusion is intentional. We've lost sight of all that salvation is designed to be and to provide. The version of salvation that is preached and widely embraced throughout the Western world has largely become only about forgiveness and justification. Don't get me wrong—forgiveness and justification are important parts of the picture, but they are not the *whole* picture.

Next time you hear an evangelistic message, listen to how people are invited to come to Christ. Typically, the language we use is all about forgiveness of sin and looking forward to heaven. There is no assumption or expectation of a change in our fundamental identity or in how we live our lives—and that omission is partly responsible for the anemic condition of the church throughout the Western world today.

When salvation is seen as primarily about forgiveness and justification, it tends to be viewed as a *past event*, a historical moment in time. This one-time experience of becoming a Christian is important, yes, but big problems emerge when people make a decision to "follow" Jesus and then do little or nothing to live out their salvation from that point on. A life of growth into greater intimacy with God is seen as optional and only for the spiritually elite. Over my years in pastoral ministry, I've seen this time and time again. Years after accepting Christ, these people may technically be Christians, but their relationship with God is, at best, far from robust, and may even be nonexistent. The certificate may be posted on the wall, but the plane is still in the hangar.

When I was a young pastor, it took me a long time to identify, understand, and articulate this problem—even in myself. As I glanced out across the congregation, I saw people who had been Christians for a long time, and I assumed they were all mature and growing. My logic was simple. They had been in church a long time, so therefore they should be walking in great obedience, and their lives should reflect their intimacy with God.

Yet, as I got to know people better, I soon found that wasn't the case. Person after person bore the tragic earmarks of spiritual immaturity. In one situation after another, I found that many of these professing Christians weren't any more advanced in their relationship with God than they had been when they first believed. It wasn't for lack of knowledge. It wasn't that they weren't hearing God's voice, receiving his guidance, or experiencing his presence in ways that one would expect would lead to a depth of relationship and personal transformation. Yet they were not growing in their faith.

My experience as a pastor is supported by much of the research today on the condition of the American church. The Pew Research Center, the Barna Group, and other researchers have discovered there is little difference between people in evangelical churches and the general population in beliefs, attitudes, and lifestyle. In *Growing True Disciples*, George Barna's book examining the quality of discipleship in the lives of Christians today, he writes, "While there are instances in which believers are different from nonbelievers, when we compare the two groups, the statistical differences are minimal."[1]

I did my doctoral project at Carey Theological College, at the University of British Columbia, on the subject of discipleship—which I defined from Scripture as the intentional process of tucking in close behind Jesus in order to follow him. At the same time, I worked as a pastor in Edmonds and encountered people in the church who desperately needed to grow in their relationship with God. During my research, I stumbled onto Dallas Willard's book *The Divine Conspiracy*, which proved very helpful in highlighting the biggest challenge facing the church in America today—and the answer was not simply to "be more relevant."

Before his death in 2013, Willard was a professor of philosophy at the University of Southern California, as well as a popular speaker and writer on the subject of spiritual formation. In *The Divine Conspiracy*, Willard concludes that too many believers live as if their Christian life is a "bar code"—an identifying mark that identifies us as children of God and will automatically scan us into heaven, whether or not we have an ongoing relationship with God, or any transformation in our character, or any conformity to the life of Jesus evident in our lives. In other words, salvation is viewed as a *change in status*—period. But this is contrary to the very nature of the gospel and the work of the Holy Spirit in transforming us into the image of Christ.

Willard writes:

> Think of the bar codes now used on goods in most stores. The scanner responds only to the bar code. It makes no difference what is in the bottle or package that bears it, or whether the sticker is on the "right" one or not. . . .
>
> On a recent radio program a prominent minister spent fifteen minutes enforcing the point that "justification," the forgiveness of sins, involves *no change at all* in the heart or personality of the one forgiven. It is, he insisted, something entirely external to you, located wholly in God himself. His intent was to emphasize the familiar Protestant point that salvation is by God's grace only and is totally independent of what we may do. But what he in fact *said* was that being a Christian has nothing to do with the kind of person you are. The implications of this teaching are stunning. . . .
>
> The essential thing . . . is the forgiveness of sins. And the payoff for having faith and being "scanned" comes at death and after. Life now being lived has no necessary connection with being a Christian as long as the "bar code" does its job. . . .
>
> [But] can we seriously believe that God would establish a plan for us that essentially bypasses the awesome needs of present human life and leaves human character untouched? . . .
>
> Or have we somehow developed an understanding of "commitment to Jesus Christ" that does not break through to his living presence in our lives?[2]

The last two paragraphs are key. An integral component of salvation is a *changed life* lived in the presence of God. The apostle Paul, who most clearly teaches about justification in the New Testament, is also the one who writes that the believer is a "new creation."[3] Professor and theologian Theodore Runyon writes on this same theme:

> If the divine intent in Christ, however, is not only to declare forgiveness and a new status for the sinner before God but to renew all things, then salvation is truncated that does not move from forensic change to actual change, from declared righteousness to actual righteousness.[4]

If we see salvation only as a static moment, a brief court appearance where we're declared innocent and freed from our guilt, then we're missing out on the totality of what salvation truly is. Our faith will only be "bar code" Christianity—a stamp of God's acceptance at a point in time, but nothing more.

Transformed by Flight

The problem with my thinking of myself as a licensed pilot after completing only the ground school classes and passing the FAA test wasn't my head knowledge. With my license in hand, you could say I knew everything there was to know about flying. In reality, though, there was a whole world of *experience* waiting for me the first time I sat in the pilot's seat, with my hands and feet on the controls, and pushed the throttle to the firewall.

Oh my word! What a difference!

I remember to this day my first dual instruction, when I actually flew a plane for the first time with an instructor seated next to me. I cannot tell you how exhilarating it was to finally get off the ground.

After ten hours of dual instruction, the next big challenge came when I had my first solo flight. The instructor taxied me out to the base of the control tower at midfield, climbed out of the airplane, and left me in the plane all alone.

He went up to the tower so he could observe and instruct from there, and I taxied to the end of the runway 28 Right and took off to do a series of (aptly named) touch-and-goes. Just me and the airplane. That was one of the scariest and most exciting moments of my life. I was actually flying on my own.

After I had another thirty hours of instruction and flight experience under my belt, my instructor gave me a flight test and signed off on my logbook. Now I was *officially* a pilot—able to fly on my own without an instructor.

Even then, my need for training and guidance didn't end. When it comes to aviation, it's too easy to get rusty and start flying unsafely. Flying requires a combination of incredible concentration and practiced responses to the airplane and the flight environment. It's something you get good at only by doing it and honing your skills with study and experience. It requires flying on a regular basis, periodic dual instruction to refresh your skills, and additional training to add more endorsements on your license.

So I flew and flew and flew, weekend after weekend. It wasn't long before the ministry saw the benefits of using aviation to get various leaders and donors to meetings all over the country. In a few years, we needed a larger, twin-engine airplane. In order to fly the new plane, I had to obtain my multiengine endorsement, which I did, and then my instrument rating, which qualified me to fly in the clouds without visual reference to the ground. That was one of the most challenging elements of my training. I had to force myself to believe my instruments, even when everything I felt and sensed told me otherwise.

So when did I actually become a pilot?

Well, throughout the process, really. I was a pilot when I received my certification, yes, but that license would have been meaningless without the experience of actually flying.

Do you see the connection to our spiritual lives?

Receiving salvation through grace by faith in Jesus Christ is not unlike passing the FAA pilot's exam. We become a Christian at that point, but that distinction is pretty meaningless if our moment of salvation isn't simply the front door leading into an *ongoing* and *growing* experience of the Christian life. Looked at from a slightly different angle, what is the point of the *new birth* if it doesn't lead to *new life*? Yes, we receive Christ through grace by faith, but that's only the first step in the ongoing experience of a *transformed life*. So we can say that salvation is both a one-time event and a life lived. We don't get to choose one or the other. The Bible identifies salvation as both justification and being born again.[5]

The concept of *new birth* as a wonderful picture of salvation is found primarily in John's Gospel and epistles. It is a different perspective on the miracle of salvation. And like the birth and development of a child, everyone in the family would be gravely concerned if two years later the baby looked just like it did at birth. New birth is a miraculous transformation of everything about us, from the inside (and including the outside). The goal of New Testament salvation is the joy of living a transformed life *now*, in the presence of God, and of being fitted for the eternal glory of God's full presence when we finally see him face-to-face.[6]

If we see salvation as only a one-time, past occurrence, then there is nothing more to the Christian life than planting a flag and never moving forward. What kind of life is that?

But if we recognize that salvation is a lifelong experience by which Jesus continually transforms our lives, then God's presence becomes an essential element of our everyday lives, as the wellspring of our salvation, and our hunger for God's presence grows as we respond to his love for us.

The Cost of Sin

I've spent a lot of time on this one point because it's foundational to our understanding of the importance of God's presence in every believer's salvation. But a lack of understanding about salvation isn't the only hindrance to our living in the presence of God. Another major obstacle is *sin*. Bold and basic sin.

The New Testament speaks extensively about the work of the

Holy Spirit in our lives. The Holy Spirit is the person of the Godhead who resides in us and, being God himself, ministers the presence of God to us. We cannot live the Christian life without the Spirit.

In Ephesians 4, Paul challenges believers with a number of specific directives to live as children of light. We are told to put off our old selves, which are characterized by deceitful desires. We're to tell the truth and not lie. We're not to let the sun go down on our anger. We're not to let any unwholesome talk come out of our mouths. And so on.

Then, in Ephesians 4:30, in the context of Paul's warnings about sin, he tells us not to grieve the Holy Spirit. If we allow unconfessed sin to continue in our lives, it grieves the Holy Spirit. The result appears to be some degree of loss in our relationship with the Spirit, and some degree of loss in his activity in our lives. To be clear, the Holy Spirit does not withdraw from us, but sin hardens the sensitivity of our hearts and deafens our ears to his voice. Hebrews 3:13-14 says, "Exhort one another every day, as long as it is called 'today,' that none of you may be hardened by the deceitfulness of sin. For we have come to share in Christ, if indeed we hold our original confidence firm to the end." Unrepentant sin hardens our sensitivities to God, which makes it more difficult for us to hear his voice, perceive his presence, and be transformed by his glory.

Unconfessed sin costs us in our relationship with God. That's always the bottom line.

I Can Stop Loving You

A third hindrance to our experiencing God's presence is apathy. This happens whenever we become indifferent to God. We are still saved, but we get caught up in the busyness of life and become inattentive to his voice and his ways. In Luke 8:14, Jesus speaks of the danger of seed falling on thorny and hardened soil. The Word takes root, but it is eventually choked out by life's worries, riches, and pleasures. What do you want most in life? Be honest! Are you more interested in your job, your home, your hobbies or other pursuits, or are you more interested in pursuing God?

When we first started our prayer meetings at Westgate Chapel in Edmonds, a fairly affluent suburb of Seattle, it became apparent after the initial enthusiasm of the first year that we lacked urgency in our prayers. Attendance started to slide. We still had several hundred in attendance each Tuesday night, but there was a hesitancy to pray out loud and to pray freely with any degree of authentic passion for God. Frustrated, I called my friend Jim Cymbala, pastor of Brooklyn Tabernacle, whose Tuesday night prayer meetings draw an average of four thousand people who pray together with a great deal of freedom and enthusiasm. I've attended several of their prayer meetings over the years, and when the people begin to pray it's as thunderous as being at the base of Niagara Falls. It's an amazing experience— just a gathering of humble people with a genuine passion and desire for God.

"It's the handicap of the location you're in," Jim said to me over the phone. "The stuff we face in the life of our congregation forces us to be desperate in calling out to God. We just had to open a second nursery for babies with AIDS. Every Sunday, we have people in our services addicted to crack cocaine or heroin. They don't need a hip service and a cute sermon. No man-made program can address those needs. Our people need to have an encounter with the power of God, and we need to call on God because we have nothing else to offer them."

Yes, our circumstances have a bearing on our desperation for God. But what if we don't feel desperate? What if life in general is pretty comfortable? A hunger for God cannot be contrived or manufactured, or else it's artificial—like the monks of old who purposely wore horsehair clothing so their skin would be irritated as a reminder of their fallen humanity. Their method of producing desperation didn't work. So what can we do?

The solution is for all people, rich and poor, to recognize the condition of their hearts as *broken* and *desperate* before God. Only the Holy Spirit can reveal to us the true depth of our need; and only the Spirit can create hunger in us. First John 2:15 says, "Do not love the world or the things in the world. If anyone loves the world, the love of the Father is not in him." We must love God more than anything else in the world. We must pursue God as if our very lives depended on him—because they do! We must love Jesus Christ with the kind of love you would expect for someone who has given his life to save yours. But how do we do this if we're surrounded by comfort and affluence?

My father, for as long as I knew him, was a car guy. In fact, he owned a car dealership before he entered the pastorate. Before that, he worked as a mechanic for a wealthy mining family in South Africa that raced Type 35 Bugattis. It was Dad's job to keep the cars in racing condition. His enthusiasm was contagious, and I grew up loving cars. Once, while I was a pastor in Iowa and my parents were visiting, a parishioner in the church offered to sell me a beautiful 1936 slant-back Ford four-door sedan. It was all original, and he wanted $3,000 for it. That was a lot of money for me in those days. When Dad and I went out to look at the car, our eyes lit up. "Dad," I said, "is it right for me to own a car that's ultimately a toy when I'm ministering to some people in the congregation who can't afford any car?"

"You and the Lord will need to sort that out," he said wisely. "Ask yourself three questions: Can you own that car and hold it with an open hand? If God ever asks you to engage in the financial needs of others, would you sell the car without hesitation? And if you discovered that the car was interfering with your love for God, would you be willing to sell it? If you can answer affirmatively to all three questions, then yes, you're mature enough in your relationship with God to have a hobby car."

I bought the car. Over the next few years, I loved and cherished that car, but I was always mindful never to let it encroach on the first love of my life. Now, if you've got a '36 Ford and one hubcap is missing, it can be time-consuming to find a replacement, and those were the days before the Internet. So there were times when my first love for the Lord was tested, but not abandoned. The Bible doesn't say we can't enjoy the things that the Lord graciously allows us, like a hobby car; but the Bible does prohibit the cravings of our sinful nature.[7] So we always need to ask ourselves a few questions. Do I want everything my eyes see? Am I too obsessive about any one thing of life? Do I crave something more than I crave the Lord? Am I scheming and manipulating to get things? Who is the first love of my life? It must be Jesus, or else something needs to go.

Years later, I started riding motorcycles and greatly enjoyed the sport. Week after week, I pored through motorcycle magazines, obsessing about chrome pipes and computer chips to increase horsepower. One morning, during a quiet time, the Lord said in almost an audible voice, "The magazines have to go." There was nothing intrinsically wrong with the magazines; it wasn't a morality issue with me. But I realized that the magazines were causing me to think more about motorcycle parts than I was thinking about the Lord. God must always be first in our lives.

Anxiety: Not the Fruit of the Spirit

A fourth hindrance that can keep us from experiencing God's presence is the worries of this life. My goodness, if all we do is watch the news, the constant bombardment we receive about the economy, the environment, the safety of our children, and the dangers of rogue world powers can fill us with fear and keep us distracted from pursuing God. When all our waking thoughts are about how dangerous the world is and how to protect ourselves, we're tempted to respond as if this life and this world are all there is. We forget that we're sons and daughters of the King of kings and that our citizenship is in a heavenly city. Worry can cancel out God's work in our lives. It generates an obsession with ourselves, our protection and safety, our future and well-being. Worry destroys faith, and faith is how we experience God. Without faith, it's impossible to please God.[8]

Being close to God, saturating ourselves in his Word, experiencing his presence, casting our cares upon him,[9] and setting our minds on things above[10] are the antidotes to worry. When we are in God's presence, we realize who he is, and we become enamored of him. The horizons of our lives become filled with the Lord and with the hope of his coming kingdom rather than with the cares and anxieties of this world.

I realize this is easier said than done. Years ago, when I received a cancer diagnosis, I'd wake up some nights in a cold sweat, worrying about how Rita would be taken care of, who would help her sell the house, and how the church would transition leadership after I was dead. It was an immobilizing fear. I had to consciously shake myself awake and immerse my mind in Scripture. The passage I continually focused on was Philippians 4:6-7: "Do not be anxious about anything, but in everything by prayer and supplication with thanksgiving let your requests be made known to God. And the peace of God, which surpasses all understanding, will guard your hearts and your minds in Christ Jesus." Another passage I meditated on was 2 Timothy 1:7: "For God gave us a spirit not of fear but of power and love and self-control." I'd repeat these verses out loud over and over again, saturating my mind and my heart in God's truth, until I could feel his pushing back the wall of fear that encroached on me.

I have always found corporate worship and fellowship with other believers to be a wonderful antidote to anxiety. Corporate worship focuses our hearts on eternal truths and celebrates the realities of God's eternal kingdom. Being with other believers offers us a reminder of our true identity in Christ. This helps bring the peace of God into our hearts and pushes back our fears.

Westgate Chapel has a choir that's a wonderful mixture of ages and ethnicities. The choir sings contemporary, upbeat worship music designed to honor God to the fullest. But the lives of the people in the choir minister to me as much as the music. Some of them are walking through unimaginable issues. One woman in the soprano section is a picture of continual rejoicing in the face of life's hardest times. A while back, she was diagnosed with inoperable cancer. There is nothing the medical community can do for her. The family still has children at home, and the mother's time is short. Yet, each week, she stands up in the choir with her face radiant and her hands raised as she worships the Lord. Her faith, so vibrant in spite of this terminal diagnosis, is a lesson to many in the church, including me. It reminds us that we are strangers on earth and our true citizenship is in heaven above, where we will live in God's immediate presence forever. That is what we were created for. That is why we are saved.

Moving On Up

Thus far in this chapter, we've spent a lot of time focused on "the problem." And there's a reason for that. When we identify and understand the things that keep us from experiencing God's presence, we are better able to reverse the process and focus on the solution. So, what is the solution? It centers on three words: *Christ. In. Me.*

Think about that amazing truth: Christ is *in* us. Our relationship with him can't get any more intimate than that. Hebrews 12:2 tells us that Jesus Christ is seated at the right hand of the Father. Yet, Jesus is not bound by space or time. If we are believers, Jesus Christ is present and active right now in each of our lives, by the Holy Spirit.

Consider how Jesus' prayer in John 17:20-21 describes the depth of our intimacy with him:

> My prayer is not for them alone. I pray also for those who will believe in me through their message, that all of them may be one, Father, just as you are in me and I am in you. May they also be in us so that the world may believe that you have sent me.[11]

All that "in" language is key. It's *in* and *in* and *in*.

- Jesus prays for all those who believe *in* him . . .
- Just as the Father is *in* Jesus . . .
- And Jesus is *in* the Father . . .
- That all believers would be *in* God.

Colossians 1:27 notes that Jesus' prayer has been fulfilled. Paul writes, "To them God has chosen to make known among the Gentiles the glorious riches of this mystery, *which is Christ in you*, the hope of glory."[12]

Paul, writing under the inspiration of the Holy Spirit, does *not* say that the glory of the mystery of salvation is heaven. Rather it is *Christ in you*. That's the hope of glory.

Think about the word *glory* for a moment. Glory is splendor, brightness, and amazing might. There's nothing passive about glory. The verse says that we are in *union* with Christ. That's location language. It speaks to the address where we live this Christian life. It's *Jesus*. He becomes our new address when we believe. No longer am I Alec Rowlands who lives in Edmonds, Washington. Now I'm Alec Rowlands who lives in Jesus. I have a new and permanent address.

Knowing our new address is important because salvation is not just positional or static or unmoving or a once-only experience. Salvation is ongoing, transformational, and continual. Instead of telling people who begin their Christian journey, "Your sins are forgiven, end of subject, you know how to fly," we invite them to see that there's an airplane waiting in the hangar. "Don't just walk around with the license in your pocket. Fly the airplane."

We can think of our salvation as a four-part harmony: (1) justification, (2) identity, (3) location, and (4) intimacy.

- *Justification* means our sins are forgiven, and our past is done away with.
- *Identity* means we're born again. We're new creations.
- *Location* means we're *in* Christ—which means full engagement with the Father, Son, and Holy Spirit.
- *Intimacy* means full fellowship with God.[13]

Gone Fishing

I've mentioned that my father had a stoic, British demeanor and disposition. When he first took on pastoral work, he approached it by rolling up his sleeves and doing the heavy lifting himself. In the Durban pastorate, all that human effort resulted in his being hospitalized with an inoperable bleeding ulcer and the church unchanged with all kinds of unresolved and serious problems.

When the presence of God fell on Dad's church, not only did the church blossom, but Dad's life also blossomed. He still worked hard, but it was with a renewed sense of faith and rest. He understood his new identity and location better—he was born again, in Christ—and because of that, he had a fuller sense of intimacy with God.

One morning when I was out fishing with my father, he told me he enjoyed fishing so much that he worried it might be displeasing to the Lord. He had prayed about it and sensed that the Lord had told him, "No, you keep right on fishing. I know you delight in me. While you're out fishing, I delight in you."

After the presence of God fell on the church, there was a new lightness to Dad's temperament that everyone who knew him could see. Though he was just as purposeful in his pursuit of God, he was far less driven in the way he approached life and ministry. He was healthier and experienced a new sense of rest in the Lord.

Friend, the Lord is *for* you, not against you.[14] What keeps you from his presence? Nothing needs to. God's presence is something you desire or you wouldn't have kept reading this far. You don't need to claw for it or clutch after it. Just welcome it. Welcome him! Remove the distractions and the apathy from your life, enjoy your new identity and location, and then go fishing with Jesus. He's always with you. You live in him. He's your new address. He surrounds you with his love. He rejoices over you with singing. Let nothing distract you from experiencing God to the fullest.

SIGNS OF REVIVAL
Revived believers become powerful witnesses, and unbelievers are dramatically converted, significantly affecting everyday life in the community at large.

CHAPTER 8

WHERE REASON KANT, EXPERIENCE CAN

I FIRST FELT God's call into pastoral ministry when I was twelve years old, but for many years I largely ignored it. I loved earth sciences and was intent on becoming a geography professor. I figured God could use me as a lay minister and volunteer in church. My undergrad degree from Wittenberg University was a double major in earth science and education. My first master's degree from the University of Miami was in urban studies. After the program finished, I was accepted at the University of North Carolina at Chapel Hill for the PhD program in geography. Everything looked to be on track.

Then I sensed again God's call to full-time pastoral ministry. This time the call was unmistakable. I needed to obey God. So I dropped out of the PhD program in geography and followed God's direction. This led first to a season of ministry with Youth Development, Inc., and then to the pulpit of the church in Cedar Rapids. There was only one problem. Most of my initial understanding of theology and pastoral work came from growing up under my dad's ministry, not from any formal theological education. So after wrestling with some of the harder issues of church leadership in the first two and a half years in Cedar Rapids, I realized I needed more theological training—and I needed it fast.

I applied to a seminary in Missouri to begin a second master's degree—this time in theology—through the extension program for full-time pastors. The seminary officials reviewed my transcripts and liked what they saw, but they concluded I needed three credits in philosophy before they would admit me to their program. I enrolled in a philosophy course at the University of Iowa, attending their extension campus in Cedar Rapids.

The class met on Tuesdays and Thursdays at 8:00 a.m., during a bitterly cold winter. Some mornings when I left for class, the temperature was anywhere from ten to twenty-five degrees below zero.

The professor who taught the class proved as cold as the mornings. It wasn't that he was dull. Far from it. His lectures were captivating. His intellect stunning. His grasp of the subject matter impressive. It was just that he hated Christians, and he made that perfectly clear early and often during the course. As we waded through Aristotle, Plato, Kant, and Nietzsche, the professor used every opportunity to make fun of Christianity. If there was a God responsible for creating the world, the professor insisted, he had long since withdrawn himself from our day-to-day lives. If there was a God, he was like a watchmaker who assembles all the intricate gears and drives, winds it up, gets it started, and then is never involved with its workings again.

This professor was treading on my territory. I didn't think I had the academic chops to debate him openly, but after class I often talked to him and asked questions about his lectures and his rejection of God. My faith remained unshaken by the speculations of these various philosophers, and in some of our conversations I had the opportunity to tell the professor as much. Unfazed, he would obliterate me with his arguments.

Even though I didn't feel as if I was making much progress, I began to pray in earnest for my professor. I prayed that the Holy Spirit would break into his life—that he would see and understand things in this world that can't be explained other than by a God who is closely and intimately involved in the world he created.

One bone-chilling February morning when the professor walked into the classroom, he seemed unusually quiet and ill at ease. He was obviously distracted by something. As he began his lecture, he stumbled over his words and seemed a bit lost with the subject of Friedrich Nietzsche's philosophy. A few minutes into the class, he stopped abruptly and said, "You know, I had the strangest thing happen to me this morning." At that moment, the entire class was surprised to see tears come to his eyes.

As he was having breakfast at his kitchen table that morning, he said, he looked outside through the single-pane window in his back door, and what caught his eye were the spontaneous ice crystals that formed on the window while he watched. He was mesmerized. On one level, it was such a simple scene—the winter sun coming up over the frozen expanse of his backyard. But what had captured his heart was the wonderment of the most intricate patterns of ice forming on the glass, enhanced by a dazzling spectrum of colors as the sun's rays illumined the crystals. Overwhelmed by the beauty of it all, he sat at his breakfast table and wept. He was now weeping again, in front of the class, as he recalled the experience. He offered no conclusion as to what it all meant or why this beauty had overwhelmed him so powerfully. Instead, he mumbled something about the surprises of Mother Nature and composed himself enough to return to our discussion of Nietzsche. No one in the class said a word, including me. The story was so out of character for him.

When the class was over, I waited until the regular crowd of students who stayed to talk with him had left. I then approached him and asked, "Would you mind if I read you a verse of Scripture?"

He nodded reluctantly, and I opened my Bible to Romans 1:19-20: "What may be known about God is plain to them, because God has made it plain to them. For since the creation of the world God's invisible qualities—his eternal power and divine nature—have been clearly seen, being understood from what has been made, so that people are without excuse."[1]

The professor shrugged, so I explained how I believed that what had happened to him that morning was a revelation of God, given out of God's love for him and just for his benefit. God's nature and eternal power had been revealed through creation. The beauty of the ice crystal formations, the majesty of the sun's rays, the colors at just the moment he was in the kitchen to observe it all—these things could not be the work of chance. Even the way that the wonder of his experience overpowered him showed there is something inside each of us that resonates with God's revealed presence.

The professor mumbled something and cleared his throat. Our conversation was clearly over. I didn't press him very hard, but he also didn't push back that day or criticize my beliefs. Normally, he would have annihilated anything I said with the force of his academic reasoning, but this day he was overcome by a strange quietness. Some may have even called it reverence.

The course came to an end a few weeks later, and I had no further contact with the professor. I don't know what happened in his life or to his beliefs. The experience he had with the ice crystals may have been just a blip that the Lord orchestrated for his life, but I tell the story to illustrate a larger point. There are times when God interrupts our lives with something dramatic, and there are also times when God reveals himself using something subtle, quiet, and filled with wonder. Sometimes God reveals himself to our intellect, allowing us to think our way toward him. At other times, he approaches our senses with a demonstration of his love for us, and we are left in awe of having experienced the wonder of his presence.

Like watching ice crystals form spontaneous patterns on a windowpane.

Truth and Presence: A Package Deal

The professor's approach to life through reason and intellect is not exclusive to the secular classroom. In fact, this love affair with reason has also taken over Christianity. Ever since the dawn of the Age of the Enlightenment, well-meaning believers have insisted that the only reliable way of knowing God, the only way that we encounter God, is through our intellectual apprehension of him in Scripture. We must *think* or *reason* our way to God, and we can only truly know him through what we study in his Word. Any *experience* we may have of God's presence is automatically suspect.

But why should it be that way?

Stanley Grenz, professor of theology and ethics at Carey Theological College, notes that much of the way people think about God today can be traced back to the Enlightenment's formative influence on the Protestant Reformation. René Descartes, the great Enlightenment philosopher, is perhaps best known for his propositional statement, *Cogito ergo sum* ("I think, therefore I am"). Wrapped up in this statement is a focus on the power of our unaided human ability to think as the means of understanding the universe. Descartes's rationale has affected how we think ever since. Grenz writes:

> René Descartes laid the philosophic foundation for the modern edifice with his focus on doubt, which led him to conclude that the existence of the thinking self is the first truth that doubt cannot deny. . . . Isaac Newton later provided the scientific framework for modernity, picturing the physical world as a machine the laws and regularity of which could be discerned by the human mind. The modern human can appropriately be characterized as Descartes' autonomous, rational substance encountering Newton's mechanistic world.[2]

Modernity, beginning with the Age of Reason, still affects how we think today, even though some of its foundations have crumbled around us. Christians are still led to believe that we need *only* to think our way to God, that we know him by means of our reason properly applied to Scripture. Propositional truth reigns supreme. Only the superstitious or uneducated would think to approach God any way other than by means of reason. Ever since the Reformation, the predominant ethos in the Christian life has been that any and all experiences of God's presence are too subjective to be relied upon.

This view relies on a false dichotomy that has serious ramifications for the Christian life and churches today. At one end of the spectrum are churches that focus solely on apprehending God with the mind and reason. The danger here is that a purely intellectual approach to God can lead to formalism, dryness, and distance. Worship and faith exist only in the creeds and in our minds. How many sermons have you sat through where there was no passion for God in the pulpit? Dr. Cheryl Bridges Johns writes,

> Moderns have so commodified the Bible that we have forgotten that revelation brings us the very presence of God and not merely teachings about God. We have forgotten what it means to be afraid. We have so objectified the biblical text that we do not recognize our own position as object under the Word of God. Therefore, we believe that it is possible to promote truth about God without realizing that God's truth and God's presence are a package deal. We believe that the truth we are somehow promoting can be neatly packaged, arranged, and presented in a form that is easy to manipulate.[3]

At the other end of the spectrum are churches that focus solely on experience. Christians in these churches are continually encouraged to "sense" God or "feel" God, and the tone of worship is often more like a high school pep rally or cheerleading contest. Little emphasis is given to scriptural teaching. Sermons are mostly topical, with strong emphasis on "relevance" and living your best life now. If church becomes nothing more than an emotional experience, we must heed the warning of Romans 10:2: "They have a zeal for God, but not according to knowledge." Another translation calls it "misdirected zeal."[4] An exclusive reliance on intellectual reason or on misdirected zeal is equally dangerous.

Knowledge and zeal must be joined together—where did we get the idea that they are mutually exclusive?—so that God may be known through Scripture by the Holy Spirit working in the mind, and by making himself known to us through our experience, as well. The Bible invites Christians to approach God with the mind *and* the spirit.[5] But how?

Open Heart Procedure

Let's begin with Scripture. God has wired us physiologically to comprehend him with our minds and to experience him with our hearts. The commandments to love God with our total being appear like bookends in the Bible. At the beginning of Israel's history, God's people are called to "love the LORD your God with all your heart and with all your soul and with all your might."[6] Clearly, a relationship with God is not purely a mental process, but also includes the body, will, desire, and heart. Then, in the Gospels, at the pinnacle of God's revelation of himself in Christ, when Jesus is asked to identify the greatest commandment of all, he repeats Deuteronomy 6:5: "'Love the Lord your God with all your heart and with all your soul and with all your mind.'"[7] And then he adds, "'Love your neighbor as yourself.' All the Law and the Prophets hang on these two commandments."[8] As we can see from these bookend Scriptures, it is clearly not just an intellectual pursuit of God that will satisfy or transform us. Rather, it is both our intellect and the affection of our hearts that must be touched by God in order for us to be conformed to his likeness.

Several other passages in Scripture show reason and experience working together in our relationship with God. For instance, Proverbs 19:2 says, "It is not good to have zeal without knowledge, nor to be hasty and miss the way."[9] Experience alone can lead us astray. In John 5:39-40, Jesus criticizes the Pharisees for having head knowledge about God without a commensurate love and affection for him: "You search the Scriptures because you think that in them you have eternal life; and it is they that bear witness about me, yet you refuse to come to me that you may have life." To be clear, I am not saying that you are a Pharisee if you currently lean toward a purely intellectual approach to God. My point is that Jesus identifies both the intellect and the experience of his presence working in tandem in our relationship with him.

Saul's conversion experience on the Damascus road[10] is nothing that could be described as *reasonable*. Saul was persecuting the church and was on his way to Damascus to do more damage. Unexpectedly, Jesus showed up in a blinding light that knocked Saul to the ground. Saul did not originate or manufacture that experience. He certainly wasn't looking for it. But the awesome presence of God intersected Saul's life for the purpose of getting his attention, drawing Saul out of himself and eventually into God's purpose for him.

In Acts 16:12-15, Paul and his companions traveled to Philippi, a Roman colony in Greece that was without a synagogue. It was the practice of God-fearers in cities without a synagogue to go to the nearest river for worship and prayer, and that is where the apostles found a group of women gathered on the Sabbath. As was Paul's custom in situations like this, he began to explain from the Old Testament Scriptures the coming of Christ and his death and resurrection for the salvation of Jews and Gentiles alike. What has always intrigued me about this story is the report that one of the group who heard the message that day was a businesswoman named Lydia. Scripture says, "The Lord *opened her heart* to pay attention to what was said by Paul."[11] She was converted and later baptized by Paul, along with her household. What's interesting to note is that in this instance, the Bible does not say that the Lord prepared Lydia's *mind*. No, he opened her *heart*.

John Wesley writes:

The moment the Spirit of the Almighty strikes the heart of him that was till then without God in the world, it breaks the hardness of his heart, and creates all things new. The Sun of Righteousness appears, and shines upon his soul, showing him the light of the glory of God in the face of Jesus Christ. He is in a new world. All things around him are become new.[12]

This is not intellectual language—neither the quote from Wesley's sermon nor the passage from Acts that describes Lydia's conversion. This is experiential language. The very nature of becoming a Christian involves our reason, certainly, as the Holy Spirit brings the revelation of God to our minds through Scripture. Yet few would say, reflecting on the moment of their own salvation, that it was their "brains" that were touched by God. Salvation typically also includes a softening and stirring of the heart in the presence of God, by the work of the Holy Spirit. Why, then, do so many Christians act as if this heart experience of God must or does end at salvation?

A Heart for the Tin Man

When I did my doctoral studies at Carey Theological College, I had the privilege of taking a course from Dr. Stanley Grenz, whom I quoted earlier in this chapter. As a Baptist, Grenz was a strong proponent of robust, reasoned biblical education. Yet this learned man would come to his classroom carrying an acoustic guitar. Before each class session began, he'd lead us in worship. He wanted his students to experience God with our hearts *and* our minds.

At Carey, I also took several classes in pastoral theology from Dr. Gordon Fee, an academic giant. He approached God the same way—with both his head and his heart—although not musically, like Grenz. I remember Dr. Fee, while discussing a passage from 1 Corinthians during a lecture on Paul's pastoral theology, leaning over his lectern with tears running down his cheeks from the sheer passion he felt for God.

In 1997, during an intensely difficult year at Westgate Chapel, Rita woke me up early one morning after having an experience with God. Over the previous twelve months, the church had been vandalized, we'd had an attempted arsonist's fire, the church landscaper had been murdered on church grounds, services had been canceled due to bomb threats, a pastoral staff member had left under terrible circumstances, and more than half of the campus had burned to the ground in a four-alarm blaze. On this particular morning, Rita had been in her normal devotional routine and God had spoken to her through one of her scheduled chapters: Isaiah 7. It was such a clear experience with God that Rita felt compelled to wake me up.

"Alec, you've got to hear this."

Bleary eyed, I swung my legs out of bed and sat in the bedside chair. In recent weeks, clinical depression had been hanging over my head, and it was getting increasingly difficult to get out of bed in the morning, much less preach and lead the church. Honestly, I wanted to quit. If I could have found something else to do to earn a living at that moment, I would have jumped at the chance. I was feeling tapped out emotionally and spiritually, and I didn't know how much longer I could continue in pastoral ministry.

The passage Rita read centered on a difficult time in the history of Judah. Two troublemakers, Rezin and Pekah, had come to Jerusalem intending to destroy the City of God. The heart of King Ahaz and the hearts of all his people "shook as the trees of the forest shake before the wind."[13] God told the prophet Isaiah to go and speak to Ahaz, who was beside himself with fear.

"Be careful, keep calm and don't be afraid," Isaiah said to the king. "Do not lose heart because of these two smoldering stubs of firewood. . . . [They] have plotted your ruin. . . . Yet this is what the Sovereign LORD says: 'It will not happen.'"[14] But this encouragement also came with a warning: "If you do not stand firm in your faith, you will not stand at all."[15]

As Rita knew, that was exactly where I was. I felt as if my ruin were already in motion. But we came to believe that God's word to

King Ahaz was also God's word to us—to me. He was not going to let Westgate Chapel come to ruin. My task was to stand firm in my faith.

Rita had not been randomly flipping through her Bible, frantically searching for answers to our problem. This passage came up in the normal course of her reading schedule, when her mind was fully engaged in the pursuit of God in his Word. Yet these verses were also a specific answer to our crisis—transcending logic and capturing her heart and mine. Logic was telling me to quit my job. Reason said that my leadership was in tatters, and I should find another career. But the Holy Spirit, through the Word of God, moved Rita's heart and encouraged me to stand fast and not leave my post, even though what we were experiencing was incredibly difficult. For the next year and a half, we stood firm on that promise. And we would not have survived without it. Rita and I quoted those verses back and forth to each other many times during those eighteen months. By the grace of God we stood strong, and God didn't allow us to be destroyed.

Some Christians, particularly if they've had any formal theological training, are inclined to be skeptical about encounters with God like this. They continue to insist that God speaks to us only through an intellectual and rational interpretation of Scripture. From this perspective, the only significance for those verses in Isaiah 7 was for King Ahaz. Surely God wasn't speaking to Rita and me through the book of Isaiah. He was simply telling a powerful story about a prophet and a king of old. The logical application of that text for us today is that God is sovereign over kings and nations. End of story.

Yet why must the story end there? Certainly, we must bring sound reason and logic to our interpretation of Scripture. But there were supernatural forces at work to destroy the church and us. Peter reminds us that Satan is a roaring lion on the prowl, with the destruction of Christians in view.[16] That's why we so desperately need the immediate presence of God in our lives to encourage our hearts and give us the strength to stand our ground. There was no verse in the Bible that addressed arson and murder on the church grounds. But what I needed was a sharp reminder to stand by faith and the assurance that God was still in control. I'm just glad Rita was listening.

Frederick Buechner describes a safe and normal truth that can best be known through reason, contrasted with a truth that's deeper, wilder—the truth found in the living and active Scriptures. Buechner laments that we are seldom offered much of this "deeper truth" in church because too many pastors have been pressured into mixing God's Word with the practicality and busyness of normal life. We dumb down the gospel to make it palatable because we are hard pressed to truly embrace that which is beyond us. He writes,

> The truth, reality, is what it is. . . . The truth is all the sounds that well up within the preacher as he sits down at his desk to put his sermon together—the sounds of the bills to be paid, the children to educate, the storm windows to put up, the sounds of his own blunders and triumphs, of his lusts and memories and dreams and doubts, any one of which when you come right down to it is apt to seem more real and immediate and clamorous to him than the sound of truth as high and wild and holy.
>
> So homiletics becomes apologetics. The preacher exchanges the truth that is too good to be true for a . . . truth that instead of drowning out all the other truths the world is loud with is in some kind of harmony with them. He secularizes and makes rational. He adapts and makes relevant. He demythologizes and makes credible.
>
> And what remains of the . . . Gospel becomes in his hands a fairy tale not unlike *The Wizard of Oz.* . . . Like a skilled psychologist, the wizard helps them to an inner adjustment that makes them better equipped to deal with the world as it is, but he is not able to open up for them or inside of them a world of transcendence and joy. . . . The wild and joyful promise of the Gospel is reduced to promises more easily kept.[17]

Time for a Gut Check

Research has shown that human beings have at least two "brains"[18]—and probably more like three. These are sections of our bodies that control our thoughts, behavior, will, and activity.

One brain, the one we're most familiar with, lies at the top of our spinal cord and typically handles cognitive perception, reasoning, language, analysis, and pattern recognition.

Our second brain is the entire enteric nervous system, a complex system of electronic circuitry, neurotransmitters, and proteins found in the gut. It typically handles self-preservation and mobilization. "The gut brain, also known as the enteric brain, contains over 500 million neurons and sends and receives nerve signals throughout the chest and torso and innervates organs as diverse as the pancreas, lungs, diaphragm, and liver. . . . Research has shown that the gut brain can learn, store memories, and perform complex independent processing."[19]

A third brain is found in the complex and functional neural network in a person's heart. It handles values and emotions such as anger, grief, joy, happiness, and hatred. This brain processes what's important to a person and affects how the person connects with others.[20]

If we are embarrassed, for instance, how do we show our embarrassment? Usually, our face turns red. But what part of the body prompts this physical change? Scientists have proven that the "first brain," the gray spongy tissue between our ears, actually has very little to do with this physiological change. Rather, it's the "heart brain" that triggers the blushing response. The power of how we feel affects our lives—and this change has very little to do with logic. We can rationally and intellectually tell ourselves not to be embarrassed, but we will blush anyway. The heart brain rules in situations like this, and our life change has everything to do with the emotions we feel.

Think of how you feel before you walk out on stage to give a speech, even to a small crowd. You can rationally tell yourself there's nothing to be afraid of. You've prepared your material well. You're a credible speaker. No one will mind if you fumble around with your notes. Yet even then, your hands grow clammy and a lump rises in your throat. Why? It's because there's a reality beyond your "first brain" that guides you—in this case, your gut brain informs you about danger, safety, boundaries, aversions, and the need to fight or flee.

So how does this knowledge of multiple brains affect us as Christians? Simply this. It's seldom through reason alone that we're changed, and the Christian life is all about change—change in status, change in lifestyle. This research is now showing that information accompanied by experience is what actually embeds new neuropathways in our brains to make lasting and effective changes in our lives.

A Rising Tide Lifts All Boats

I'll close this chapter by calling you to live with the tension—hold on to it, wrestle with it, and do not let it go. *Reason* and *experience* are the two seemingly opposing forces that create the tension—and we need both. What we *know* of God and what we *experience* of God are both necessary for maintaining and building our faith-based relationship with him.

If all we allow in our spiritual lives is *reason* as a means of knowing God, the most we can expect from our faith is a lifeless formalism. Where is the hope, where is the adventure in that?

Conversely, if all we allow is our *experience* of God, how easily we will be drawn into what a friend of mine calls "this present weirdness."

But if we pursue God with both reason and experience—with our heads *and* our hearts both involved, both available to the work of the Holy Spirit—how rich our faith will be.

A nationally known evangelist was invited to hold a weeklong series of meetings at an Episcopal church on the East Coast. His first meeting at the church was scheduled for a Sunday night, but the priest wanted the evangelist on the platform at the Sunday morning service so he could be introduced to the congregation. It was Easter

Sunday and the priest preached from a lectionary, as he was accustomed to do. Throughout the service, the evangelist sensed a dryness pervading the congregation, like dust settling over a well-traveled road after a car passes.

The evangelist began to pray for the priest and for the meetings to follow that week. As he was praying, the Holy Spirit spoke to him and said, "I am about to pour out my Spirit on this priest."

At that point in the sermon, the priest was reading from Luke 24:6: "He is not here. He is risen."[21] After he read the line, the priest stopped, looked puzzled, and took a longer-than-normal breath. The evangelist noticed that the priest, who up to this point had been standing absolutely motionless behind the pulpit, had begun to tap his right toe.

Oh boy, here it comes, he thought.

The priest reread the text: "He is not here, he is risen!"

At that very moment, it appeared to the evangelist as if the text moved from reason to experience, from the priest's head to his heart. The priest stepped away from the pulpit with a look of surprise on his face. He looked out at the congregation, and repeated, "He is not here, he is risen!" It was as if he were hearing it for the first time.

"HE IS NOT HERE! HE IS RISEN!" the priest repeated, louder than the congregation had ever heard him speak from the pulpit. At this point he reached down, grabbed a fistful of his robes in each hand and began pacing back and forth across the platform, shouting the same phrase over and over again. He was fully in control of his body, and even though it caught the priest and his parish by surprise, it wasn't a chaotic moment. He was simply gripped anew in his heart by the power and depth of the truth he was reading. The truth welled up with a wildness he had not felt in years.

Just then, the presence of God swept through the normally stoic congregation and they jumped to their feet. Some wept. Some prayed out loud. Some lifted their hands. Everyone began to worship.

That's the journey of faith—the response of both head and heart—that I pray this book draws you to step into for yourself. We have a God who longs to be near to us, longs to be known, and longs to be experienced. If we make it our life's goal to draw near to him, we can be sure that along the way, God will take us by surprise. It may be in a prison cell or on a Damascus road; while sitting in church on Easter Sunday or simply while gazing out at the backyard on a cold winter morning, marveling at ice crystals forming on the window pane. But God promises that our search for him will be rewarded.[22] In whatever way he may choose to make himself known to us, we can be certain that it comes from his heart of love for us, in order to draw us closer to him and transform us into his likeness.

STAGE 1 OF REVIVAL
Prosperity and ease divert the people of God from their first love, making them spiritually lethargic and powerless.

CHAPTER 9

WE ARE WHAT WE LOVE

emotions

To say that John Wesley grew up religious would be an understatement.

As a small boy, he was rescued by his father from their burning rectory, and from that point on was known within his family as a "brand plucked from the burning."[1] Sent by his parents to the Charterhouse boarding school in London, he was trained in the spiritual disciplines that also characterized his home life. As a young man, Wesley studied theology at Oxford University and participated in the Holy Club, a group of young men who met regularly to discuss Scripture and various religious topics, and who ministered in prisons and to the needy in the community.

Wesley's father was the rector of Epworth in the Church of England, and soon after graduation, Wesley followed in his father's footsteps and was ordained as an Anglican priest.

Up to this point in his life, he had been immersed in religion, yet despite all his intellectual knowledge about God, he still wasn't confident that he'd had a saving experience with Christ. The solution, he concluded, was to pursue God by serving in a place of hardship and personal deprivation. So at the age of thirty-two, John, along with his younger brother, Charles, traveled by ship from England to Savannah, Georgia, where he was appointed to pastor an Anglican congregation in the colonies and evangelize the Native Americans.

On the ship bound for Georgia, the Wesleys and the rest of the passengers encountered a severe, life-threatening storm. Hurricane winds and mammoth waves tossed the oceangoing vessel about. Sails were ripped to shreds. The mast broke off. Seasoned sailors were convinced that all hands would perish at sea. Everyone panicked—that is, except for a group of German Moravian missionaries on board, who calmly sang hymns and prayed while the storm raged. Wesley was unnerved by the experience. On one hand, he was drawn to the missionaries. They appeared to have the spiritual peace he so desperately wanted. On the other hand, he was upset, even angry, that all his experience with God up to this point had not produced the same peace he saw in the Moravians. He knew he lacked something, but he couldn't put his finger on it. For all of his learning, and for all of his good works, Wesley didn't feel as if he had ever truly experienced God. Fortunately for everyone, the storm died down and the ship wasn't lost. Wesley began to query the Moravians about the source of their peace. He received a few answers that resonated in his heart, but he still arrived in Georgia unhappy and disquieted in spirit.

From the outset, the work in Georgia did not go well. John and Charles had no success in evangelizing the Native Americans. Charles soon returned home, leaving John alone in Savannah. There he encountered a variety of relational problems within the church and was eventually sued by a jilted ex-girlfriend and her new husband for refusing them Communion. Wesley's manner drew the ire of his congregants to such an extent that he actually fled Savannah under cover of darkness one night, crossed the river into South Carolina, and took a ship back to England to escape their anger. The experience in Georgia left him exhausted and further disillusioned about the authenticity of his faith. His experiment had failed.

Back in England, still deeply troubled, Wesley began to study the Moravian faith and their experiences of God. He received personal tutelage from Peter Boehler, a young German missionary on leave in England. At Boehler's insistence, Wesley read Luther's commentary on Romans, and for the first time grasped the reality of salvation by faith alone and the promise of receiving assurance of salvation from the Holy Spirit.

On May 24, 1738, at a Moravian meeting on Aldersgate Street in London, Wesley had the now-famous encounter with God that left his heart feeling "strangely warmed."[2] From that point on, he experienced what he described as "heart religion,"[3] by which he meant the revelation of God's love, in Christ, communicated by the Holy Spirit to a person's heart—that is, to the center of our humanity, the core of who we are, from which all of life is ordered according to the things we love or hate. This appeal to the human heart elicits a response of the heart to God in faith.

After his Aldersgate experience, Wesley preached to huge crowds throughout Britain about having a heart experience of the love of God that "reorders the loves and fears of our everyday existence."[4] Professor Randy Maddox of Duke University expands on this idea:

In the interactions leading up to Aldersgate Wesley's focus sharpened on the importance of "feeling" the love of God. But this time it was not so much *his* love for God that he longed to feel, it was *God's* reconciling love for him—an experience which he described in the biblical terms of "having the love of God shed abroad in his heart, through the Holy Ghost which is given unto him."

From that point on in his preaching Wesley consistently encouraged his hearers to expect and pray that they might experience the love of God shed abroad in their hearts.[5]

Why is this important?

Because some of the most impactful and transformative moments in our lives are characterized by deep feelings that often beggar description. Like the first time your eyes connected with your future spouse. Or watching your loved one step off the troop transport returning from war. Or seeing your newborn baby emerge into the world. Or walking your precious daughter down the aisle and into the arms of a man you hope will cherish her as much as you do. We are moved deeply by our experiences and the emotions they evoke—and sometimes we're changed forever. No one can deny the reality of these emotions. Few would deny their lasting impact.

So why should the Christian life be any different?

I don't believe it is. In our natural humanity, before we are saved, our "senses are not competent to comprehend or respond to God," writes Theodore H. Runyon.[6] According to the apostle Paul, the god of this world has blinded the minds of unbelievers.[7] Isaiah describes the Israelites as spiritually insensitive, having blinded eyes and hardened hearts.[8] Only the initiating grace of God can open our eyes to his love and enable us to respond.[9]

John Wesley, as a result of his Aldersgate experience, came to believe that Christians are given "spiritual senses" that connect us with divine reality, equivalent to how our physical senses connect us with physical reality.[10] I believe that is what Jesus tries to explain to Nicodemus in John 3.

One of the ways that the Bible describes the Christian life is as being "born again." In Jesus' words, we are born again only by the Spirit's activity in our lives.[11] Not only are we forgiven of our sins, but the metaphor of new birth means we become brand new at our core—spiritual people with new hearts capable of receiving and discerning spiritual things mediated to us by the Holy Spirit, who has taken up residence in our lives. As Runyon explains, "The quickening of the spiritual receptors by the sense impressions written on them constitutes the reawakening of the image of God . . . and marks the crucial difference between the 'almost a Christian' and the genuine Christian."[12]

For instance, the assurance or confidence that we are "a new creation" is confirmed by the Holy Spirit: "The Spirit himself bears witness with our spirit that we are children of God."[13]

When we become born again, we are able to comprehend God and experience him because it is by the Spirit that he is discerned. In 1 Corinthians 2:13-14, Paul says that the words he teaches cannot be received by human wisdom. They're foolishness, in fact, to someone not yet born again. But when we are born again, the Holy Spirit enables us to receive and respond to spiritual truths because we are now spiritual people.

All of this means that believers can live with a brand-new set of spiritual sensibilities provided by the Holy Spirit. So though it's important for us to be cautious about being controlled by our feelings, we are able to experience God with the confidence that the Holy Spirit breathes new life into our entire born-again beings—including our emotions. It is completely appropriate to expect to experience God through our new, sanctified, spiritual sensibilities and to have those encounters affect us at every level of our being, including our feelings.

Does that rule out reason and logic in our faith? Absolutely not. Faith itself, writes theologian Henry Knight, is "the gift by God of a spiritual sense whereby the things of God can be discerned and experienced. . . . Faith as a spiritual sense thus cooperates with the five senses in such a way that the reality of God is experienced when Scripture is read, the Word proclaimed, and the Eucharist celebrated."[14] What separates this "spiritual sense" from spurious, subjective spiritual encounters is that the object must always be the God whose character is revealed in Scripture. And the end must always be our transformation into his likeness.[15]

In any discussion today about experiencing the presence of God, some critics will still look askance at people such as John Wesley. If we open our hearts to experiencing God, these Christian leaders warn, we are living on our feelings and checking our brains at the door. Feelings can never be trusted, they insist, particularly feelings that lead us to make decisions or that confirm decisions we've made in our pursuit of God and godly lives. It's best to lead with your head, always and only.

But is that accurate?

In our pursuit of God, can we ever trust our feelings?

Holy Hostages

James K. A. Smith, who teaches philosophy at Calvin College in Grand Rapids, is presently causing quite a stir in Christian academic circles. Smith rejects the notion that we are primarily *thinking* beings. He criticizes Protestant worship services that are based on Descartes's philosophy of reason, calling them a "heady affair fixated on 'messages' that disseminate Christian ideas and abstract values (easily summarized on PowerPoint slides)."[16]

In his book *Desiring the Kingdom*, Smith presents a convincing argument that, by God's design, we are "not primarily . . . *thinkers*, or even *believers*. Instead, [we] are . . . fundamentally . . . *lovers*. . . . The point is to emphasize that the way we inhabit the world is not primarily as thinkers, or even believers, but . . . more by feeling our way around in it."[17] In simple terms, this means we are shaped throughout our lives primarily by our *relationships*—the love that ultimately defines us.

Is this correct? Of course it is! Look at who created us! The essence of God is *relational* and *loving*—rooted in the selfless, self-sacrificing, transparent, unconditional love between Father, Son, and Spirit.[18] This is huge! Precisely because God himself is relational and loving, "it shapes our language about God to shape our heart[s] so we might share in the life of God," writes Stephen Seamands, professor at Asbury Theological Seminary.[19] "The trinitarian circle of Father, Son, and Holy Spirit is therefore an open, not a closed, circle. Through faith in Christ, through baptism *into* the name of the Father, Son, and Holy Spirit (Matthew 28:19), we enter into the life of the Trinity and are graciously included as partners."[20]

We were created in the image and likeness of God specifically for relationship with him, for intimacy, for love. Is it a faith-appropriated, faith-based relationship? Absolutely. But wouldn't it be ridiculous to think that our *emotions* would not be affected by so great a love? After Adam and Eve's sin of rebellion, God immediately set about to restore them to relationship with him. And it was love for all humanity that motivated Jesus' death and resurrection as the means of redeeming us from the sin that separated us from him and restoring us to relationship with him.[21] What love!

In light of our being invited into so great a love, it's no surprise that Jesus summed up the greatest of commandments by saying, "You must love the LORD your God with all your heart, all your soul, and all your mind."[22]

The apostle John explains the motivation and power behind our love for God: "We love because he first loved us."[23] How can we experience all of this love without any involvement of our emotions or feelings? The Christian life is far more than a faith-based decision that makes sense only to our minds. It is a lifelong love relationship with God that encompasses our entire being.

At the same time, when God manifests his presence, it's never for the mere purpose of creating a certain feeling within us. It's not for our entertainment, to give us goose bumps, or simply for dramatic effect. It is always to draw us into a more active love response to God. It is to let us know we're not alone, abandoned, or forsaken. It is to reassure us that he loves us, he is sovereign, he is trustworthy, and he always works everything for the good for those who love him and are called according to his purpose.[24]

Yes, when God shows himself to us, we can be certain that the experience will have some impact on our emotions. We need to allow this truth to sink into our minds and hearts. We were created with a huge capacity to experience and respond to the God of love.

Unchained by Love

John Wesley warned of the dangers of being misled by some of the more fickle emotions associated with the human heart—emotions that can lead to irrationality, self-deception, self-absorption, and manipulation.[25] I have seen these at play often enough. At the same time, it would be impossible to truly experience the glory of God in this life and not feel the impact of his glory on our hearts and emotions. It would be completely artificial to even try. "Some of Wesley's sharpest rebuttals [to his critics]," writes Randy Maddox, "concentrate on the importance of keeping emotions like joy, peace, and love central to religion, lest it degenerate into a 'dry dead carcass.'"[26]

The word *feelings* has come to be associated with any sort of fickle emotion that comes and goes. But both John Wesley and Jonathan Edwards, the famed New England revivalist, identified the indispensable importance of a heart encounter with God that touches the whole person, including the feelings or emotions.

Though feelings might indeed be transitory, they nonetheless shape the affections of the heart in lasting and transformational ways. "He that has doctrinal knowledge and speculation only, without affection," writes Jonathan Edwards, "never is engaged in the business of religion."[27] For both Wesley and Edwards, experiencing the touch of God established godly affections that were more akin to *dispositions of the heart* than fickle feelings of elation or exuberance. I believe this distinction establishes safer ground for our discussion.

Examples of these *affections*, as identified by both Wesley and Edwards, include fear, hope, love, hatred, desire, joy, sorrow, gratitude, compassion, and zeal.[28] These affections, Wesley maintained, are built out of, shaped, and formed by our experiences with God, and provide a consciousness of the reality of God and his presence with us. They are *from* God, God-initiated, and God-centered, and these criteria comprise arguably the strongest test today to confirm whether a feeling can be trusted or not. Experiences with God will likely include an emotional feeling, but the test is whether they result in a change of affections, or character. Ask yourself: Is this particular emotion directing me toward God and to serve others, or is it just a pleasurable feeling providing personal satisfaction?

Or think of it this way: Wesley and Edwards did not negate the role of head knowledge in the pursuit of God, but they broadened the concept of "knowing God" so that it more accurately reflected its biblical definition, not simply a strict dictionary definition. *Knowing*, in this sense, is not just *knowledge about something*. Rather, knowledge is *experiential*.

The word for "know" in the Hebrew Old Testament is *yâda*, the same word used to describe the intimacy between a husband and wife—as in "Adam *knew* Eve,"[29] which communicates much more than that Adam knew *about* Eve. The concept of "knowledge" as a purely cerebral understanding of facts about something is strictly a modern connotation. The biblical understanding of "knowing" is a knowledge that includes and embraces *experience* and *connection*.

We see this distinction clearly elsewhere in Scripture as well. For instance, when God declares in Jeremiah 9:24, "Let him who boasts boast in this, that he understands and knows me." In Hebrew, the word for "understands" here means "has insight or comprehension." That would be the comprehension of the mind. By contrast, the word for "knows" used in this same verse is *yâda*, the word used in the Bible for the way a parent knows a child or a husband knows his wife. This type of knowing cannot be achieved across long distances or with a casual detachment, but only "by active and intentional engagement in lived experience."[30]

The New Testament parallel of the Jeremiah passage is found in the words of Jesus, as recorded in John 17:3: "This is eternal life: that they know you the only true God, and Jesus Christ whom you have sent." Here, the Greek word for "know," *ginosko*, means "a special participation in the object known."[31]

This can mean only one thing: According to the Bible (both the Old and New Testaments), we cannot have an experiential intimacy with God without our emotions or affections being touched and changed. When it comes to *knowing* God, we need to think of the word *knowledge* in a broader sense. We want to *know* God in a way that awakens and restores a love for him in our hearts. When we love God in this way, we can expect true transformation. Our intimate, loving knowledge of God will produce godly living. In other words, our obedience to Christ comes from the overflow of our transformed hearts.

A few Sundays ago, my son-in-law and I were sitting side by side on the front row of our church during a time of tremendous congregational worship. The presence of the Lord was so evident as our young people led the worship that day. In the middle of a chorus about God's power to break chains, my son-in-law leaned over with tears in his eyes and whispered to me, "Dad, I just realized that it was ten years ago today that I came back to Christ. I'm so glad I'm not white-knuckling this transformation, but that God has delivered me and is clearly sustaining me. His work is being completed."

That phrase gripped my heart: "*I'm not white-knuckling it.*" Not having walked the same path as my son-in-law, I can only imagine how difficult and discouraging it is when sin has such strong control over us as to almost destroy our lives.

My son-in-law was raised in a Christian home, but that didn't keep him from some emotionally and spiritually crippling circumstances during his teenage years. He managed to cope with the fall-out until early in his adult life, when he plummeted into a lifestyle of drug abuse and promiscuity. Fortunately, God got his attention through the love of some friends, who broke down his pride and brought him to a place of true repentance. Over the next two years, God completely reclaimed his life—filling his heart with godly love and supernaturally transforming him from the inside out. Having witnessed some of this miraculous transformation firsthand, I can attest that my son-in-law was restored by *experiencing* the loving *presence* of God. Now, a full decade later, he still revels in God's abundant and unmerited grace. His gratitude to the Lord is so great. He senses God at work in his mind, his heart, and his affections. As he encountered and responded to God's love, it changed his character from the ground up. He no longer feels compelled to go back to his old behavior. There is an ease to his spiritual walk and his ongoing victory that is contagious. He recognizes that his peace is directly connected to his intimacy with God—not unlike the peace that John Wesley observed in the Moravians on board that ship in the midst of a storm.

A Heart-to-Heart Affair

In some Christian circles, emotions are seen as the enemy. Some Christian leaders go so far as to say that emotions are evil, will get us into trouble, and are thus to be mistrusted or avoided altogether.

Well-meaning Christian leaders often point to Jeremiah 17:9—"The heart is deceitful above all things, and desperately wicked; who can know it?"[32]—and use this as proof that the Bible mistrusts feelings. But a careful reading of the larger context of Jeremiah 17 makes it clear that the "deceitful and wicked" heart describes an idolatrous, rebellious person who trusts in human strength and "whose heart turns away from the LORD."[33] Later in Jeremiah, God promises to give new hearts to his people—hearts that aren't intrinsically deceitful or wicked: "This is the covenant that I will make with the house of Israel after those days, declares the LORD: I will put my law within them, and I will *write it on their hearts*. And I will be their God, and they shall be my people."[34] He doesn't say, "I will impress it upon their minds." No, "I will write it on their hearts."

Ezekiel 36:26 also describes the changes that happen to a person's heart under the new covenant. God declares, "I will give you a new heart, and a new spirit I will put within you. And I will remove the heart of stone from your flesh and give you a heart of flesh." A regenerated heart of flesh is capable of a range of healthy experiences and responses to the love of God, including our emotions or affections.

Still the suspicion remains.

We can all remember times when our feelings have been faulty or misled us. We dated someone we were convinced was the right one—only to have the relationship sour. We took a job because we had a gut feeling it was going to be good, only to have it turn into one of our more troubling life experiences. Maybe we felt certain that going to a particular church was going to be right, but the leaders there ended up preaching heresy. Or perhaps we felt right about buying a certain car only to have it end up being a lemon.

Our suspicion extends beyond the decisions we make. Perhaps we went to a Christian retreat and came back on a spiritual high that didn't produce fruit in our lives and didn't last. The problem was not the experience. The real problem was that our encounter with God was not properly stewarded when we came down off the mountain. Too many people aren't taught how to walk out a sustainable faith, one that includes and celebrates mountaintops, so they flounder in the valleys, left longing for the next high.

We don't pursue God for the sake of experiencing a "high." We pursue him just because he is God and draws us to himself. Unfortunately, certain segments of American Christianity have catered to "experience junkies"—Christians who run from one fix to the next, looking for whatever spiritually excites or energizes them. The danger of depending on an approach to God based on emotional experience is that it militates against faith—it can alleviate our responsibility to wrestle with and grow in our faith. And without faith it is impossible to please God.[35]

More often, intense experiences with God are like emergency room paddles, intended by the Holy Spirit to bring a cold, dead heart back to life. Yes, we need to have the wisdom to see that living at intense emotional levels is unsustainable, yet retreats and powerful Sunday mornings can be like God's gracious emergency room, where after our encounter with God we are encouraged and enabled to walk by faith at a new and higher level than before. Those mountaintop experiences are part of genuine discipleship.

One final caveat. God is and must always be the Actor and Initiator in any relationship of intimacy with him. Any experience of God is *from* him and *for* him. We cannot manipulate God into manifesting his presence. Worship and other faith practices only *prepare our hearts and minds* for God to pour out his grace and make his presence known. But just as the wind "blows where it wishes"[36] and no one knows where it goes, so too does God decide when, where, and how to show himself to us. He remains in charge. We have no assurance that if we sing all the right songs in the right order at the right volume we will experience God's presence. God is always the ultimate Designer of how and when he will be experienced. We are the gracious recipients of his presence, humbled by the fact that he would make himself known to us at all.

Faces of Love

Consider all the emotions that Jesus demonstrated during his life on earth. He was *moved with compassion* when he saw sick and hurting people, and he healed them. He was *incited to holy anger* when he saw the Temple desecrated by money changers. Jesus *wept* over Jerusalem, expressing his longing to gather its inhabitants to himself. He wept when his good friend Lazarus died and he saw Mary and Martha grieving. In the midst of a storm on the Sea of Galilee when his disciples were frantically rowing their boat and trying to get to safety, Jesus exhibited *perfect peace*—even sleeping in the middle of all the shouting, the waves, and rushing wind. He exhibited *determination* when he fixed his eyes like flint to go to Jerusalem for his crucifixion. In the upper room, he showed *humility* by washing the road-weary feet of his disciples. In the garden of Gethsemane, he displayed *anguish* as great drops of sweat fell like blood from his brow.

All these emotions were *felt by God*. Stop and think about that for a moment.

God feels.
He has emotions.

Though Jesus felt a full range of human emotions, it's important to keep in mind that his responses to these feelings, or his actions as a result of these feelings, were always focused on his mission and resulted in advancing the priorities of the Kingdom of God. If our experience of God's presence doesn't make a difference in our affections and actions, then it really doesn't matter what we feel. But if we respond as Jesus did, with actions consistent with our calling and purpose, then our emotions become a helpful motivator to the good works that God has set before us.[37]

Galatians 5:22-23 identifies love, joy, peace, patience, kindness, goodness, faithfulness, gentleness, and self-control as marks of a sanctified, mature believer. These emotions, affections, and attributes are the goal of any experience with God. That's why they are called the fruit of the Holy Spirit. Sermons have been preached, seminars have been conducted, and books have been written on the subject. But this is all for naught if our experience of God's presence doesn't produce the affections and actions that give evidence of the love of God within us.

What does it mean to love somebody? Is it just a warm feeling? Is it just something we might write a blog about? No. God's love in us compels us to *share* that love with the *least*, the *last*, and the *lost*. "As you did it to one of the least of these . . . , you did it to me," said Jesus.[38] So, moved by God's love, you go down to where the homeless hang out in your city and offer them coffee and a sandwich. Or you lean over the wall of the cubicle and invite your coworker to lunch—the same coworker who is shunned by the rest of the office because he is difficult to get along with. Or you maintain the yard of a widow nearby who has no family in town to help her. What moves us is the love of God experienced first in our hearts and then worked out in us (producing love, joy, and peace) and through us (resulting in patience, kindness, goodness, faithfulness, gentleness, and self-control), or else the works we do will all be for the wrong reasons.

The love we show is the result of God's love for us, and not because everyone we meet is so lovable. Joy is the result of being redeemed by God's grace and not because everything is perfect in our lives. Peace is a settled assurance in the midst of the storm because we know God is in charge. Patience with others emerges because we have been the recipients of God's persistent love and unmerited grace. Kindness and goodness and faithfulness and gentleness to others result because God has captured our hearts, and life is no longer about *us* and our own self-interest. Self-control is evidence that the Holy Spirit, who resides within us, is greater than our temperaments.

Changed hearts make righteous choices. God's objective in every one of our encounters with him is to produce changed hearts resulting in changed lives that bring praise and glory to his name.

A Two-Way Street

Back to our original question: Can feelings be trusted?

Ultimately, the answer is a resounding *yes*—provided our hearts are surrendered to God, we are watchful of the dangers we've mentioned, and our feelings are bringing us closer to God and shaping the affections of our hearts for God and others. That is why God lets us experience him in our *hearts* and not only in our minds; it's why he calls us to love him with all our heart, soul, mind, and strength. The work of God must engage our hearts, which includes our feelings. May we drive that important truth home time and time again.

A woman we interviewed on the island of Stornoway described how, years earlier, in 1949, when she was a teenager, she was invited to the revival meetings in her community. Having been catechized as a child, she had a *head knowledge* of God. She knew of God's existence and nature; she had even given lip service to the creeds while growing up; but she wasn't living for God. She agreed to go to the meetings, but she knew she was going only as a critic. She wanted to make fun of Duncan Campbell, the preacher from Edinburgh.

Instead, while she was at the meeting, she experienced the presence of God at a heart level. At a gathering in the Church of Scotland at Barvas, she was suddenly overcome with a sense of God's presence and a deep conviction of her sins. This strong sense of God's love for her stayed with her throughout the service, and she felt a joy beyond anything she had ever experienced.

At first, she said, she resisted the feelings because she feared being seen by her friends as too emotional.

But on her way out, just as she reached the front door of the church, she was overcome by the Holy Spirit, fell to her knees, and began weeping in repentance.

"I didn't care who was there or who saw me," she whispered during our interview. "All I wanted was Christ for my soul."

That's what I'm talking about. Search for God with all your heart and cry out to him for a closer relationship.

He is good.

In his time, he will answer.

Let God touch your emotions.

Allow him to create—and satisfy—a deep hunger in your heart for him.

STAGE 2 OF REVIVAL

The church's witness is eventually lost as the church becomes more and more like the world.

non-traditional spiritual experiences

CHAPTER 10

THIS PRESENT WEIRDNESS

ONE SUNDAY MORNING, after I'd been at Westgate Chapel for a few years, a woman came up to me after a service and told me she was new to the church and excited to be there. She added, "The congregation my husband and I just left was not open to my sharing words I receive from the Lord."

How would you handle a situation like that?

Now, I must add that Westgate Chapel is the kind of congregation that is open to experiencing God in the wonder of his presence, but I admit it does come with the risk that things may get out of hand.

I must also add that I grew up with an out-of-the-ordinary mix of conservative and Pentecostal theology and witnessed a few out-of-the-box experiences while growing up in my father's church.[1]

Even so, when this woman introduced herself to me in that way, all kinds of alarms went off in my head. I welcomed her kindly but walked away worried about what would happen next.

About six months later, the same woman came up to me after

service and said, "Pastor Alec, I have a word from the Lord for Westgate Chapel."

"And what would that be?"

"God told me to tell everybody they must get rid of all their credit cards. This is urgent and must be shared with the congregation as soon as possible."

Although I had no doubt that credit cards could be a stumbling block to some people, I told her I did not believe it was a message from the Lord for our congregation at that point. I assured her I would consult with the other leaders and get back to her, but in the meantime I politely declined her request to speak to the congregation. At Westgate, we're open to the presence of God, but to prevent things from getting weird or leading people astray, we also have filters through which we evaluate people's experiences with God.

She was obviously not happy with my answer.

One Sunday a couple of months later, when I saw the woman and her husband at our 9:00 a.m. service, I noticed she had a strange look of determination on her face during the entire service; but fortunately nothing happened. I went back to my office relieved, but just as the second service was set to begin, I heard a knock on my door. It was one of our ushers.

"Pastor," he said, "you're going to want to see this. There's a woman standing in the front below the pulpit, facing the church with her arms crossed. She's got her Bible drawn to her chest, and she looks like she's waiting to announce something."

Instantly, I knew who it was. I called in our senior associate pastor and executive pastor, explained the situation, and said, "The two of you go to her before the service starts and do whatever it takes to get her out of the sanctuary. If she wants to talk or argue, get her into one of the empty classrooms so we can start the service."

I gave them what I thought would be an appropriate amount of time to handle the situation, slightly delaying the start of the service. At five minutes after 11:00, I walked onto the platform along with the choir and worship pastor. To my surprise, the woman was still standing down below the pulpit, engaged in what was now a heated conversation with our two pastors.

To buy them more time, I disregarded the order of service, went straight to the pulpit, announced a hymn, and asked the congregation to stand. While the people were reaching for their hymnals, the woman's husband, still seated in the congregation, began to shout repeatedly, "Let her speak! Let her speak!" Fortunately, two ushers appeared out of nowhere and escorted him to the lobby while he continued to shout over his shoulder.

We launched into the hymn, but no one was worshiping. We were all too distracted. Halfway through the hymn, I glanced down in front and noticed—much to my alarm—that our two pastors were both gone and the woman was still there. (I learned later that she had said, "God told me that this would happen and that I would need to be carried out." She was a woman of considerable size, and realizing they were outmatched, the two pastors had gone to the lobby to look for ushers to help them.)

All I knew at the moment was that the pastors were gone and there was nothing left to do but take matters into my own hands. I was not feeling much like a loving shepherd right then. I was angry. I handed the hymnal to my wife, who was standing in the front row of the choir just behind me, and she stepped forward to lead the singing while I stepped down to the altar area. I got within an inch of the woman's nose and said firmly, "You are not in the Spirit, you are in the flesh, and you are leaving with me right now." Because there are no side doors out of the sanctuary, I took her by the elbow to lead her down the aisle toward the lobby. To my surprise, she responded and walked with me, but all the time cursing me: "God did not put you in this church! Man did! And a wasting disease will take you out!"

The hymn was still being sung, but every eye in the building was on me. I escorted the woman to the lobby, where the pastors and ushers had her husband corralled. After a brief—or shall I say *terse*—conversation, the couple left the building and the situation was resolved. But I realized it made no sense to try to continue the service as if nothing had happened. I went back to the pulpit, relieved my wife of her song-leading duty, stopped the hymn, had the congregation sit down, and said, "Okay, we need to talk about what just happened."

I shared the background to the story and reaffirmed the responsibility of church leadership to sense what God is doing in a church service and obey the Lord. I told them that none of the leaders believed the woman had a message from the Lord, and that was why she was denied the opportunity to speak. We prayed as a congregation and then continued in worship. To my relief, it turned out to be one of the more energized worship services we'd had for months.

When I compare notes with pastoral colleagues around the country, I find that stories like this aren't uncommon. So I raise the question again in its larger context: What do you do if you are pursuing God's presence and things get weird?

Is Anything Too Weird for God?

Comedian Richard Pryor, in one of the few comedy routines of his clean enough to be repeated here, offered a snippet of wisdom that has a surprisingly deep theological application for the subject matter of this book. He quipped, "I was walking down a street one night, past a dark alley, and out of that alley came the voice of God saying, 'Richard, come here!'" Pryor paused for dramatic effect, then added in a worried voice, "I did not go down that alley—because it might not have been the voice of God."

It makes for great comedy, but it also highlights the reality that we are always vulnerable to misinterpreting what may or may not be an actual experience of God's presence. We want to be people in pursuit of God, yes, and we want to be open to the expectation that he will make himself known to us. That is the kind of faith that pleases him. But is it possible that a genuine spiritual experience may appear to be out-of-the-box, against the grain of our tradition, or even uncanny?

The simple answer is *yes*—absolutely yes.

But think about the flip side. Are spiritual experiences any more apt to become weird than pursuing God with only our intellect? Think of all the weird doctrines and bizarre interpretations of Scripture that have arisen out of people's *minds*. Consider the damage done in the nineteenth century by higher criticism, an intellectual bias of philosophers and liberal theologians against the plain interpretation and application of Scripture. The result for many has been to strip God of his power and glory. Confidence in God's Word has been shredded, belief in the miracles of Jesus undermined, and any notion of a personal relationship with God eviscerated. And it all came from a purely intellectual approach to God.

Look to those times in church history when God has revealed himself in such a way as to grip the passions of his followers, and you'll find stories of awakened spiritual interest, repentance for sin, increased conversions, more passionate worship, widespread confession, deeper appreciation of the Word of God, families strengthened, broken lives restored, increased social justice, more love for God and fellow man, and communities transformed. So let's not be too quick to throw out the baby with the bathwater.

One of the startling characteristics of the 1904 Welsh revival was a powerful sense of God's presence over the whole nation. It brought such wholesale conviction of sin in the mining communities that miners who had stolen company tools over the years brought them back and laid them at the entrance of the gates of the mines. The next morning, workers had difficulty getting to the gates past piles of returned tools. Donkeys that pulled the carts in the mines had to be retrained. They didn't know how respond to commands when every other word was no longer a curse word.

Were there instances of excess during that revival? Yes, but my concern is that some people make a life's work of pointing out perceived or real spiritual excesses simply as a way of buffering themselves against encountering the presence of the living God. J. I. Packer, the renowned Bible scholar, writes that the reason for the weakness of the church today can be attributed to "ignorance both of [God's] ways and of *the practice of communion with him*."[2] Packer places the fault at the feet of "churchmen who look at God, so to speak, through the wrong end of the telescope, so reducing him to pygmy proportions . . . [and resulting in] pygmy Christians."[3] Satan will do everything in his power to keep a distance between God and us. It works out better for him that way.

Simon Says

Just because it's weird doesn't mean it's wrong.

In fact, far from it. In Scripture, God often reveals himself intentionally in ways designed to get our attention and refocus our lives on him. So it's okay to be open to spiritual experiences that may not fit our traditional model of the Christian life. Why? Because the narrative of Scripture is full of them. Let's look at some perfectly legitimate examples of people who encountered God in out-of-the box ways.

- How about being instructed by God to lie on your left side, tied with ropes, for 390 days in front of a makeshift model of the city of Jerusalem? Okay, that is weird, but that's what God told the prophet Ezekiel to do.[4]

- How about encountering Jesus in a blinding light on your way to Damascus, hearing an audible voice and falling to the ground in front of all your friends? That's what happened to Saul.[5] Has anything like that ever happened in your church?

- How about leading an Ethiopian court official to Christ, and in the next instant being transported nineteen miles away to another city? That's how Philip's encounter with God turned out in Acts 8:26-40. "Beam me up, Scotty!"

- How about being "caught up to the third heaven," where you hear amazing things you are forbidden to talk about? That's what happened to the apostle Paul (formerly Saul, of the Damascus road experience), which he mentions in 2 Corinthians 12:2-4.

These experiences don't fit the three-points-and-a-poem Sunday morning routine that is typical of so many churches today. Please understand that I'm not trying to build a case for seeking weirdness for the sake of weirdness. And we mustn't pursue out-of-the-box spiritual experiences simply for entertainment. As my good friend, theologian Steve Land, says, the manifest presence of God is not a remedy "for the bored and impatient."[6] Yet there are believers across North America who spend their lives running from church to church looking for the next big thing. We must avoid that temptation.

My point is simply that if God *does* show up outside of our expectations, then scripturally speaking, we need to be open. God is God, and he may choose to operate in ways that do not fit our routines or limited expectations. But if an experience results in self-absorption, self-promotion, or arrogance that causes us to become unteachable, it's time to question whether the experience was truly of God's presence. If the experience draws attention to *itself* rather than prompting deeper worship, reverence, and respect for God, then whatever it might be, it's most certainly not a manifestation of God's holy presence.

I realize this creates a tension for many Christians. But tension isn't always a bad thing. It calls for wisdom and discernment, both of which the Holy Spirit provides. Any time in history when the people of God have opened themselves to experiencing God's presence, the challenge has always been in interpreting and moderating the experiences.

In the case of the 1904 Welsh revival, we have an example of this tension in the life of Evan Roberts, the leader God used as a catalyst for the revival. The enemy used Roberts's vulnerability and doubt to permanently remove him from his position of leadership in the movement. As a result, some historians believe that what potentially could have been the largest movement of God in the modern era was prematurely aborted.

Roberts was initially a coal miner who attended Bible school but dropped out because of a limited capacity for study. Nevertheless, he devoted himself to the Lord and specifically to the ministry of prayer, spending most evenings—and often all night—on his knees. At a moment of desperation in his pursuit of God, Roberts began to pray one phrase, "Bend me, Lord," which was an appeal for the Lord to deliver him from himself. As Roberts went on to speak to house churches throughout Wales, that phrase—"Bend me, Lord"—became the cry of the revival movement. The Lord swept into people's hearts and lives through the simplicity of Roberts's messages, which focused chiefly on the centrality of Jesus Christ and our need for salvation.

The Welsh revival was characterized by an unusual sense of God's presence and by tremendous worship, and it soon involved more leaders than just Roberts. Although the revival lasted for only little more than a year, some 100,000 new Welsh converts were counted for Christ during that time. Later, the revival spread to Scotland, England, and Southern California, with some one million converts.[7]

A few years ago, I interviewed Dr. Richard Owen Roberts (no relation to Evan Roberts), an expert on the 1904 Welsh Revival. He noted that the demise of the revival began when Evan Roberts became too focused on visions, revelations, and experiences, and in the process began to deemphasize biblical preaching.

One night when Roberts went to the pastor's vestry to pray before the evening service, the room filled with light and a strong sense of God's presence. Roberts went out charged for the service and saw a widespread response. The following Sunday, in a different town and church, he again went to the pastor's vestry to pray before the service. This time, he experienced an almost debilitating heaviness and darkness. The results of that night's meeting were slim.

In the months following the two experiences with the light and darkness, Roberts began to question his ability to rightly interpret the events. Previously, he had rejoiced in the light and spurned the darkness, but now he wasn't quite as certain.

He came to the conclusion that both of his experiences, the light as well as darkness, had come from the enemy.

He could scarcely believe it. Yet he could not escape the conclusion. Before this, every victory had been won on the basis of faith alone in dependence upon the Holy Spirit. The strategy of the enemy to bring defeat at that important meeting was to switch him from the basis of faith and direct his attention to impressions and feelings. The unusual light accomplished the enemy's purpose.

[Roberts] confessed that after the experience of the supernatural light he began to look for more manifestations, and his position of faith was thus weakened. The experience of darkness came after he had already weakened himself by turning from the basis of faith to that of impressions.[8]

The sad conclusion to this story is that these events caused Evan Roberts to so doubt his own discernment that he withdrew from leadership in the revival and spent the rest of his life as a recluse. He lived in the tension, and the tension won!

How can we distinguish between genuine manifestations of God and the counterfeit? How are we able to tell if something out-of-the-ordinary originates from God, the Father of Lights, or from the devil, who masquerades as an angel of light?[9]

Terms and Conditions

The following "filters" have been developed through much prayer, thought, and Scripture searching. Among others, I have Emory University professor Theodore Runyon, in particular, to thank for his influence in the development of this list.[10]

"Beloved, do not believe every spirit," writes the apostle John, "but test the spirits to see whether they are from God, for many false prophets have gone out into the world."[11] If, while seeking God's presence, you come across an experience that seems off-kilter, ask yourself the following questions:

1. *Does it have clear, telltale marks of being from God?* For an experience to be valid, it must clearly come from God, whose nature and being are revealed in Scripture. It must plainly be initiated by God and have the God of the Bible as its focus. Runyon explains: "Experience . . . must transcend subjectivism. It must come from a source that is external to us, our feelings, and imagination. . . . There is no true knowledge of God apart from God's own active participation in that knowledge."[12] This is why Scripture, our primary source of God's revelation, must be the final authority over all experience.

On a TV show I watched recently, the leader of a so-called revival flopped down on the ground in front of thousands of audience members, supposedly to receive his sermon directly from God. When he got up some time later and delivered the message, it was an unintelligible rambling of clichés and Scripture ripped from its context. I'm confident that message did not come from the Lord. The whole episode made the evangelist and his so-called experience with God the center of attention. When God manifests his presence, his presence will always be the center of attention.

2. *Is it in line with Scripture?* A genuine encounter with God will elicit responses that align with God's revealed Word—humility, repentance, confession, contrite hearts, gratitude, worship, a deepened hunger for Scripture, a greater passion for evangelism, the fruit of the Spirit, and a growing love for God and others. That's just for starters.

In the mid-1990s, I encountered people who had been influenced by what was called the Toronto Blessing. This was at about the same time that the Holy Laughter movement ran its course in North America.

When some of the leaders of the movement came to Seattle to conduct a series of meetings, they asked for my support. Skeptical of what I had heard about the movement, I researched what was reported to be happening in Toronto and watched the video clips that accompanied their promotional material. Participants were seen laughing hysterically, jerking, twitching, shaking, rolling on the floor, roaring like lions, barking like dogs, and undergoing a vomit-like "crunching" that was said to cleanse and release negative experiences. In one expression of the movement, some participants even purposely relieved themselves in their pants as a sign of complete abandonment to God. When comparing these often-degrading manifestations with what occurred during historic revivals such as in Wales and Stornoway, it's hard to see how this movement could be a manifestation of God's holy presence.

3. *Does it make me want more of God, or simply more of the experience?* An experience with God will result in a longing for more of God, not simply more of the experience. "The focus in religious experience is upon the Other, and upon the self only as it serves as the object of the Other and the necessary receptor of experience."[13]

A true encounter with God will leave us hungry for more of God—a longing for God to be the center and focus of our lives and a yearning to be more like him. Paul tells the Philippian church that everything he is and owns is rubbish by comparison with the "surpassing greatness of knowing Christ."[14] Not content with that, two verses later Paul cries out again, "I want to know Christ!" Paul's experience of the love of Christ leaves him wanting more.

A genuine experience of God's presence always causes us to want him more, to want to be more like him, and to be about his business in the lives of others. If the experience does not "constrain" us to be more loving toward God or "compel" us toward greater holiness and being a blessing to others, we can conclude that the experience was just weirdness.

4. *Does it make me more selfless or more selfish?* A genuine experience with God is "inevitably transforming."[15] How can it not be? Yet it should also give me greater compassion for others. If the experience makes me more selfish or arrogant, it is either not of God or I am abusing God's grace. "'Knowledge' puffs up," Paul reminds us in 1 Corinthians 8:1, "but love builds up [others]." That is the test!

When I spoke with Dr. Richard Owen Roberts about the Welsh revivals, he noted that a spirit of pride spoiled some of the revival's results. Some of those who were saved in the powerful conviction and move of God's manifest presence later came to disdain and disparage the salvation experience of subsequent generations who did not come to Christ in the same kind of fervor. Even parents were concerned about their children because they were suspicious of their conversions. This kept the first generation from having a positive influence on subsequent generations.[16]

5. *Am I teachable and open to correction?* One of the concerns I had with the woman at Westgate who stood at the front of the church and insisted we allow her to share her "word from the Lord" was that she was standing in direct rebellion to church leadership. A truly godly person is teachable, and open to correction and guidance from spiritual leaders and other spiritually mature Christians. If that isn't the case, then the person's experiences are largely discredited. By contrast, "fanatics are marked by harshness towards those who don't fall in line with them."[17]

This is why if we seek to experience the presence of God, we need to be in active community with other godly believers—people walking together through life and helping each other discern the voice of the Spirit and their experience with God. Certainly, a person outside the community of faith can experience God's presence. The danger is that in isolation, with only one's own interpretation of the experience and of Scripture, it is too easy to be deceived or misled.

"Faith experience is always open to comparison with, and correction by, other faith experiences—biblical, historical, and in the present community—and is not threatened by this rational process of 'testing the spirits' to see 'whether they are of God' (1 John 4:1)."[18] To be safe in our experience of God, we must be under authority and in community.

The Summer of '92

It started out as just another sleepy summer Sunday in Seattle—August 23, 1992. I remember the date well.

Rita and I had been at Westgate Chapel for four years already, and I had started to experience discouragement and frustration. The honeymoon phase was long over. My emphasis on prayer and the presence of God wasn't nearly as successful as I'd hoped. We were running about 1,300 in attendance, but try as I might, I couldn't coax more than about thirty people to come out to weekly prayer meetings. To make matters worse, the church was made up of fairly wealthy people, many of whom owned vacation homes in warmer climates. So during the summer months, church attendance would drop by one-third. Ministries shut down. Leadership for Sunday worship was reduced to me, an elderly organist, and an occasional soloist singing to tracks.

I hated summer. It could last well into October if the sun stayed out.

By August 1992, my faith was at an all-time low. I was in maintenance mode, holding on until school and the rain brought the congregation back and we could resume God's business. The 9:00 a.m. service went off as planned. We sang some worship songs. We introduced visiting missionaries. We took the offering. Someone sang a song to a sound track that obviously hadn't been rehearsed with. I delivered the sermon. It was nothing to write home about. I could tell by the faces in the congregation that most were on autopilot. Including me.

The 11:00 a.m. service began the same way. A hymn was sung. A couple of choruses. Exactly like the early service. But after the choruses, as people were being seated, I noticed that up in the balcony one man remained standing. I knew him to be a godly man. He and his family had been involved at Westgate for several years. He was in community with others in the church and clearly under authority in his relationships with the pastors. I also knew him to be a man of prayer with a great heart of worship.

When he saw that I had noticed him, he began to speak. Now, people had spoken out before during our services, though it was not a regular occurrence, so I let it continue. His demeanor wasn't frantic or ecstatic. It wasn't even overly emotional or passionate. He simply spoke, with reference to Luke 8:4-15, about how various "soils" were present in our congregation. Some soils were hard and crusty and resisted the sharp edge of Scripture's plow. Some seed fell on fallow ground and wasn't fruitful. Yet some soil was receptive.

He encouraged us that the receptive soil in our congregation would find reason to rejoice. He spoke of God's Word breaking through, how our congregation would melt in spirit and heart, and how God would bring forth fruit from that. He encouraged us to seize the moment and put it in our memory because we would never be the same after that. He said it was a day of rejoicing and breakthrough. And then he sat down.

That was when a miracle happened in front of our eyes. As I mentioned, we'd had people speak out before in our services, but very seldom did the words land with such gravity and urgency. Everyone knew that God had interrupted our routine. Many who were present that day felt that God wasn't simply interrupting the service, he was interrupting the direction of the entire church.

When the man sat down, I looked out across the congregation— and to this day I find it hard to explain what I saw. Most in the congregation, main floor and balcony, were weeping. Some had spontaneously gathered into small groups across the sanctuary and begun to pray. Some stood to their feet, eyes closed, faces directed to heaven. Others lifted their hands before God, like a toddler reaching for a parent's love. Several hundred left their seats and streamed into the altar area, where they knelt to pray. No one had given any directive from the pulpit. I was concerned that anything I might do or say would disrupt the work that God was so obviously doing. After a long while, I went to the microphone and said, "God's not done, and we're not going to interfere with what he's doing. Please just keep your hearts open and surrendered to him." And then I sat down.

For the next forty-five minutes, God took charge. I didn't preach. I didn't introduce the missionaries. The soloist didn't sing. We didn't take an offering. We all just went to prayer. Finally, when those who had been in the altar area headed back to their seats, I went to the microphone and gave an altar call for those who had never given their lives to Christ. Twenty-five people came forward.

The 11:00 service would normally end by 12:30. But at 1:00 p.m. that day, the sanctuary was still full. Nobody wanted to leave. By 2:00, it was still more than half full. The people continued in quiet prayer and worship. God's presence broke through in an unusual way that day.

The next night was our regular monthly board meeting. Not everyone had been in the second service, so the people who were there explained to the rest of the board what had happened. After an animated discussion of the previous day's events, a lingering sense of the awe of the Lord pervaded the board meeting. A few men on the board at that time were ex-military, so I asked them, "If we were generals of an army, and our commander in chief informed us of a breakthrough, what would we do?"

"We would throw all our personnel and resources into the breach before it closed back up," one of the men replied.

So that's what we did.

The next Sunday, with the board's backing, we called for a solemn assembly to take place at the church on the following Wednesday night. Based on our track record as a church, I remember thinking I'd be happy if a hundred people showed up. You can imagine my surprise on Wednesday night, when I walked out of my study and into the sanctuary to find the main floor and balcony packed. It was such a confirmation for me that this was a God thing.

I explained to the congregation that the church leaders believed we had heard from the Lord. We wanted to take God's words to us seriously. We would humble ourselves in that meeting and not presume we knew what was next. We would ask God what came next. That was the pressing question: *What do we do now?* The presence of God in the sanctuary that night was incredible. Everyone was worshiping. Everyone was praying. There were no spectators.

For the next six months, we canceled everything on Westgate's calendar except Sunday services and Wednesday evening prayer meetings. We needed that amount of time for a true spirit of prayer to permeate the life of the church. Everything changed. Worship changed. Prayer changed. The atmosphere in the congregation changed. The pastors changed. I changed. Hundreds now attended our midweek prayer meetings.

I tell this story because this was definitely an experience I'd classify as "out of the ordinary." It certainly wasn't expected or planned. There was no way it could have been manipulated into existence. From then until now, the emphasis on prayer has remained a constant, not just midweek but throughout the life of the church. And we have certainly changed, just like the Lord said we would. We went from being a mostly Caucasian congregation to a multiethnic congregation, with thirty-nine nationalities now represented. We've changed from being a wealthy congregation to a mixed socioeconomic congregation. People still take their normal summer vacations, but there's no sense of abandonment of the church and its ministries during the summer months. Ministry continues strong all year long. Hearts have been softened. Lives forever changed. People have been humbled. The gentleman who spoke from the balcony was not afforded some sort of elevated status. Overall, the life of the church changed for the good from that Sunday onward.

Maybe you long for a similar breakthrough, either in your personal life or in the life of your church. To all who are seeking a breakthrough, my simple encouragement is to shift the focus away from the breakthrough itself and back onto God. Make God the focal point of your search, not the experience.

Seeing a vision from Macedonia was not the focal point of Paul's life. But Paul's mission was redirected by it.

Philip wasn't looking for a Star Trek teleporting experience when he witnessed to the Ethiopian eunuch. He just wanted to preach the Good News of the gospel wherever God sent him.

John the Baptist wasn't looking to launch a new line of clothing for aspiring evangelists. He just wanted to prepare the way for the Lord.

At Westgate Chapel, we didn't go looking for a dramatic interruption of our Sunday service. We just knew we were desperate for God.

That's my word of encouragement to you. Make God the focal point and the priority of your life. Make drawing near to God the main activity of your life. And let God reveal himself to you in whatever ways he knows will advance his purposes in you.

STAGE 3 OF REVIVAL
Without the church's influence as salt and light, society grows increasingly evil.

CHAPTER II

A HOLY TAILWIND

WHILE I WAS working for Youth Development in San Diego, the president of the organization encouraged me to fly their plane at least two hours a month in addition to ministry trips, for the purpose of increasing my logged hours and proficiency as a pilot.

One Sunday morning, after leading worship at the church we attended, I made a spur-of-the-moment decision to fly Rita and my brother-in-law, Bill, to Lake Havasu for lunch. Lake Havasu is a resort city on the Arizona side of the Colorado River, on the eastern border of California. The old London Bridge, shipped all the way from England and reassembled to connect the city with an island in the lake, is one of the main tourist attractions there. I had flown to Lake Havasu several times with my instructor and knew of a great restaurant on the river that operated a fleet of old English taxis to shuttle guests to and from the airport.

Our plane was kept in a hangar at Montgomery Field in San Diego, less than two miles from our home church. It was a typical Southern California day, with blue skies and warm temperatures.

Under normal conditions, the flight took an hour. I needed to be back at the church in time to lead worship for the evening service, but I calculated that with an hour there, an hour back, and an hour for lunch, we'd be home by 4:00 p.m. at the latest. Rita and Bill were excited to join me, so we drove out to the airfield, jumped into the Cessna 182, fired it up, taxied to end of the runway, waited for clearance from the tower, and took off. I dialed in the headings for the route to Lake Havasu, and we settled in for a pleasant flight. Things couldn't have been better.

As a low-time pilot, it didn't even register with me that the flight out to Havasu that day took only forty minutes. I wrote it off to my world-class navigational skills. We landed, taxied the plane over to the fixed-base operator, tied up, called for the restaurant taxi, and fueled the plane while we waited. When we reached the restaurant, beautifully situated at the river's edge, we enjoyed a leisurely lunch. I congratulated myself on the brilliant idea as we rode in the taxi back to the airport with plenty of time to spare.

Unfortunately, by the time we arrived back at the airport, surface winds had picked up significantly and had shifted direction. Because the wind was now blowing out of the northwest, we were directed to use the airport's alternate gravel runway. Even then, the wind was crossways to the runway. This concerned me quite a bit because of the compounding complications of taking off on gravel with crosswind. But I made the decision to fly anyway.

We obviously couldn't see the wind, but we could sure feel it buffeting the plane from left to right during the run-up before takeoff. With a brief prayer, I rolled on power and pulled the yoke all the way back to my chest. We were airborne very quickly, but things got dangerous right away. We weren't five feet off the ground when the crosswinds blew us completely off the runway and on a course toward some old outbuildings at the edge of the airport. There was nothing to be done at that moment except fly the airplane and try to squeeze out as much altitude as possible. It felt like we rose inches at a time rather than feet, but in the nick of time we cleared the top of the outbuildings and continued climbing to the appropriate altitude for our westbound trek back to San Diego.

High over the desert floor, the stiff crosswind at takeoff was a distant memory. We all relaxed after our harrowing experience, and Bill and Rita began to point out various interesting topographic features below us, such as the dry lakebeds and Granite Mountains. Twenty minutes went by, and I was silently beginning to congratulate myself on my flying prowess when Rita tapped me on the shoulder and spoke with a worried voice. "Alec," she said. "I think we're standing still."

Sure enough—the same features we had noticed below us fifteen minutes earlier were still below us now. We were barely moving. The instruments indicated we were doing 120 knots, but I now realized our problem. The reason we had arrived so quickly in Lake Havasu was because of a strong tailwind. That same wind was now preventing us from getting back to San Diego. I increased power and pushed the plane as hard as I could, but with the clock ticking, we struggled all the way home.

This was in the days before cell phones, so we had no way to contact the pastor or worship staff. As we entered the traffic pattern at Montgomery Field, our inbound leg took us directly over the church. We all three looked down to see the parking lot already full. The evening service was moments away from beginning. By the time we got the plane landed and in the hangar and raced over to the church, the service was well under way without us. So much for my brilliant planning and world-class navigational skills.

As I think back on this story, I'm reminded of what Jesus told Nicodemus during their nighttime conversation. The prominent Pharisee wondered aloud how a grown man could possibly be born again.[1]

"Unless one is born of water and the Spirit, he cannot enter the kingdom of God," Jesus explained to him. "The wind blows where it wishes, and you hear its sound, but you do not know where it comes from or where it goes. So it is with everyone who is born of the Spirit."[2]

Think about that line—*the wind blows where it wishes*. The whole principle of flight is based on the activity of moving air (wind) over aerodynamic flight surfaces. You can't see the wind, and you can't always feel it, but it's there all right—accelerating or slowing your progress, pushing you along, even changing your intended direction. In similar fashion, the invisible force of the Holy Spirit makes our journey possible and more efficient as the Spirit moves, empowers, and directs us when we're in alignment with his purposes.

It is impossible to live the Christian life without the Holy Spirit. He applies the saving work of Christ and "initiates and administers the Christian life within us."[3] He is the agent and mediator of the presence of God in our lives. When he is present in us, "absolutely all of the Godhead is present and operative."[4] John Wesley identified the Holy Spirit in us as "God's breathing into the soul . . . an unceasing presence of God, the loving, pardoning God, manifested to the heart and perceived by faith."[5] We cannot get anywhere in life without him.

When we were flying home from Lake Havasu, we found ourselves in the unfortunate predicament of flying against a strong headwind. The course we chose to our destination positioned us unavoidably against the wind. With the wind against us, the traveling was much harder and we made far slower progress. How, too, like our spiritual lives whenever we try to take a course that positions us against the Holy Spirit's leading and empowerment in our lives.

That's the big question for us to explore: Are we flying *with* or *against* the Holy Spirit?

A Breath of Fresh Air

Sadly, the Holy Spirit has been marginalized by much of contemporary Christianity. We have well-constructed doctrinal positions that include him on paper, and we give him lip service in the major creeds; but far too often we live as if he's distant at best, nonexistent at worst.

The truth about this third person of the Trinity is that he is very much real and anything but distant.

In the Old Testament, the word translated "Holy Spirit" is *ruach*.

In the New Testament, the word is *pneuma*. In both instances, the word means "breath of the mouth, breath of air, air in motion, breeze, wind, storm," and all are attributed to the activity of the Holy Spirit (where dictated by context).[6] When we read the Scriptures from Genesis to Revelation concerning the presence of the Holy Spirit and his activity in the lives of God's people, we come to understand that the movement of the Holy Spirit is sometimes a gentle breeze and sometimes a life-altering hurricane.

Gordon Fee writes, "For Paul, and [in] the rest of the N[ew] T[estament], the way God is now present is by his Spirit."[7] From salvation to the grave and our eventual resurrection, we need the Holy Spirit at work in us. But he is also what some theologians today call the "shy member" of the Trinity, not drawing attention to himself. He always points away from himself to the love of the Father and the saving grace of the Son. But that doesn't mean we can or should ignore him.

The closer we get to God and the greater our sensitivity to spiritual things, the more we recognize the Holy Spirit's activity in our lives. The more we invite his guidance and power, the quicker we're going to move toward God's purpose and destination for us. The Spirit of God is a Holy Tailwind behind us. That's great news!

Bad News, Good News

Recently, I invited Dr. Rob Wall from Seattle Pacific University to preach at Westgate Chapel a series of sermons I had heard on the university's website. Dr. Wall spoke from John 13–14, where Jesus announces to his disciples that he isn't going to be with them much longer. Think about that for a moment. Up to this point, Jesus has been with them day and night for three years. He has loved them, taught them, fed them, washed their feet, and done miracles to reassure them that he indeed is Immanuel—God with us. They have left everything to follow him, and now he is going to *leave* them? Jesus' announcement undoubtedly sounded counterproductive to the disciples, even frightening. Just when they were starting to feel comfortable in this relationship, Jesus was leaving.

Typical for Peter, he speaks up first and blurts out, "Lord! Where are you going? . . . Why can't I follow you now?"[8]

Thomas's reaction is more plaintive: "We do not know where you're going. How can we know the way?"[9]

Philip responds with pragmatism: "Lord, show us the Father, and we will be satisfied."[10]

But Jesus answers all three questions in ways the disciples could never have anticipated. He doesn't tell Peter where he is going or why Peter can't follow. He doesn't explain to Thomas how to get there or tell Philip how to discover the Father. Jesus also doesn't allay their fears by promising to stick around and help them. Instead, he promises to "ask the Father, and he will give you another Helper, to be with you forever, even the Spirit of truth, whom the world cannot receive, because it neither sees him nor knows him. You know him, for he dwells with you and will be in you."[11]

That answers all three concerns: The Holy Spirit will be with us forever and will show us the way back to the presence of the Father.

That's God's solution for every disciple of Jesus Christ. Yes, we would love to have Jesus with us physically, but that's not an available option. So how can we live our lives without feeling abandoned like orphans? How will we know the presence of Christ as if he were physically present today? How will we experience Jesus like the disciples did when they walked alongside him, ate with him, and were led and taught by him two thousand years ago?

The answer is the Holy Spirit.

Jesus said, "In that day [when the Spirit comes] you will know that I am in my Father, and you in me, and I in you."[12]

Jesus will always be the source of our salvation and the focal point of our lives here on earth. Paul puts it this way: "It is no longer I who live, but Christ who lives in me."[13] It is miraculous that Christ lives in us. Yet the only way to realize and *activate* that miracle is by the work of the Holy Spirit.

We must not forget—though it seems we often do—that the Holy Spirit is fully God, the very means by which God makes his presence and power known in our lives. To say that the Holy Spirit is the third person in the triune Godhead is not to say he is a *third wheel*. Not at all. Like Jesus, the "whole fullness of deity dwells"[14] in him, waiting to bring the fullness of God's presence and purpose into our lives. He will not force his way in, violating our God-given free will. Instead, he waits for us to commune with him, to ask him to fill us with God's presence and guide us in every decision or interaction. As Steve Land reminds us, "The Spirit's filling must be invoked daily because the point is to live out of his fullness and by his direction and not that of the world, the flesh, or the devil."[15]

What might this look like in everyday life? We can rely on him in the middle of a board meeting; while correcting our children; while deciding what college to attend, whom to marry, or how many children to have—everything! He is just waiting to be invited to give input into our lives.

At Westgate Chapel, a member of the choir serves as an administrative assistant at an engineering firm that subcontracts for one of the top aerospace companies in the area. She recently told the choir the following story:

Our company was asked to design a critical piece of equipment for a new aircraft. The engineers kept working at it, but try as they might, they were stumped by the design and function of a particular small component.

Month after month, they worked to try to solve the problem, only to run into a dead end time and time again. Two or three of the chief engineers on the design team were Christians, including the one I work for. The rest of the team were not believers.

Finally, after months without any progress, one of the Christian engineers went home for the weekend and decided he had tried everything else—except prayer—and it was now time to commit the matter fully to the Lord. All that weekend, he fasted and prayed and asked the Lord for guidance.

Friday went by without a solution.

Saturday went by without a solution.

Sunday went by without a solution.

By faith, the man kept praying and fasting.

In the early hours of Monday morning, he woke up with a start. He had the answer. The conundrum had unfolded. The solution now lay clearly in his mind. He leapt out of bed, ran into his home office, grabbed a pencil, sketched a prototype for the new piece of equipment, and then went back to bed. When he arrived at work that morning, he called a special meeting of all the engineers. As the team gathered around the conference table, he unrolled the sheet of paper with the design sketches for the product. He explained it, answered questions, and described its function. It was the perfect solution. The rest of the team was blown away.

One of his colleagues asked the obvious question: "Where did you get this?"

Somewhat tentatively, the engineer said, "God."

"No, I'm serious," said the first engineer. "We have been stumped by this design for months. Where did you get this?"

The Christian engineer answered, "I had exhausted everything I knew, trying to solve the problem. None of us had come up with anything close. So I prayed all weekend. And I woke up at three o'clock this morning with the answer. I got it from God."

I was in the conference room for this meeting, and I saw what an incredible witness this event was to the whole team. Everyone realized that the best of their brilliant thinking had been confounded by the problem. And no one could say that the Christian engineer hadn't received the solution from the Lord.

What do you think about that?

Why should a story like this surprise us? The Spirit knows the mind of God, and God knows all things, including solutions to aeronautical design problems. We don't know what he is doing or where he's taking us all the time, but as Jesus tells his disciples in John 14:17, "You know him, for he dwells with you and will be in you."

Think about the power in that phrase for a moment. "To know," in Greek, is *ginosko*, a word that captures the same idea we discussed in chapter 9: *knowledge as experiential intimacy*. The same way that Adam knew Eve. We could paraphrase John 14:17 like this: "You experience God's presence, for the Holy Spirit dwells inside of you."

Oh, may we rest in this amazing truth! The same God who created the universe, the same God who took on human form and walked this earth for thirty-three years before dying on a cross for the sins of humanity—this is the same God who lives in you. The same God who communes with you. The same God who leads and guides you. This God, embraced by faith, can be known experientially—*by you*.

Let that truth astound you.

In 1 Corinthians 2:12, Paul underscores the reality of this truth for us: "Now we have received not the spirit of the world, but the Spirit who is from God, that we might understand the things freely given us by God."

Caution: Construction Zone Ahead

We know that the Holy Spirit lives in us. When we are walking in fellowship with him, what can we expect the Holy Spirit to do in our lives? How do we recognize his work in us?

The Bible is clear. The Holy Spirit draws people to God. Without his activity in our lives, none of us would have any desire to know God, love him, or be saved. The simple fact that you are drawn to a book about the presence of God is evidence of the work of the Holy Spirit inside of you. Those desires are not in any of us naturally.

So consider this partial list of the Holy Spirit's activity in our lives:

- The Spirit gives life.[16]

- The Spirit is our counselor and helper. He comforts, counsels, and defends.[17]

- The Spirit teaches all things and brings truths to our remembrance.[18]

- The Spirit guides us into all truth.[19]

- The Spirit convicts the world of sin, righteousness, and judgment.[20]

- The Spirit tells us what is yet to come.[21]

- The Spirit provides spiritual power for ministry.[22]

- The Spirit commissions us and gives us a job to do.[23]

- Our relationship with the Holy Spirit now is a foretaste of things to come—of the type of direct and intimate communion that will be experienced with God throughout eternity.[24]

- The Spirit intercedes in prayer for us.[25]

- The Spirit provides us with a new nature.[26]

- The Spirit seals our salvation. He makes it secure. He is the guarantee our salvation is accomplished.[27]

- The fruit of the Spirit is evidence of the Spirit's presence and activity in our lives.[28]

- The Spirit provides joy.[29]

These verses are not a cold collection of intellectual facts about the Holy Spirit. They describe the work of a living and active *person* of the Godhead. They describe how the Holy Spirit operates in us today. Oh, if only these words could leap off the page! I'm reminded of Job's doxology: "These are but the outer fringe of his works; how faint the whisper we hear of him! Who then can understand the thunder of his power?"[30]

I must warn you that these benefits come with a strong caveat: The Holy Spirit can be *grieved* by our sins,[31] which means he will withdraw from working in our lives if we persist in ignoring his grace and the conviction that should lead to repentance. The activity of the Holy Spirit can also be *quenched*[32] whenever we persist in doing things our own way and in our own strength. He can be *resisted*,[33] *lied to*,[34] and *blasphemed against*,[35] though not without dire consequences. If we ignore the Holy Spirit or allow unconfessed sin to continue unattended in our lives, it's like trying to fly from Lake Havasu to San Diego with an eighty-knot headwind pushing us in the opposite direction. We will run out of fuel before we arrive at our destination.

The Corinthian Christians struggled with all kinds of sinful issues: division, pride, love of the world, lawsuits, abuse of the Communion celebration, even sexual immorality. In 1 Corinthians 3:16-17, Paul appeals to them collectively with a stark foundational truth: "Do you not know that you are God's temple and that God's Spirit dwells in you? If anyone destroys God's temple, God will destroy him. For God's temple is holy, and you are that temple."

That's as strong as it gets.

We are God's temple.[36]

The idea of being God's temple may sound foreign to us. We don't have many readily available modern-day images of temples to identify with. The temple is primarily an Old Testament concept, so what does it represent? In simple terms, a *temple* is where God chooses to dwell with his people.

God has always wanted to be with his people. In the Old Testament, the Temple was a physical structure in a physical location chosen by God. In Israel's early days on their way to the Promised Land, God's presence dwelt in a Tabernacle, a tent whose structure, furnishings, and forms of worship were made according to very specific instructions from God. It was a big deal. God's glory rested between the wings of cherubim over the Ark of the Covenant in the Holy of Holies. God revealed his presence there in the form of a visible cloud by day, which the entire camp of Israelites was able to see, and a pillar of fire at night. During the Exodus, God's people moved only when the cloud above the Ark lifted and moved. They moved in the direction that God moved. So it was God's presence that moved them.

After the people of God had settled in the Promised Land, the first Temple was constructed during the time of King Solomon. At the dedication of the Temple, the glory of the Lord—that is, a powerful manifestation of God's presence—came down and was so overwhelming that the priests could no longer stand up to minister.[37]

It is no coincidence that Paul borrows Temple language from the Old Testament to teach the Corinthians (and us) about the place where God has now chosen to make his holy residence. Today the dwelling place of God is not in buildings made with human hands,[38] not in human structures or institutions. Now, by his Spirit, God dwells in a people made up of every language and nationality—a people no longer identified by race, gender, or socioeconomic status. Now God dwells wherever two or three are gathered together in Jesus' name.[39] Wherever local churches gather, God dwells by his Spirit— whether that church is in an isolated barn in rural China or is a large community of faith in North America. We, the church, are now the living stones of God's temple, and by his Holy Spirit he dwells in us. The Holy Spirit is the one sent by the Father and the Son, without whom we cannot live the Christian life. Holy Spirit, we need you!

Getting the Wind at My Back

If you find yourself struggling against the wind in your flight path, where might you get some relief? The simple answer is *on your knees*.

After I had been in Cedar Rapids for a little more than two years, trying to pastor the church in my own strength, I had succeeded only in becoming tired and discouraged. Church life looked fine on the surface, and the people seemed happy with their new pastor, but I knew that nothing much of any spiritual significance was happening beneath the surface.

I began to search for remedies, reading all the church-growth books I could get my hands on and rushing to various seminars to learn new strategies and methods for creating a successful church—and then trying all these solutions on the church. The poor people! After a flurry of activity, I had to admit that still not much was really happening in the church—except we had a lot of tired people from all the new activities we had added to the calendar.

I knew something was missing, but for the life of me I couldn't put my finger on it. All I knew for sure was that I couldn't continue like this. Leading a lifeless church was not what I had signed up for. Honestly, I wanted out of the ministry. My calling had become tedious and boring.

Thinking that more theological training might be the answer, I signed up for a graduate program at a seminary in Missouri, which meant a seven-hour drive from my home in Iowa for a one-week intensive course. The first class I enrolled in, called "Guidance and Power in Luke and Acts," was taught by Dr. Stanley Horton. There were about thirty other students in the class, mostly pastors.

Throughout the week, in a series of all-day lectures, Dr. Horton led us through the various Greek words that Luke used in his Gospel to describe the person and work of the Holy Spirit in the earthly ministry of Jesus. Then he showed us how Luke used the very same words to describe the ministry of the Holy Spirit in the body of Christ, the church, in the book of Acts. What jumped out at me time and again was the glaring absence of those words to describe my life or the life of our church in Cedar Rapids.

Dr. Horton was well into his seventies by that point, and a seasoned teacher. He taught the entire class using only an open Greek New Testament. No notes. He taught with such a humble, winsome spirit that I had to move from the front row, where I usually sat, to the back row of the classroom because his presentations on the Holy Spirit made me weep. I was under such deep conviction. It felt as if the Holy Spirit had orchestrated this class just for me at this time in my life. I had been trying to fly the church on my own energy and against a headwind, and we weren't getting anywhere.

During that week, the Holy Spirit convicted me about two things specifically:

1. I had been putting far too much faith in the church-growth experts and in all the ministry and marketing strategies and techniques they promised would make our church thrive. My own ministry did not recognize the Holy Spirit and was not dependent on the Holy Spirit.
2. I wasn't praying. I literally had no prayer life. Oh sure, I prayed before meals and offered a perfunctory prayer before sermon preparation. But I had no real prayer life where I was deeply and actively engaged in communion with God through the Holy Spirit. I was not inviting the Holy Spirit to actively lead me, my family, or the church.

On Friday at 5:00 p.m., when the class finished, I hopped into my car and drove the seven hours home, in hopes of getting some sleep before the next day. I still needed to prepare a sermon on Saturday and preach on Sunday.

On Saturday morning I got up and hit the books, but nothing came to me. It was as if my mind went completely blank. I tried to dig up an old sermon in hopes of reworking it into something usable for the next day, but again I came up empty. All day Saturday I could not prepare even the faintest glimpse of a sermon.

On Sunday morning after our time of worship was finished, I hesitantly went to the pulpit and told the truth. I said, "The Holy Spirit has not allowed me to prepare a sermon, and I need to tell you why. I need to confess to you that I've been a prayerless pastor. I need to ask you for your forgiveness. How could I possibly lead you spiritually into places I haven't been? I need to invite you to walk through some changes with me. From now on, we're going to be a church focused on prayer. I am inviting the Holy Spirit to take charge of me and of this church. We are going to meet for prayer every morning from six to seven, right here in the sanctuary, and also from noon to one o'clock, to call on the Lord. Will you join me?"

That's about all I said. I was pretty broken, still feeling the deep conviction of the Spirit from the class. The people seemed genuinely moved. I dismissed the service. We sang one last song and went home.

On Monday morning, we held our first prayer meeting. Our congregation consisted of about three hundred people in those days, and nearly a third came to that first prayer meeting. I was blown away. The prayer was real and passionate, and almost everyone participated during the course of the hour.

That prayer meeting marked the start of a new season at the church. Everything changed from that day on. People came to church with anticipation, expecting God to work because they had prayed, and he did not disappoint us.

That one-week course also marked a major turning point in my own life. That one faithful, godly professor was the catalyst for a whole new understanding for me of how the Holy Spirit works and moves in us today.

Looking back, I can see that it was the Holy Spirit himself, inside of me, leading me where I needed to go.

You could say he turned my plane around and I began to fly *with* the wind rather than against it.

STAGE 4 OF REVIVAL

At some point in the decline of the church, God intervenes, either with judgment or with a prophetic voice, awakening a holy dissatisfaction among certain of God's people.

CHAPTER 12

TOGETHER WE ARE

AN ANTHROPOLOGIST STUDYING the habits and customs of an African tribe devised a game for the children of the village to play. He put a basket of candy at the base of a nearby tree with a solitary ribbon attached, drew a line in the dust some distance from the tree, and called the children to join him behind the line.

"When I say *go*," he announced, "the first one to the basket wins all the candy."

The children nodded excitedly in agreement as they swarmed around the starting line.

When the anthropologist shouted, "Go!" much to his surprise the children all joined hands and raced toward the tree together, where they happily shared the candy with one another. Stunned, the anthropologist asked them why they had all run together, especially since the first one to arrive at the tree could have won all the candy in the basket.

One young girl replied, "How can one of us be happy if all the others are sad?"

I *love* that story. What the anthropologist witnessed that day was a worldview that is foreign to the "me first" culture of North America. The Africans call their worldview *ubuntu*, which means, "I am because we are." And it's a worldview that has powerful spiritual implications for us today.

In stark contrast with *ubuntu*, our Western culture is centered on individualism. Our relentless search to find meaning as individuals is exhibited in everything from our hairstyles to the brand of coffee we drink. Everything in life is interpreted in light of its impact on us as individuals. Our tastes in clothing. Our choice in universities. Whom we date and why we get married. Where we live. How we raise our children. We're taught to think of ourselves as solitary brands; as isolated runners who race against time to acquire possessions and status; as competitors whose mantra is "he who dies with the most toys wins."

But this preoccupation with self leads only to social isolation. Instead of producing the intended results, it takes us down a pathway to excruciating loneliness, increased disillusionment, deep despair, and eventually anger and rage.

As human beings, we need each other. This deeply intrinsic need goes to the heart of who God is and why he made us in his image and likeness.

"Hear, O Israel: The LORD our God, the LORD is one."[1] In this famous call to prayer, the Hebrew word translated as *one* "stresses unity while recognizing diversity."[2] Bible scholars believe that the word allows for the doctrine of the Trinity. God is one in essence, one in purpose, and one in truth. And in a mystery we will never fully understand in this life, the God who is one has revealed himself to us in three distinct persons of Father, Son, and Holy Spirit. Before there was an earth, stars, galaxies, time, or the universe as we know it, God existed in eternity as Father, Son, and Holy Spirit. God is a community of mutual interdependence and love. Before there was even an African continent, the identity of God was *ubuntu* (I am because we are).

So why do we need the church in our experience of God's presence?

Because privatized experiences of God, open only to personal interpretation, are contrary to God's design for his people. To put it bluntly, they're dangerous. As believers, we need the balance, perspective, encouragement, and wisdom of other Christians. Our experiences of God and our understanding of his ways are best lived out in a community of faith. Only in relationship with God and each other do we find out who God is and who we truly are.

God in Our Genes

Have you ever considered how God's very identity, revealed to us in Scripture by the Holy Spirit, springs from relationship within the Godhead? God is one, yes, but God also exists in the loving relationship of three.

Let's begin with the first person of the Trinity, God the Father. The meaning of *father* only makes sense in relationship with offspring. Paul points out this divine relationship in 2 Corinthians 1:3: "Blessed be the God and *Father of our Lord Jesus Christ*, the Father of mercies and God of all comfort."[3] This means that God reveals himself to us as Father because of his relationship with his Son, Jesus Christ. That is God the Father's identity.

Identity within the Godhead is tied directly to *relationship*. It's never about an isolated self.

Second Corinthians 1:3 also refers to Jesus as God's Son. The word *son* derives meaning only in relationship to *father*. Jesus could not possess the identity of the Son of God unless God the Father was his father. The disciple whom Jesus loved identifies this love relationship between Father and Son in his Gospel. "The Father loves the Son and shows him all that he himself is doing."[4] And "I do as the Father has commanded me, so that the world may know that I love the Father."[5]

The third member of the Trinity, God the Holy Spirit, also receives his identity from his relationships—with the Father and the

Son. Acts 16:7 refers to the Holy Spirit as "the Spirit of Jesus," and several other verses in the New Testament refer to him as the "Spirit of God."[6] In these instances, the Greek nouns for "of Jesus" or "of God" are in the genitive case, which refers to the "kind of relationship that one noun has to another noun."[7] From these and other Scriptures, theologians conclude that the Holy Spirit is in relationship with the Father and the Son and is sent by the Father and the Son to be in and with believers today.

God's very identity springs from relationship. The members of the Trinity draw meaning from relationship with one another. God does not exist in an isolated vacuum, devoid of relationship, and neither should we. This is important for us to know because when you and I were created, God the Father, God the Son, and God the Holy Spirit said, "Let us make man in our image, after our likeness."[8] If God, who exists and functions in relationship, created us in his image, then it only makes sense that we, too, were created for relationship.

Our sense of who we are and why we exist comes from our being in relationship—in reconciled communion—with the Father, Son, and Spirit when we are saved; and in communion with other believers. These two anchors of our identity cannot be separated. They are at the root of the prayer that Jesus offered in the upper room: "I pray also for those who will believe in me through their message, that all of them may be one, Father, just as you are in me and I am in you. May they also be in us so that the world may believe that you have sent me."[9]

God in us, and us in God. It can't get any closer than that.

But wait, there's more. The apostle Paul points to the reality of our relationship with *one another* as another undeniable component of our salvation: "For as in one body we have many members, . . . so we, though many, are one body *in Christ*, and individually *members one of another*."[10]

Friends, this is so much more than a doctrinal statement concerning the local church. It is foundational to knowing *who we are* now that we are in Christ. We find our identity in relationship with God *and* in relationship with one another. Seen in the light of the New Testament, we can each say that our true identity is *ubuntu*: "I am because we are!" The quality of our connection to one another, as we travel the Christian life together and experience God together, is vital and indispensable to our identity and our well-being.

This connection to other believers is so much more than a *place* to spend ninety minutes on Sunday morning!

Consider the example of the apostle Paul. As a Jew reared in the Jewish religious system, his identity came from his place in the synagogue, from studying the Torah with his family and in the synagogue, and from holding fast to the Jewish rituals and celebrations (such as the Sabbath and the Feast of the Tabernacles). It was all designed by God to create a sense of community—which includes a sense of both *identity* and *belonging*—for his covenant people. Prior to Paul's conversion, everything he was and knew about himself was wrapped up in his Jewish heritage and shared religious experience. That was what he was fighting so hard to protect before Jesus interrupted him on the road to Damascus.

After his conversion, Paul's sense of identity was no longer found in Judaism, Torah observances, and the synagogue. Now he belonged to Christ and his church. Paul left behind one community, from which he drew identity and purpose in life, and immersed himself in a new identity and purpose—planting and establishing new communities of faith in the cities of Ephesus, Corinth, Thessalonica, and Philippi, to mention just a few. This is why Paul was obsessed with the quality of life in each of those churches. These gatherings, these communities, were now where Paul and countless others would learn and experience their identity as the people of *God's presence*— indwelt by the Holy Spirit and grafted into the vital relationship of the Trinity.[11]

Paul's letters to the churches and his appeals to them to live holy lives are not just for the sake of personal transformation or personal holiness. His concern in each city was to establish a new community of faith that clearly embodied "an alternative order that stands as a sign of God's redemptive purposes in the world."[12] For that to be, we must all *together* know God, *together* be transformed, and *together* do God's work.

Why together?

Because we are supernaturally joined to Jesus and to one another. And because the local church is the community of God from which we now draw our identity in worship, discipleship, and pursuing the mission of God.

As evidence that our relationships with others in the body of Christ are important to God, there are more than fifty Scriptures in the New Testament that address the nature and quality of those relationships. Here is a brief sample:

> They devoted themselves to the apostles' teaching and the fellowship, to the breaking of bread and the prayers.
> ACTS 2:42

> Love one another with brotherly affection. Outdo one another in showing honor.
> ROMANS 12:10

> Live in harmony with one another. Do not be haughty, but associate with the lowly.
> ROMANS 12:16

> [Do] not pass judgment on one another any longer, but rather decide never to put a stumbling block or hindrance in the way of a brother.
> ROMANS 14:13

> Welcome one another as Christ has welcomed you, for the glory of God.
> ROMANS 15:7

Instruct one another.

ROMANS 15:14

Care for one another.

1 CORINTHIANS 12:25

Comfort one another, agree with one another, live in peace.

2 CORINTHIANS 13:11

Through love serve one another.

GALATIANS 5:13

Bear one another's burdens.

GALATIANS 6:2

[Address] one another in psalms and hymns and spiritual songs.

EPHESIANS 5:19

[Submit] to one another out of reverence for Christ.

EPHESIANS 5:21

Let the word of Christ dwell in you richly, teaching and admonishing one another in all wisdom, singing psalms and hymns and spiritual songs, with thankfulness in your hearts to God.

COLOSSIANS 3:16

Encourage one another.

1 THESSALONIANS 4:18

Show hospitality to one another without grumbling.

1 PETER 4:9

> Clothe yourselves, all of you, with humility toward one
> another.
> 1 PETER 5:5

It's a staggering list, isn't it?

God is *with* us and *in* us by his Holy Spirit, and by his grace we are formed together with other believers through meaningful relationships in the local church to be the people of God in that locale. Perfect? No. But God's countercultural people nonetheless.

No wonder the writer of Hebrews warns us not to neglect being with one another.[13] Look at all we would miss! The question we must ask ourselves is this: Are we connected to the lives of other people in our local church community, such that these experiences of the body of Christ can shape and form our identity?

Temple R Us

What is the result of our gathering together in Christian community in the local church? The apostle Peter paints a remarkable picture. "As you come to [Jesus], a living stone rejected by men but in the sight of God chosen and precious, you yourselves like living stones are being built up as a spiritual house, to be a holy priesthood."[14] In other words, God is building for himself a new temple, one not made with human hands, and Christ is the cornerstone. A few verses later, Peter adds, "Once you were not a people, but now you are God's people."[15]

From the days of the Old Testament to the present, God has always had for himself a people who could clearly be identified as the people of his presence. When God moved his people across the wilderness to the Promised Land, he made his presence known to them as a pillar of fire by night and a cloud by day. It was his presence that protected them from the Egyptians and guided them very specifically along the route he had for them. It was God's presence that reassured them that he was with them. In fact, God's presence was such a defining reality of their relationship with him that when they disobeyed him by worshiping the golden calf, the Lord threatened to send them along on their journey, but without his presence.[16]

Moses immediately responded by begging the Lord not to do such a thing: "If Your presence does not go with us, do not lead us up from here. For how then can it be known that I have found favor in Your sight, I and Your people? Is it not by Your going with us, so that we . . . may be distinguished from all the other people who are upon the face of the earth?"[17] Moses was clearly ready to forgo the Promised Land and everything it stood for . . . if it came at the expense of God's manifest presence.

In the New Testament, God is still committed to having a people for himself, only now it's a people without geographic borders, a holy nation made up of "every tribe and language and people and nation."[18] But unlike the Old Testament, where God's presence with his people was experienced in the Tabernacle or the Temple in Jerusalem, now it is the people of God themselves who are the temple. It's not a physical temple, but a "spiritual house."[19] It is the people of God gathered in Jesus' name. It is the church.

Throughout the centuries they have gathered in homes, they have gathered in caves, they have gathered in buildings of all sizes in rural communities, suburbs, and cities. "They" are *we*, and we are called the church of Jesus Christ. In 1 Corinthians 3:16, Paul calls the assembled believers in Corinth "God's temple . . . [where] God's Spirit dwells."

In Greek, the article and verb translated "you are" (*eimí*) in this verse is second-person plural,[20] which means Paul is saying that the local expression of the body of Christ in Corinth is, in a collective sense, the temple of the Holy Spirit. So the presence of God is something we should expect whenever we are together with God's people. In fact, as Moses suggests in Exodus 33:16, God's presence should be the main thing that assures us of God's pleasure with us. It should be what sets us apart.

Jesus is still doing one thing in the world. He is building his church. It is what he will be doing until the day he reappears and the last days are at an end. Until then, our salvation involves not only a personal faith response to his saving work on the Cross, but also a supernatural joining of our lives to the lives of the other believers in our local fellowship.[21] We're saved not simply to have an isolated, personal experience with Jesus. Rather, we're saved to become part of the body of Christ, which finds expression in a local assembly that experiences the presence of God *together*.

Please note, I'm not suggesting that the church is the proprietor of salvation. The church does not dispense saving grace. But the church is certainly more than a building we go to on Sunday morning. It is more than a random gathering of people with similar tastes, interests, and lifestyles—that's what social clubs are for. Instead, the church is a gathering of people who are together joined to Christ and to one another in a congregation where our experiences with God are shaped and tested.

The local community of faith is where our hearts are moved by God's presence when we gather, and where the likeness of Jesus Christ gets worked deeply into our character and makeup. The real stuff of the Christian life can't happen without the vital functioning of the church, the body of Christ. If we're simply attending Sunday services with the mind-set that we can pop in for an hour of entertainment and then slip home and live our lives disconnected from other people, we are living a dangerous, shallow, and anemic version of what Jesus intended. The robust life of experiencing God, being transformed by him, and doing his work only happens through the interworkings of the people of God in relationship with one another in the local church.

Sadly, too many local church gatherings today have everything going on except the presence of God. The music and musicians are the attraction. Or the preacher and his unique style of delivery or his personality. Or some innovation in church ministry methods catches our attention—but not the presence of God.

We have, unfortunately, established a church culture in the Western world where the congregation is viewed as a clientele rather than a community. A clientele requires programs, services, and enter-tainment. The presence of God would be an unwelcome interruption in the carefully orchestrated service order. So church leaders occupy themselves with research on what the clientele wants, and every Sunday the church staff bends over backward to provide just the right music in just the right style, with just the right building, just the right temperature, just the right volume, and leaving just the right impression. The sermon and service must be short enough to get everyone out of church in time for the big game or to usher in the next "seating" of clients. Pastors today are required to be magicians pulling rabbits out of hats rather than shepherds guiding the flock into a dynamic and living relationship with God.

I'm a pastor, so I'm not against church-growth strategies or being sensitive to a congregation's needs, but my point is that we're saved to experience and be changed by God's presence . . . together. In fact, without his presence, the most significant things that need to happen in our lives and in the life of the church won't happen. The local church is not a clientele, sampling the wares set before it every Sunday. We are not an audience. We are participants together in the divine life of the living and active body of Christ.

No, the local church is not perfect. It never has been and never will be. Don't fall for the temptation to dismiss the idea of church because of bad experiences you may have had. Life in the church of Corinth, for instance, was far from ideal. That's why Paul wrote two epistles and at least one other letter to the believers there.[22] Yet even then, with all the difficulties in Corinth, Paul could still say, "When you are assembled in the name of the Lord Jesus and my spirit is pres-ent, with the power of our Lord Jesus . . ."[23] In other words, when you assemble, even with the problems in the church, Jesus will be present with you in power. That's key.

The presence of God doesn't guarantee a perfectly functioning and attractive church. Yet the local church is still God's temple for his presence today.

Why the Lone Ranger Needs Tonto

I know the Lone Ranger is making a comeback in the movie industry today, but as a cultural icon, the Lone Ranger is a dangerous metaphor for Christianity. Errors and personal excesses can creep into people's experience with God (or their understanding of that experience). And that's another reason why the local church is the safest place for those who experience God's presence.

When the so-called Toronto Blessing was crossing North America and came to Seattle, people here flocked to the meetings, looking for the latest spiritual high. Three women from my congregation went to the meetings, which took place on a Friday night and Saturday. On Saturday evening, they telephoned me—all three were on the phone at the same time—and were laughing so hysterically that they could barely get through an entire sentence. They said that God had told them this laughter was what was going to occur the next morning at Westgate Chapel, that I would be flat on my back caught up in the experience, and that the worship pastor would need to take charge of the service.

I asked them to meet me in my office half an hour before the first service, along with one of our elders. They arrived, still visibly affected by their experience, and recited again to me, in the midst of breaking down into hysterical fits, what was going to happen in the services that morning.

When they were finished, I said, "All right, I am the first to acknowledge that Jesus is the Lord and head of this church, and he doesn't need my permission to do with this church and congregation whatever he desires. The problem is that I do not see the biblical framework in Scripture for this movement. So you need to know that while I am perfectly willing for God to do whatever he wants in this service, you may not jump-start this experience here at Westgate. I have a question: Do you believe that the three of you can sit through this service without breaking into laughter? If you can't, I forbid you from being in the service. Let's let God be God. If you can't contain yourselves, then wait and pray in one of the classrooms."

They concluded that they could not be in the service without breaking into laughter. They weren't terribly happy with me or the elder for putting boundaries around their experience, and they and their families soon moved on to other congregations. I remain convinced that if the Lord had intended for "holy laughter" to break out in our congregation that morning, he would have had his way even without the three women in attendance. I'm equally convinced that, as leaders in our congregation, the elder and I exercised appropriate caution that did not "quench the Spirit" but prevented our congregation from being manipulated. There will always be a tension between our being open to the work of the Holy Spirit and the presence of God and the "sober-minded [and] watchful" diligence required to avoid and resist distractions from the devil, who "prowls around like a roaring lion, seeking someone to devour."[24]

The church is absolutely essential in our walk with the Lord because it is a safety net. The community of faith provides a healthy context for mutual submission and for living out our experience of God openly with other believers. It is in this place of safety that we submit our understanding of God and our experience of his presence to the collective wisdom and discernment of the community of faith and its leadership. The Christian life is not the product of an individual's experience with God; it is the responsibility of the community of faith. It is within the local church that our motivations are best discerned, our track record is known among the people, and God's Word can be properly applied.

We really do need each other!

God in the House

How might we encounter God's presence within a community? I have always been intrigued by John Wesley's Aldersgate experience. After years of the finest theological training at Oxford and ministry experience in the church parish and prisons, Wesley came to realize he had no assurance of ever having been saved. He pointed to a single meeting in Aldersgate, London, as the point of his true conversion. After listening to a teaching from Romans, he experienced God's presence to such a degree that he later likened it to a "baptism of love."

For some reason, the phrase *baptism of love* captured my attention and prompted two questions in my mind: What did Wesley mean by a "baptism of love," and how could I explain it to the people of my church in Seattle so that they could understand and experience a baptism of God's love in ways that would change them forever, from the inside out?

I scheduled a meeting with Wesley specialist Dr. Steve Land and flew down to Oakland, California, where he was lecturing for a week. We met over the course of two days, between classes and in the evenings, and I asked him my two questions.

Dr. Land's answers were strangely vague. In hindsight, I think he intended it that way. He commended me for pursuing my questions so intently but gave me no concrete answers, inviting me only to encourage the people of Westgate Chapel to experience God's presence for themselves and not just through the lens of Wesley's experience. I flew home appreciating my time with the man and his wisdom, but frustrated nevertheless. I was looking for an easy, how-to solution.

When I arrived home that evening, I drove straight from the airport to our regular prayer meeting, which had been switched just that week from Wednesday to Tuesday. I was anxious to see if the change would affect attendance. By the time I arrived at the church, the prayer meeting was already underway. To my surprise, about six hundred people were in the sanctuary—adults, children, and teenagers—and Rita was already leading worship. During my two-hour flight home, a worship song from the Brooklyn Tabernacle had been running continually through my head: *"Jehovah Jireh, my provider, you're more than enough for me."*[25] When I slipped into the prayer meeting through a side door, I motioned to Rita and asked if she would transition to this chorus.

As soon as the congregation began to sing this song, a remarkable sense of the presence of the Lord came down on that prayer meeting in a way that still beggars description. A feeling of awe and wonder descended on our people. Most stood with their hands lifted in worship at the thought that God alone is *more than enough* for us. Some were singing, some were standing silently with their eyes closed. Some were weeping tears of thanksgiving and joy. I didn't do anything. I just stood there, watching, soaking it all in.

After a few repetitions of the chorus, I felt compelled to go to the microphone and say, "If God has been speaking to you through this song—and whether he answers another prayer or not, whether you receive the things you're longing for or not, if he's simply more than enough for you—then would you come forward as we sing again? Would you come forward so that your presence in this altar area is a public acknowledgment that regardless of anything you have or want to receive from God, he and he alone is more than enough?"

About two-thirds of the congregation streamed forward and filled the altar area. There was nothing weird or ostentatious. No shouting or screaming out. No demonstrations of anything grandiose. People were simply lost in worship around that one thought—that God is more than enough.

After about twenty more minutes of worship, people gradually and quietly filed back to their seats. I continued to stand off to the side of the platform, praying, worshiping, taking it all in. I felt compelled to go to the microphone one more time, and I said, "We are sensing the presence of God in such an amazing way tonight, so if you feel there is anything in your life that has created a barrier between you and God, hindering your ability to be free in his presence, this would be a great time to come forward and allow the Holy Spirit to work repentance in your heart. Don't let anything stand between you and God's presence." Another wave of people came forward, filling the altar area. We spent the next twenty minutes in the unmistakable presence of God with singing, prayer, quiet weeping, and intercession, while corporate worship continued. As I again stood to the side, watching in amazement what had just happened, the Lord said to me, "Okay, Alec. I've just shown you a baptism of my love."

It wasn't an audible voice, no. But it was a distinct and worded impression that leapt into my mind. Some would call what happened that evening simply a good time of worship, but—and this is where it's hard to explain—it had been a long time since we had experienced a prayer meeting like that. God made his presence known, and his presence that evening communicated his love for us. His presence revealed his love. And that love melted people's hearts and transformed the lives of many.

It Grows on You

Just how much do we need the local church, when it comes to experiencing God's presence? The simple answer is . . . *desperately*. We all need the church, yet some of us need it more than others. For some, it comes close to a matter of life and death.

"Angie" is one such person.[26] She lives in the vicinity of our church, and several years ago, she was at the lowest point of her life. She'd come from an extremely abusive background, and after a painful divorce from an abusive husband, she was asked by her former church to leave, without any discussion. She had fallen into a deep suicidal depression, was taking a variety of medications for emotional issues, and had such severe agoraphobia that she seldom left her house, where she lived alone. She couldn't visit friends. She didn't feel safe buying groceries, except at 2:00 a.m., when no one else was shopping. She lived alone. Basically, she was completely cut off from family and God's people.

In Angie's own words, she lived in "absolute isolation . . . the perfect place for darkness and despair to reside." But at the same time, she knew she had to be in church, so she looked for a large one where she could hope to go unnoticed.

At about 7:45 one Sunday morning, when very few cars were in the parking lot, Angie happened by Westgate Chapel and could hear music coming from inside the church. The first service wouldn't begin until 9:00, and our choir was still practicing. Even though the thought of being around people scared her, Angie felt compelled to go inside.

As she walked into the lobby, she sensed God's presence, and a peace came over her. She slipped into the back of the sanctuary where it was dark and she could sit alone with no one nearby. She told us afterward that the songs of the choir were like oil flowing over her, like a balm for her wounds. The lyrics ministered so deeply to her that she sat there caught up in the presence of the Lord for the remainder of the choir practice.

The next Sunday, she came back again and sat in the dark, staying to take in the worship service.

As soon as the benediction was completed, she ducked out before she had to talk to anybody.

Soon she started coming to our Tuesday night prayer meetings as well. She always sat in the back and didn't speak to anyone. Finally, during a Sunday morning service when I invited people forward for prayer, Angie waited for a long while and then cautiously moved out from her seat. She was terrified of being exposed to those around her, but she knew she needed to stand in the presence of God. She had no words to offer, just the need to be in God's presence.

As she approached the altar area, she shut her eyes tightly and stepped into the midst of a hundred or more people who were there—and she began to weep. She later said, "With every tear, I felt the washing of God's presence and God's love over me."

Another woman quietly slipped up and put her arm around Angie's shoulder. She didn't say anything and didn't pray audibly; she simply stood alongside Angie and cried with her. She had no way of knowing that Angie had thought to herself as she walked forward, *I don't want words. I just need the presence of the Lord.*

A couple of weeks later, Angie saw the woman who had stood next to her that day, and she shared what God had done in her. The woman said, "When I was walking toward you, God told me not to say a word—that *he* was doing the work."

Angie marks that encounter with God as the beginning of the turnaround in her life. From that point on, she started reaching out to people and integrating more into the conversations and community of the congregational life.

The healing continued in significant ways. Angie began to reconnect with her family and friends. She had been struggling at work and wondered every day if it was going to be her last. Instead, after her experience with God, she advanced quickly in her position with a leading computer company in town. Today, she is totally integrated in her work environment—the very thing her psychiatrist said she would never do.

She attributes all this healing to the presence of God, experienced in the regular life of a local church.

Our experiences with the local church may not be as dramatic as Angie's, but rest assured, we still all need the local church. It's the temple of the Lord for today—the community of believers where God's presence rests.

We really do need the church!

We need it like we need our next breath.

STAGE 5 OF REVIVAL

An awakened core of believers catches a vision of what the church could be, praying to God and speaking to people about the need for revival.

CHAPTER 13

GOD'S POSITIONING SYSTEM

IN THE LATE 1970s, Rita and I were happily working for Youth Development in San Diego and planned to stay there for a long time to come. We supervised the organization's residential youth ranches and produced their national radio show, *Reality*. We also developed a five-piece vocal ensemble for them, called Master Design, and toured the country giving performances in churches and civic service organizations. We were busy and loved everything we were doing. We had just bought a new house in Rancho La Costa, and Rita had just given birth to our first child. For all intents and purposes, life seemed perfectly stable, perfectly on track.

Funny how things can change so quickly.

In 1979, an economic recession swept the country. Unemployment soared. Interest rates went double-digit. Everyone waited in lines at gas stations. Fortunately, we still had solid jobs and felt secure in our finances, enough to take our vacation that year to Northern California. We drove to the San Francisco Bay area and spent two weeks with friends. We returned home on a Friday, and on the following Monday, our boss informed us that because of the recession, the organization was cutting back in all areas. We were laid off immediately and needed to have our offices cleared out by the end of the week.

To say I panicked is an understatement. It's human nature. Unemployed, with a new baby and a new mortgage, I scrambled to find work. A month went by without anything turning up. And then another. Pretty soon, five months had passed, and we were still out of work. Instead of following the incredible example of faith my father had modeled for the family and trusting in the Lord, I basically gave God lip service as I frantically looked for a job. I failed to turn to the Lord in any sort of focused manner to seek his direction and will, and instead began calling friends for favors and chasing down every new lead. Every day, it seemed, I read about something or heard something I was convinced would be a perfect fit. Every opportunity that came to my attention I attributed to the Lord's leading, but every last one turned out to be a rabbit trail.

For a while, I pursued DJ work for a Christian radio station in Los Angeles. When that didn't pan out, I contacted a TV producer friend in Van Nuys and explored doing a Christian news program patterned after *60 Minutes*. We spent days brainstorming the concept, and even started working on a pilot episode to show investors, using a Christian stunt pilot based in Orange County.

When that didn't work out, Rita and I chased outside funding to go on the road full-time with our music ensemble. We had a brandnew album produced by Ralph Carmichael, then a well-known music mogul who ran Light Records. When that didn't work out, we contemplated moving ten hours north to Merced, where a good friend, Dr. Wayne Hill, was the head of counseling for the county school district.

At Dr. Hill's house one evening after the kids were in bed, our good friend sat us down and asked some probing questions. He could see the frenetic pace of our lives and sense our lack of direction.

"Have you taken time to seek the Lord about this?" he asked simply.

At first, I was offended. Of course we had! We were in Christian ministry. I'm the son of a pastor. I'd been praying all along: *God, please help us.* Offhandedly, I dismissed Wayne's question, but he probed further.

"Yes, but how serious have you been in seeking God's will for your life? It's obvious you have no peace. You've spent weeks chasing every lead, convinced that each one was God's direction in your life. Explain to me exactly how you've been pursuing the Lord." He was very direct with us, almost intrusive.

We were finally completely honest with him and ourselves. I admitted that other than an occasional prayer before a phone call, there was no consistent pattern in our lives of drawing near to God— none now and none in the previous several years. Oh sure, we worked for a Christian organization. We led worship and taught Sunday school at our church from time to time. I preached sermons when called upon. Our Christian music ensemble sang all over the country. During one stretch, we had performed an exhausting 253 concerts in a single year. Our lives were filled with Christian activity, but we had not developed any discipline or practice of consistently and deeply drawing near to God.

I wonder if you might be feeling a twinge of recognition right now. I believe that my story describes a situation that a lot of Christians can relate to. We are spiritually busy, busy, busy, and our lives are filled with good activities; but we're not doing the one thing we really need to be doing—the thing most needful.

That Necessary Thing

You've heard of Mary and Martha, the two women in Luke 10:38-42 who invited Jesus over for supper. Martha was a regular Martha Stewart. She prepped and cooked and cleaned and flew around the house at a brisk pace, trying to make everything perfect for the Lord. The text describes Martha as *distracted*. Mary, by contrast, was focused, relaxed, in tune. She sat at Jesus' feet, soaking in the goodness of his presence and hanging on every word. When Martha complained to Jesus that Mary wasn't helping enough in the kitchen, Jesus rebuked her gently, saying, "Martha, Martha, you are anxious and troubled about many things, but [only] one thing is necessary."[1]

Jesus doesn't say directly what that one thing is. He leaves the phrase hanging in Martha's ears—as well as in ours. Scholars think he may have been alluding to Psalm 27:4, where King David says, "One thing have I asked of the LORD, that will I seek after: that I may dwell in the house of the LORD all the days of my life, to gaze upon the beauty of the LORD, and to inquire in his temple." At its core, the psalm is a call to worship, an invitation to draw near to God's presence.

It is what Jesus rebuked the church in Ephesus for not doing. They had abandoned the one thing. Oh, they were *doing*. They were a busy church, those Ephesians. They excelled in hard work, in perseverance, in protecting orthodox doctrine, and in pursuing righteousness. Nevertheless, in Revelation 2:4, Jesus says, "But I have this against you, that you have abandoned the love you had at first."

What does it mean to abandon our first love?

Today, looking back at the time when Rita and I were let go from Youth Development, our lives fit the pattern of the church in Ephesus. We were busy, busy, busy, serving the Lord in all kinds of spiritual activities, but we spent little or no time sitting at his feet, seeking him with our whole hearts. We were Marthas.

Why do so many Christians today fit the Martha/Ephesus profile? Because it's easier to work than to sit. It requires less faith to *do* something tangible than to wait on God's wisdom, timing, and direction. And the feedback and rewards are much more immediate. We're convinced that because salvation is by faith alone (which it is), there is nothing else required of us spiritually. For some, the lack of attentiveness to Jesus is pure carelessness.

The vitality and health of our salvation requires that our attention stay fixed on Jesus, the *"founder and perfecter* of our faith."[2] Apparently there are some things he intends to *perfect* in us that are a continuation of our being saved. In Philippians 2:12, Paul clearly instructs us to "work out [our] own salvation." Jesus instructs the church in Ephesus to have their first love for him restored by doing the things they did back when their love for him was white hot.[3] He puts the responsibility back on the church. There is *action* required, he says, action that will put us in the place where the grace of God gets poured out, renewing our love and passion for the Lord.

Richard Foster writes,

> We are tempted to believe there is nothing we can do. If all human strivings end in moral bankruptcy . . . , and if righteousness is a gracious gift from God . . . , then is it not logical to conclude that we must wait for God to come and transform us? Strangely enough, the answer is no. The analysis is correct—human striving *is* insufficient and righteousness *is* a gift from God—but the conclusion is faulty. Happily there is something we can do. . . . The Disciplines allow us to place ourselves before God so that he can transform us.[4]

So how do we fix our attention on the Lord? As Richard Foster suggests, we "place ourselves before God" by practicing spiritual disciplines.

As much as I admire and respect Richard Foster and the concepts he teaches, I don't much like the word *disciplines* in this context. It tends to evoke images of pain or punishment, of getting teeth pulled, or going for a run on a cold winter morning when you'd rather stay in bed. Instead, I prefer the term *faith practices*, by which I mean habits and exercises embraced by men and women of God in the Bible that helped them draw closer to God. We undertake these practices by faith, but they also require some degree of effort on our part if they are going to be effective in our lives.

Pursuing Faith Practices

The responsibility for pursuing the faith practices is on us, but they must also be empowered in us by the Holy Spirit or they can quickly become lifeless rituals. In the words of Hebrews 4:16, we draw near to God's throne of grace with confidence, holding fast to the promise of James 4:8 that when we draw near to God, he draws near to us.

There are several great resources available on faith practices, and it would be difficult to provide a definitive or exhaustive list.[5] But I've identified a few "best practices" of a lifestyle lived God's way, based on Jesus' instructions to the church in Ephesus for how they could recapture their passion for him.[6]

He told them to *remember* what it was like when they really loved the Lord.

Then he told them to *repent* for the condition of their hearts and to choose a path to remedy their predicament.

Finally, he told them to *return* to the things they used to do.

Jesus doesn't specify what those things might be for the Ephesian Christians, but it seems reasonable to draw conclusions about possible answers from the narrative of the earliest practices of the church (in Jerusalem) in the book of Acts. Acts 2:46 says they met daily in the Temple courts (because they had no building yet to meet in) and in homes, "and they devoted themselves to the apostles' teaching and the fellowship, to the breaking of bread and the prayers."[7] The word *devoted* in the original Greek (*proskartereō*) means they "became one" with the apostles' teaching, fellowship, communion, and prayer.[8] The idea is akin to supergluing two pieces of something together—they become so closely conjoined as to be inseparable.[9]

Let's look closer at several faith practices to see how we might benefit from them today as we respond to the invitation from the Lord to draw near to him. Perhaps we'll regain our first love for him. We'll start with the four categories mentioned in Acts 2:42, and then I'll add a few more representative faith practices embraced by the people of God in the early church.

The challenge for us is to "superglue" ourselves to these practices.

Hearing the Voice of God in the Word

The early believers gave their full attention to the Word of God from the Old Testament Scriptures and the apostles' teaching (which was likely based on their personal experience as disciples of Jesus and later became part of the New Testament in the Gospels and apostolic epistles). They believed that all Scripture was "breathed out by God and profitable for teaching, for reproof, for correction, and for training in righteousness," as Paul writes in 2 Timothy 3:16. They believed Scripture was written by men "carried along by the Holy Spirit."[10] They believed it was the very voice of God speaking, and culminating in Jesus.[11] How can you and I expect to navigate our lives, and to survive the strategies of the enemy against us and our families, if we are not regularly hearing from the Author of life? The Bible is the voice of God spoken by the Holy Spirit into our lives, and we need to continually immerse ourselves in its pages with our ears and hearts open.

The danger is that we view the Bible like any other book. We pick it up and set it down at will, or read the text as if it's merely black ink on paper. But reading the Bible is not the same as reading Shakespeare, Clancy, or Grisham. The Bible is the voice of God, different from any other book on our shelves. When we pick it up, we are to pay attention to the one whose words are eternal life to us.

When we read Scripture, we should say, "Holy Spirit, I welcome you right now as the one who will make the voice of God real to me as I read this text today. Help me apply what I read to my life." The Holy Spirit will keep our reading from becoming a purely academic pursuit. The Holy Spirit causes the strings of our hearts to vibrate and resonate with the sounds of God's voice. Does it happen every time we read Scripture? No. But if we seldom or never read the Bible, we're guaranteed to hear God's voice even less.

As a faith practice, the goal is never to get through the Bible in a certain amount of time. That's the opposite of what I encourage people to do. Like a conversation with a friend, it isn't the length or the speed of a conversation that matters; it's the quality of the communication that brings life to the relationship. Personally, I divide the Bible into five sections—history, poetry and wisdom writings, the Prophets, the Gospels, and the Epistles—and I read a chapter from each section per day. This gives me access to the full range of God's counsel.[12] When I start my reading each day, I consciously invite the Holy Spirit to give me ears to hear, and to speak to me from God's Word that day. As I read, I keep a journal close by to make notes of what I hear God speaking to me. Sometimes I hear his voice in the first chapter and take all my time with that passage, not reading any further that day. Other times I read only one or two chapters because of time constraints.

When I share the Bible reading plan at Westgate Chapel, I emphasize that the goal is not to read five chapters a day, but rather to listen for the voice of the Lord. The benefit of the five-chapter plan is that even if you can only read one chapter a day, by the end of the week you will have a more balanced view of the whole counsel of God, rather than getting bogged down in only one book of the Bible.

Far too many Christians are making do with the Scripture they hear in their pastor's sermon on Sunday. Romans 10:17 tells us that faith comes to us by hearing and hearing by the Word of God. When we're not in the Scriptures on our own, reading, meditating, and listening, we hear less from God and our faith is diminished.

The faith practice of being in the Word is one way to "place ourselves before God so that he can transform us."[13]

Finding God in Fellowship

We've spent some time already in this book on the importance of engagement in the local church for spiritual growth. Regular fellowship with other believers is a faith practice because being with other believers is where iron sharpens iron when Jesus is the focal point.

It's in Christ-centered, consistent, regular fellowship with other believers that our blind spots can be pointed out—either lovingly or sometimes in the context of confrontation. In fellowship, our tendency toward selfishness is revealed, and we're forced to deal with our true motives: "Do nothing from selfish ambition or conceit, but in humility count others more significant than yourselves."[14]

Marvelous things happen in the context of godly relationships and godly counsel. And to be clear, Christian fellowship involves much more than Christians riding motorcycles together or fly fishing or playing softball. Those activities can be beneficial, but true fellowship focuses on the things that draw us closer to God. Intentional fellowship involves praying together, studying God's Word, sharing one another's burdens, encouraging one another, and spurring one another to love and good works.[15]

The faith practice of Christian fellowship is another way to place ourselves before God so that he can transform us.

Experiencing God in the Breaking of Bread

In New Testament times, the breaking of bread typically involved a fellowship meal followed by what we call Communion. Today, these meals have been separated in church life. Communion is the regular physical act of putting ourselves into the very heart of our salvation. It's a reenactment, a reminder, of the foundation of our Christian life in Jesus' death and resurrection. And it is so important to God that when the practice was being abused in the church in Corinth, Paul reprimanded them and said that their carelessness was the reason many were sick and some had even died.[16]

Communion unites us spiritually with Christ's death and resurrection in a then, now, and ongoing kind of way. That is why it is so powerful in our lives. When Jesus says, "Remember me," in the context of Communion,[17] the word in Greek for *remember* is different from merely remembering the historical details of a past event. The word means to "climb back into the event itself."[18]

This way of remembering is seen in some of the Old Testament festivals and celebrations as well. For instance, during the Feast of

Tabernacles, the Israelites living in the Promised Land took branches and made temporary shelters in their backyards. There they spent time outside of their homes, living in these shelters as a way of climbing back into the memory of the years their forebears spent living in tents while wandering in the wilderness.

The faith practice of Communion is another way to place ourselves before God so that he can transform us.

Communing with God in Prayer

Prayer is as indispensable to our relationship with God as conversation is to a marriage or close friendship. How can we say we have a relationship with God if there is no communication with him? Without communication, a marriage will fail in short order, yet some of us can go weeks, months, or even years without a serious conversation with God. How sad that church life today is characterized by everything but corporate prayer. In both our private lives and our church lives, we plan and do everything else first and then tack on a quick prayer at the end, asking God to bless our efforts. That has to change!

Eugene Peterson writes,

> One of the indignities to which pastors are routinely subjected is to be approached, as a group of people are gathering for a meeting or a meal, with the request, "Reverend, get things started for us with a little prayer, will ya?" It would be wonderful if we would counter by bellowing William McNamara's fantasized response: "I will not! There are no *little* prayers! Prayer enters the lion's den, brings us before the holy where it is uncertain whether we will come back alive or sane, for 'it is a fearful thing to fall into the hands of a living God.'"
>
> I am not prescribing rudeness: the bellow does not have to be audible. I am insisting that the pastor who in

indolence or ignorance is politely compliant with requests from congregation or community for cut-flower prayers forfeits his or her calling. Most of the people we meet, inside and outside the church, think prayers are harmless but necessary starting pistols that shoot blanks and get things going. They suppose that the "real action," as they call it, is in the "things going"—projects and conversations, plans and performances. It is an outrage and a blasphemy when pastors adjust their practice of prayer to accommodate these inanities.[19]

Prayer is not a shopping list of things we want. James 4:3 says we don't get answers from God when we ask him for things we intend only to spend on ourselves. Prayer is also not merely bending God's ear with words. It is a two-way conversation. It requires the Holy Spirit to be invited to facilitate the conversation. He is the Spirit of prayer, who brings us into the council chamber of God, attentive to his voice and poised to do his bidding.

Through the blood of Jesus, we all have access to God. Hebrews 4:16 says, "Let us then with confidence draw near to the throne of grace, that we may receive mercy and find grace to help in time of need."

The faith practice of prayer is another way to place ourselves before God so that he can transform us.

Serving God in Works of Mercy

Taking care of the needs of others is a means of drawing close to God. Jesus himself said that he did not come to be served but to serve, and he lived his life that way, caring for the last, the least, and the lost around him. In Acts 2:44, Luke notes that all the believers were together and had all their goods in common so that no one was without. Likewise, Paul, in Philippians 2:3, instructs us to consider the needs of others as more important than our own. Doing works of mercy is a powerful means of communion with Christ. Jesus said that what we do for the *least of these*, we are actually doing *to* him.[20] You can't get any closer to Jesus than that.

When we regularly minister to the physical and spiritual needs of those around us, it puts us in close proximity to Jesus.

The faith practice of mercy is another way to place ourselves before God so that he can transform us.

Discovering God in Hospitality

In Acts 2:46, Luke mentions that the believers were regularly in each other's homes. Hebrews 13:16 reminds us not to "neglect to do good and to share what you have, for such sacrifices are pleasing to God." Peter says we're to "show hospitality to one another without grumbling."[21] Why did he say that? Because when we show hospitality, we are put out of our routine. We're inconvenienced. My parents were firm believers in offering hospitality to all, and I can't tell you how many times I had to sleep on the couch as a child because I had surrendered my bedroom to visiting pastors, friends, or family.

Hospitality goes both ways. It can be difficult to give, but a blessing to receive. I would not be in America today had not it been for my folks showing hospitality to an American evangelist who stayed in our home in South Africa for six weeks. In turn, he and his wife opened their home to me, years later, and helped facilitate my coming to America.

Unfortunately, the busyness of our schedules has made hospitality a lost art and practice, but it's one we should seek to recover—"for such sacrifices are pleasing to God."[22]

The faith practice of hospitality is another way to place ourselves before God so that he can transform us.

Drawing Near to God in Worship

The early believers were said to meet regularly in worship.[23] God is looking for worshipers.[24] Hebrews 13:15 reminds us to continually praise the Lord with "the fruit of our lips." So in this context, our worship needs to be vocalized, speaking of or singing about the love of God and his marvelous works. It doesn't matter *how* we praise him—it could be with a song, a word, or a prayer—what matters is that we recognize God's worthiness with our whole hearts.

The faith practice of worship is another way to place ourselves before God so that he can transform us.

Seeking God in Fasting

Right before Paul and Barnabas were sent out to Cyprus, the church worshiped the Lord and fasted.[25] In Acts 14:23, we find that elders were appointed, set apart, and entrusted to the care of the Lord with prayer and fasting. Fasting is an indispensable part of encountering God's presence.

Abstaining from food or drink helps to focus our hearts on God by eliminating distractions that demand our attention. When we fast, we set aside those things for a specified time, and in their place our goal is to pursue God. When we fast and pray, our objective is to align ourselves with God's purpose for us. Fasting shows *us* that we're serious about following God. God uses our fasts to grace our lives with change.

The faith practice of fasting is another way to place ourselves before God so that he can transform us.

Reading the Fine Print

Surely there are many other practices that provide a means for drawing near to God. Times of solitude and silence. Times of celebration. Times of service, confession and repentance, or submission. The list goes on and on. But we must always remember the importance of faith and the Holy Spirit in any of our faith practices. Without faith and the Holy Spirit, these activities are merely activities. The emphasis is not so much on our doing a particular set of practices as it is the opportunity they provide for us to enter into communion with God.

That's what keeps us coming back to them. We draw near to God, confident that he will draw near to us.[26]

Faith practices are never a guarantee that God will reveal his presence in any particular way or time. He remains sovereign, and his will and wisdom will prevail. In other words, faith practices are never a cause-and-effect, one-for-one relationship. God promises to draw near, but what that looks like from one time to the next, or one person to the next, will vary based on God's superior knowledge, wisdom, and love. Nevertheless, if we place ourselves before God, he *will* transform us.

During the time when God's presence came powerfully on the church in Cedar Rapids during my first pastorate, I took extended periods of time for fasting at the beginning of each year. I wrote a letter to my father about it, telling him what God was doing, about my fast, and my anticipation for ministry in the upcoming year.

In those days, it took about two weeks for letters to travel between Cedar Rapids and Africa. When my father replied, he encouraged me to be cautious.

"Be careful not to be unduly affected by how you feel during the fast," he wrote, "or by whether or not you feel God's presence or whether he has heard you. A lot of times the benefit of a fast will not be apparent to you for a long time afterward. That's God's blessing to keep us from feeling like we're in the driver's seat."

I love that last line from Dad's letter. Indeed, faith practices never put us in the driver's seat. We are drawn to them by the Holy Spirit in the first place. What's required of us is a faith-filled *response*. The Spirit provides grace for that, as well. He invites us to engage in the practices and put in the necessary work. Then God decides how he will pour out the blessing of his presence into our lives.

Recalculating the Route

So there we were, Rita and I, unemployed, frantic, and desperate, visiting our friend Dr. Wayne Hill in Merced, California. And there he was, giving us counsel. I remember his words like it was yesterday. He sat us down and said, "Here's what I want you to do."

We nodded and began to take notes.

"God has given you and Rita multiple avenues for your ministry gifts," he said, "and that may be part of the problem. You've experienced success in a variety of callings. So I can see why you would interpret any little door opening in any one of those areas as an indication of the will of God in your lives. Could you do any of the things you just outlined to me? Yes. But are they God's will for you? Maybe. Maybe not. I believe the only thing that stands between you and stepping into the will of God for your life is your own will. When you're driven by what you want and what makes sense to you, it becomes an obstacle to discerning God's will. You just admitted to me right now that you don't have a consistent lifestyle of faith practices—which means you have no way to discern the difference between God's will for you and your own willfulness."

Rita and I both knew he was speaking the truth. And he wasn't done yet.

"Right now," he continued, "I wouldn't chase down any more leads. Go back to San Diego and carve out two weeks for yourself and Rita where all you do is develop a daily practice of being in Scripture, listening for the voice of God, being in prayer, and fasting as you are able. Use that time to draw close to God, but don't make your first priority asking him for direction in your life. Make it your first priority just to be close to him. In the process, totally surrender your hearts and your wills to God. Lay down all of your desires and ambitions and focus on being near to God—period."

We nodded. We were open to anything that would help.

"At the end of the two weeks," he concluded, "when you've done everything you can to lay your life and your will before God, then take a big piece of butcher paper and write down across the top each of the various avenues for ministry you're interested in: Christian radio, Christian TV, Christian music, teaching public school. Because of your background, I'd add pastoral ministry to the list. Draw vertical columns for each heading. Then, underneath each of those headings, write a list of pros and cons for each one. When you've finished with each column, cover it up so it doesn't influence your thoughts about the other columns. By faith, believe that during your time of drawing close to God he has given you the mind and heart of Christ, as it says in 1 Corinthians 2:16. You might not feel any different, but God will already have begun to deal with your desires, with your will, during the time of drawing near to him. When you get done with this exercise, uncover all the columns on the butcher paper and see what you have. I'm confident you will clearly see God's guidance in front of you. Your decision will be clear. God will guide you with his wisdom, according to James 1:5: 'If any of you lacks wisdom, let him ask God, who gives generously to all without reproach, and it will be given him.' After you've made your list of pros and cons, act in faith."

Dr. Hill said this to us with a great deal of confidence. I'm sure the Holy Spirit was speaking to us through him. It was intriguing to me that he told us to add pastoral ministry to the list because I had long since put that idea out of my mind. I'd seen my father work too hard at it, and I was running from the call. I was certain that if I agreed to become a pastor, God would stick me on the backside of nowhere and I'd be stuck changing the oil in the church bus and cleaning the bathrooms.

"One last thing," Dr. Hill said. "When you've made your decision, don't waver. Drive a stake in the ground. Go to someone you trust, a mentor, and tell him you want to be held accountable. Be prepared for your decision to be tested over an extended period of time. The enemy will come against you and try to get you to waver. But believe that God has led you in this process and hold fast to what he says to you."

Rita and I drove back to San Diego pretty much in silence, pondering what Dr. Hill had said. For the next two weeks, other than taking care of our one-year-old, all we did was pray, fast, and seek the face of the Lord. At the end of the two weeks, we did the exercise, and oh my word—when we finally looked at the sheet, the list of pros for pastoral ministry ran three times the length of any other category. Our calling was just so obvious.

Just as Dr. Hill had warned us, there were nine months of testing still to come. But we had driven a stake in the ground and believed the Lord. During those months of unemployment, we received occasional calls from people associated with other career path options, but we said no to every one. We also actively sent résumés out to churches all over the country, but received nothing but rejection notices. To stay afloat financially, I did odd jobs. We sold our house and moved in with friends.

Then in February 1980, through a remarkable set of circumstances, we received a phone call from a church looking for a new senior pastor. I sent a résumé to them on a Monday. By Thursday, Rita and I were on a plane flying to Cedar Rapids, Iowa. We went through a hectic week of interviews and were voted on immediately by the congregation. One week after that, we were in a rented moving truck on our way to assume our first senior pastorate.

What will your story look like when you pursue the presence of God?

Faith practices will put you on the path to where God pours out his grace—and it is God's grace that saves us, equips us, preserves us, and transforms us. It is *all* by God's grace. The faith practices guard against presumption. When we're consistent in them, they keep us in a place of humility and dependence on God. That they are *practices* means they should not be one-shot deals done only in a burst of enthusiasm. No, they must be integrated into our lives on a consistent basis. As one final, cautionary word, I wish I could say that I've stayed close to God ever since that experience in San Diego. But I haven't. You'll remember the story from a previous chapter where it wasn't long before the busyness of church life in Cedar Rapids crowded out the faith practices in my life, and I needed to learn the lesson all over again. I'm so grateful for God's patience with me. But he must be sought continually. It is in times of seeking that our intimacy with him grows.

Faith practices also counteract despair and hopelessness. They put us in a consistent place of intimacy with God where we become aware that he is indeed engaged in our lives every day, has our best interests on his heart, and is working his purposes in and through us, whether we feel it or not. That is "a sure and steadfast anchor of the soul, a hope that enters into the inner place behind the curtain."[27]

Your story will undoubtedly look different from Rita's and mine. But the pathway is the same: Draw near to God by means of the faith practices. Come to him in faith. Invite the Holy Spirit into the process with you. Be open to transformation. Draw near to God, and he will draw near to you.

STAGE 6 OF REVIVAL

An increased sense of God's presence begins to fall on a core of believers, and God uses their obedience as a catalyst to open the door for his work in that congregation, city, or region.

CHAPTER 14

FORGED IN THE FIRE

WHEN I ARRIVED at Westgate Chapel in the late 1980s, I inherited a challenging personnel situation that became evident as soon as I started making changes in the direction of the church. One particular staff member struggled with aligning his ministry department with the new overall vision of the church.

Although it created a problem, I didn't want to let him go. Nor did I want to micromanage him. I wanted him to catch the vision and become part of the team. So for the next four years, I prayed and worked hard to that end. I offered support. We spent time together. We played racquetball together. We water-skied. We talked, and I listened and offered suggestions for change. We flew cross-country together to visit different churches with a similar vision. I pointed him to a variety of effective resources for his department.

Still, I was met with passive resistance. Along the way, I realized that the problem was much deeper than stylistic differences. This man's heart and vision were in a different place. He was moved by a different agenda, and he was not going to respond to my leadership.

At the end of my first four years, nothing had changed, and I was faced with the very same quandary. I really did not want to let him go. It would cause him, his family, and many people in the church a lot of pain. It would have been highly disruptive to the life of the church in that season of ministry. But if he remained in his position, I knew we could not continue forward in the direction God had called us to go. So, what to do?

I resigned myself to the status quo and decided to grin and bear it. When I look back on that time now, I know my decision was based on fear, not on effective leadership, and certainly not on obedience to God. My heart was firmly inclined toward safety—mostly my own. For the sake of peace-at-all-costs, I resisted what I knew I needed to do. My heart became hardened to what I knew was God's leading, and by not taking action—as difficult as it would have been—I believe I was in sin.

One weekend, just after my four-year mark at Westgate Chapel, I happened to pass through New York City after attending a conference in Washington, DC. I decided to stay over in New York and attend a service at the Brooklyn Tabernacle on Sunday morning. Jim Cymbala, the senior pastor, is a friend of mine, and I always love to hear him preach, but I hadn't contacted him before I arrived to let him know I was stopping by. In those days, about fifteen hundred people attended each of their four services. I sat off to one side in an inconspicuous place and immediately sensed the presence of the Lord as Carol Cymbala led the choir and congregation into worship.

It just happened that the choir debuted a song that day called "It's Not in Vain." The song spoke of faithfulness in serving the Lord, of perseverance in the face of difficulty, and of the rewards from God for staying the course. It's a powerful song and I was deeply moved, but I didn't immediately make a connection between the words of the song and what I was going through back at Westgate Chapel.

After the song ended, Jim stood to preach. In the middle of some introductory comments, he stopped cold, looked straight toward where I was sitting, and said, "I see my friend Alec Rowlands is here. Congregation, would you please stand. Carol, we're going to sing that song again, and Alec, I want you to come forward and stand here in the altar area."

To say I was surprised was an understatement. I was in shock. I had no idea what was going on. I began to search my heart, thinking perhaps I'd done something wrong and God was going to publicly bring correction through Jim. Still, I walked forward and stood in the altar area as requested. The choir started the song again, and the congregation joined in. This time, the lyrics overwhelmed me, especially the line, "What you do for Jesus Christ is not in vain."[1] But even more than the lyrics, God's presence enveloped me as I stood in the altar area. My heart was immediately softened. I started to weep. I know it may sound strange, but in that moment, I felt as if I were the focal point of God's love.

As the choir reached the end of the song, and the congregation was still standing and worshiping spontaneously, Jim stepped back to the microphone and said, "Alec, the Lord has given you a direction you need to go. Do not turn to the left or to the right. But follow him wholeheartedly."

In as many years as I have known Jim Cymbala, and as often as I have been in Brooklyn Tabernacle services and prayer meetings, as far as I know he has never done anything like that before or since. The minute the words were out of his mouth, a transformation happened inside me. In a word, I became *courageous*. I knew what I needed to do, and I knew it was the right direction to go. I needed to fly home and let the out-of-step staff member go. Even though the thought of it still frightened me, the word I received that day emboldened me. Experiencing God's presence produced courage in my heart and solidified my course of action.

I came home from the trip, called for a special board meeting, and explained the situation in greater detail to the elders and deacons. We outlined a generous severance package and resolved to do all we could to help the man find another place of ministry. A week or two later when everything had been arranged, I went down to his office and told him we needed to part ways.

It was the hardest thing I had done up to that point in my leadership at Westgate Chapel. This man had some highly vocal supporters who were extremely unhappy to see him let go. Things turned ugly in a hurry. One of our elders was pinned to the wall and physically threatened by one of this man's supporters. Our preteen daughters were confronted by several irate church members. The next Sunday evening, someone slashed the tires on my car in the church parking lot. These were people who loved the Lord but had been blinded by their allegiances and were acting in line with the enemy's intention to disrupt the work of God in our congregation.

In the long run, the decision to let this man go proved to be the right thing for all parties involved. The former staff member eventually found a job that was a better fit. Our church was able to move forward with a renewed and deepened vision for the presence of God.

Though the circumstances were difficult, I tell this story for a reason. It's something I learned when I stood in front of the Brooklyn Tabernacle while the choir sang "It's Not in Vain." When we draw near to God and experience his presence, our hearts are touched and our lives transformed.

God Doesn't Make Small Change

Whenever God reveals his presence, it's always for the purpose of transforming our hearts. He doesn't simply "show up" so we can feel good, experience a thrill, or have something to talk about. It's not to enliven our worship or make our church services more powerful than those of the church down the road. God's purpose in sending his Spirit and making himself known is always to change us from the inside out.

We're all familiar with the concept of the heart as the wellspring of our lives, the center of our will, emotions, and intrinsic motivations.

Even though we fancy ourselves as logical and rational beings, we make decisions and act out of our *hearts* even more than out of our brains. That's why we experience our emotions—joy, fear, sorrow, contentment—in the core of our being and not in our heads. God reveals his presence to us in order to touch our hearts, so that everything else in our world fades to the background, and we experience his love and grace in ways that arrest our attention, capture our hearts, and leave us fundamentally changed for the experience. To *know* God is to be intimately connected with him at the level of the heart.

Jonathan Edwards, the great American theologian, absolutely believed in this process. It wasn't just a theory for him. He witnessed it firsthand in thousands of lives and hundreds of congregations during the first Great Awakening in New England during the mid-eighteenth century. Edwards used a different word for "heart." He called it our *affections* and taught that God's objective in any encounter with us is to reach into and transform our affections. Only then can we expect Christlike actions to flow out of our lives. Anything else is simply behavior modification.

Although I like both "heart" and "affections" as descriptors of our inner being, I'd prefer to offer a more colloquial phrase to describe the internal work that God does in us by his loving presence. In describing the transformation process, I like to say that God changes our *want to*. Most of the problems I've created in my own life have happened when I said, "I'm going to do whatever I want to." Our *want to* is what drives us—our motivations, desires, and longings. Our *want to* reflects the climate of our hearts. Consequently, any significant, lasting change in our lives must begin with our *want to*.

The process of transformation is described by the apostle Paul in Philippians 2:12-13. He starts by encouraging us to "work out [our] own salvation with fear and trembling," a sobering charge that is open to much misunderstanding. But before we have time to panic, Paul adds, "for it is God who works in you, both to will and to work for his good pleasure."

The two infinitive verbs in verse 13 are key: "to will" and "to work."

To will, in the original Greek of the New Testament, means an action in process with no indication of the action's completion.[2] Accordingly, God is constantly working in us to cause us to want to do the things that please him. He is continually active in our lives to transform our will, our desires, our *want to.*

To work, in the original Greek, means to bring about, to produce, to grant the ability to do something, or to cause to function.[3] God is always active in our lives to transform not only our will, but also our actions. He causes us to want what *he* wants and graciously provides the power for us to act according to his purposes. This truth is amazing, freeing, and encouraging! No wonder the writer of Hebrews calls it "such a great salvation."[4]

The connection in Philippians 2:12-13 between *heart* and *action* is clear—actions flow from the heart. (Which is not to say the process is strictly unidirectional. There are times when my heart is moved in the act of obeying the Lord, in the doing.) What *doesn't* change is that God is the initiator. He works on both our *desire* (heart) and our *doing* (actions).

This truth is important for us to absorb. Too often, as Christians, we operate with the faulty assumption that we will do what we *know* to do. The emphasis is on knowledge. If we *know* something, we'll do it. It's certainly not wrong to educate people from God's Word, but if all we do is educate our minds, then we haven't done enough. Knowledge alone won't produce lasting results because ultimately our actions flow from our hearts.

Consider the popular yet controversial DARE antidrug program. Nearly eighty percent of the school districts in the United States use this program, and it has been taught in fifty-four countries around the world. Yet scientific studies (including those done by the US Surgeon General, the National Academy of Sciences, and the US Department of Education) "have consistently shown that DARE is ineffective in reducing the use of alcohol and drugs and is sometimes even counterproductive—worse than doing nothing."[5] In other words, we can inform young people all we want about the danger of drugs; we can even scare them with "shock films" of kids overdosing; but a significant percentage of these kids will use drugs anyway, because their hearts have been taken captive by a love of the thrill, for the escape, and for social acceptance within their culture. They succumb to peer pressure and thumb their nose at authority. Why? Whatever their specific reason, ultimately they are "lured and enticed by [their] own desire."[6] Their only hope for real change is through an encounter with the God who loves them.

There's a Way That Seems Right

At one time or another, every parent has come to grips with the ineffectiveness of "head knowledge" alone in raising children. My learning moment occurred when our daughter Kathryn was about ten years old. I'm sure I had encountered it before, but this particular illustration sticks in my mind. Kathryn, you'll remember from an earlier chapter, was our strong-willed child. She's the same daughter we worried about when she left home to attend college in another state, and yet her walk with the Lord has turned out beautifully today.

When Kathryn was ten, we were homeschooling our girls for a variety of reasons. One day while Rita was upstairs teaching American history to Kathryn and I was downstairs in my study doing sermon prep, I heard an argument brewing. It started slowly, but Rita's and Kathryn's voices grew louder and louder to the point of distraction. Finally, I set my notes aside, closed my books, and went upstairs to intervene.

It turned out that Kathryn had discovered a picture of an early 1900s Sears & Roebuck mail-order catalog in her textbook. It had an advertisement for a firearm that cost only fifty cents. She knew my interest in guns and wanted to drop everything right then and there and show me the picture. In one sense, it was a sweet gesture, but Rita knew I didn't want to be interrupted and that Kathryn didn't need the distraction, and so she had told her no. Rita told Kathryn she could show me the advertisement when I was finished with my sermon prep, but Kathryn put her ten-year-old foot down. She wanted her way, and she wanted it exactly when and how she wanted it. Kathryn's heart condition at that moment was the problem. It was willful, and she was determined to triumph over her mother. We could have switched that advertisement with anything. Whatever her mother told her to do, she was going to do the opposite.

So Dad to the rescue.

I went up the stairs two at a time.

"I've got this," I said to Rita as I stepped authoritatively into Kathryn's bedroom.

I sat Kathryn down, thanked her for her interest in showing me the advertisement, and then led her through a lengthy, fact-filled sermonette on the dangers associated with disobedience. I remember referencing King Saul at one point and explaining how Saul had tried sacrifices to please God, even though Samuel had forbidden him from doing so. I leaned heavily on Samuel's line in the story that "obedience is better than sacrifice." I elaborated on the disastrous results in King Saul's life. Yes sir, I did three points and an altar call, and I was certain that Kathryn's willfulness would succumb to my pointed, impromptu sermon.

"Do you understand what Dad is saying, sweetheart?"

"Yes, Dad."

"I don't want to hear any more argument with your mother."

"Okay, Dad."

I stood up to head back downstairs, thinking all was solved, but Kathryn had one more line to offer.

"Now can I show you the advertisement?"

I gave up and went back to my study, shaking my head and wondering whether sermons make any difference at all.

Though Kathryn gave intellectual assent to the principles of obedience, her heart was still set on doing what she wanted to do. And by George, she was going to do it.

In some way and to some degree, we are all like Kathryn, even with our grown-up sensibilities. We sit through countless sermons that urge us to change our behavior and follow Christ's example. We attend seminars that fill our heads with information about how to lose weight, manage our finances, or become better parents. But how much does all that head knowledge truly change our actions?

Head knowledge is not wrong. It's just limited. Unless we pursue God's presence to touch and change our *hearts*—which, in turn, changes our desires, will, and emotions—nothing will ever really change.

Consider the many places in Scripture where the powerfulness of the heart is described. The clear implication is that the heart must be addressed if lasting change is ever to result.

- King Rehoboam "did evil, for *he did not set his heart* to seek the Lord."[7] Did the king know the truth? Sure he did. But his *want to* was not aligned with the truth he knew.

- Jesus called the Pharisees a "brood of vipers" and questioned how anything good could come out of their evil hearts. Then he added, "Out of the abundance of the heart the mouth speaks."[8] Sooner or later, whatever is in our hearts will come out in what we say.

- Jesus lamented about the hypocrites of his day. "This people honors me with their lips, but *their heart is far from me*."[9] They mouthed praises to God, but in their hearts, their *want to* was bent on evil.

- Jesus' disciples were beside themselves with fear when they saw him walking on the water toward their boat. Mark records that they did not understand the significance of Jesus' miracles because "*their hearts were hardened*."[10]

- Jesus, in telling his disciples to be ready for his return in the last days, warned them, "Watch yourselves lest your *hearts be weighed down* with dissipation and drunkenness and cares of this life, and that day come upon you suddenly like a trap."[11]

- When Ananias and Sapphira lied to God and the church about the amount of money they had given for benevolence ministry, Peter rebuked Ananias, saying, "Why has Satan *filled your heart* to lie to the Holy Spirit?"[12]

- Simon the sorcerer, even though professing to be a Christian, was controlled by his entrepreneurial spirit. He offered money to the apostles to give him the power to perform the same miracles as they were doing. Peter rebuked Simon, saying, "Your *heart is not right* before God."[13]

- Paul declared that "circumcision is a *matter of the heart*, by the Spirit,"[14] which means that walking with the Lord begins with a surgery of the heart, with a transformed *want to*.

Scripture offers example after example of the importance of our hearts in our pursuit of God. In Ephesians 1:18, Paul prays for the eyes of our hearts to be enlightened—because that is where understanding of the Christian life takes root. In Ephesians 5:19, Paul tells us to sing and make music in our hearts—because it is not notes and lyrics that impress God. God seeks worshipers who worship in spirit and in truth.[15] Colossians 3:1 urges us to set our hearts on things above. First Thessalonians 3:13 encourages us to strengthen our hearts so they're blameless and holy. Hebrews 3:8 and 3:15 warn us to not harden our hearts when we hear the voice of God.

The point is that our hearts must regularly be engaged with and captured by the presence of God. That's how our hearts, our affections, our dispositions, our *want to* get shaped to reflect the character of the one whom we worship. Theologian Henry Knight writes concerning the presence of God, "The experience is transformative because it is an experience of the identity of God."[16]

The Name of the Game

Do you see what a paradigm shift this is from what's taught and preached in many North American churches today? Far too often, we're encouraged to change our *behavior*, as if that were all that mattered. But we cannot change our behavior in any significant or lasting way without first having our hearts changed. All we're left with is simply a choice to suppress evil inclinations and harmful behavior. Because the heart is the wellspring of our actions, it's absolutely necessary for us to encounter God on a regular basis and let him transform our hearts.

Several years ago, to illustrate this very theme in a sermon I was preparing to preach, I went to a nearby amusement arcade and rented one of those pop-up gopher-and-mallet machines. They are probably antiques by now, but I'm sure you've seen one. Except this particular machine didn't feature gophers; it actually had something far more sinister: little horned cartoon demons with red capes and forked tongues. I had seen it a few days earlier on a trip to the arcade with my girls. When I told the arcade manager that I was a pastor, he couldn't believe I wanted to rent the machine—until I explained what it was for. The opportunity for an object lesson was too good to pass up.

Just like the more traditional pop-up gopher machines, the demons popped up randomly, and the idea was to knock them back down by bashing them on the head with the mallet. You can imagine the eyes of the congregation on Sunday morning when the ushers rolled this machine out on the platform at the start of the sermon and plugged it in with a long extension cord. I started feeding in quarters while talking about the futility of trying to deal with sin by suppressing evil desires whenever they pop up.

At first, I was marginally successful at beating the demons down. But after a while, as the game is programmed to do, they started popping up faster than I could bash them. After a while, all I could do was concentrate on just one or two. I pounded and pounded, but whenever I managed to strike one, others would pop up somewhere else.

Finally, the lights flashed and the siren sounded. I had lost the game. I threw the hammer down and said, "This is exactly how many of us try to live the Christian life, fighting a losing battle to keep sin under control. We can manage to knock down a few illicit desires for a short while. But inevitably others pop up to take their place. Eventually, they pop up faster than we can bash them. It's a losing proposition. There must be a better way to live than by simply using our own willpower. There is. And it has proved itself over and over. It is the victorious life that flows out of a heart transformed by love from close proximity to God."

Theologian Randy Maddox wrote that John Wesley "was convinced that the Christian life did not have to remain a life of perpetual struggle. He believed that our sin-distorted human lives can be responsibly transformed through God's loving grace to the point where we are truly freed to love God and others consistently."[17]

A while back, representatives of a national ministry came to Westgate Chapel to give a special Friday night presentation for our teens about sexual abstinence. As I sat in the congregation, I grew increasingly irritated. The entire program was focused on changing behavior by what appeared to be aversion therapy. The focus was on the physical consequences of promiscuity—everything from the risk of sexually transmitted diseases to the emotional bankruptcy of multiple sexual partners—good teaching, yes, but stuff our kids probably already knew. The facts alone would never be enough of a deterrent to keep them from experimenting with their sexual appetites.

To be clear, I'm not against behavioral deterrents. I'm for putting every weapon available in people's hands. But these weapons are useless without a transformed heart. Teens are not going to reject promiscuity because they're afraid of an STD. They will choose to live a life pleasing to God because they have a strong love relationship with him and experience the reality of his love for them. Our young people need encounters with God's presence that consistently touch their hearts. Then they won't want to risk grieving the God they love with activity they know grieves his heart.

Theologian Steve Land writes, "To relate rightly to God—that is, to know and to follow God—require[s] a progressive transformative development . . . an 'affective transformation in which lives [a]re formed and shaped' by their experience of God."[18]

We don't need more information or even better accountability. Our hearts are bent and broken and can only make wrong choices. These choices cannot be suppressed or restrained by natural means. We need an experience of the love of God—one that warms our hearts and convinces us at the core of our being that God is love. As our hearts grow in the love of God, we will discover a transformation taking place that enables us to love God in return and to love our neighbor as ourselves. The seeds of this transformation are planted in the heart of every believer, but they require nurture in the grace of God to affect the heart and change our lives.

Fired with Enthusiasm

What ultimately happens when we draw near to God? We can expect a transformed life. When we draw near to God, our *want to* gets changed.

To be clear, I'm not saying that our behavior is not important. In fact, I'd say the exact opposite. Changed behavior is vitally important. Yet lasting change—the kind that becomes a *lifestyle*—can only arise from a transformed heart. As John Wesley said, "Real religion does not consist in words, but in the power of God ruling the heart."[19]

So, what can we expect? When we draw close to God and God comes near and we experience His presence, what are the main changes that result?

Love

When we encounter God, one of the first things to happen is an awareness of his great love for us. It overwhelms us. This is why deep emotions often accompany an experience of God's presence. The thought that the great and awesome God, full of unapproachable glory and power, would make himself known to us? Inconceivable. We know ourselves. Sometimes even we don't want to be with ourselves. But when God comes near, we are dissolved and dismantled by his love for us. When that happens, our capacity for love is increased. We will love God more in response and love our neighbor more as well. An experience with God supernaturally connects us to the character and identity of the God who is making himself known. This is why our encounters with him are about more than just feelings. God is love, and when we encounter him, we cannot help but love in response.

Humility

Rita and I were at the Brooklyn Tabernacle one Friday night just to observe choir rehearsal. No one knew we were there. The only lights in the sanctuary were on the platform. We were sitting in the back in the dark, amazed at the sense of God's presence even during a rehearsal. It was not uncommon at the end of a song for the choir to spontaneously move into worship. At the end of the rehearsal, Carol Cymbala asked a young woman to come to the microphone and close in prayer. I will never forget how simply she began, "Lord, where would we be without you?" That was as far as she got. A spirit of worship came over the choir and continued unabated for the next fifteen minutes as everyone responded to that one humble expression of utter dependence on the Lord.

When we truly encounter God, one of the first appropriate responses is a genuine humility. The young prophet Isaiah responded by crying out, "Woe is me! For I am lost; for I am a man of unclean lips, and I dwell in the midst of a people of unclean lips; for my eyes have seen the King, the LORD of hosts!"[20] There is no room for bragging or strutting in God's presence.

Courage

An encounter with God often precipitates immediate and courageous action. The impossible becomes possible because God is with us. Biblical stories abound with models of courage. David and Goliath come to mind. Jonathan and his armor bearer, who took on a thousand Philistines with one sword between them. Esther boldly presenting herself to the king to save her people. Paul and Silas singing worship songs at midnight, in prison, after being severely beaten.

The presence of God shapes the disposition of our hearts, and in the process changes who we are at our core. It is far more than just a feeling. It molds us and empowers us. God gives us courage to live for him and take bold steps under his direction that would naturally cause us to recoil in doubt or fear. The psalmist explains, "I will run in the way of your commandments when you enlarge my heart!"[21]

Here's the bottom line: When we experience God, he touches our hearts and brings change there, at the wellspring of our lives. In addition to a changed disposition of the heart, we can also expect to see transformation in our affections, such as gratitude, compassion, joy, kindness, and peace. Our entire hearts get changed toward the things of God, and out of a new heart of courage will flow courageous acts of witness and ministry. Acts of love and mercy to others will flow out of a heart of compassion. Acts of service and preferring others will flow out of a heart of humility. And a joyful approach to life will flow out of a heart of joy.

Talking the Walk

In Cedar Rapids, we brought in a guest speaker who'd been a long-time missionary in Central Africa. He described how, growing up in Pittsburgh in the 1930s, he had a reputation as a street-fighting troublemaker. Let's just say he was known around town. When he was fifteen, his mother dragged him to a church service during a week of revival meetings. He went reluctantly to the first meeting but soon found himself under conviction and was saved that night.

The next evening, his mother took him to the service again. Mother and son sat behind two prim and proper churchwomen. In that particular region and tradition, it was an outward sign of godliness for women to have their hair pulled back tightly in a bun. According to the missionary, "These two old women had their hair pulled back so tightly that I was convinced they needed to let their hair down at night just so they could close their eyes and sleep."

The boy overheard one of these women ask the other, "How are the meetings going?"

"Oh, pretty good, I guess," answered the second.

"Have there been any results?"

"Not really," answered the first woman with a scoffing sneer. "That Greenaway kid went forward last night, but I don't put any stock in that. I'm sure his faith won't last."

The missionary told us that he determined right then and there he was going to serve God the rest of his life—if for no other reason than to spite those two old women.

The story, while humorous, contains a strong lesson for us. People are prone to place too much emphasis on outward appearances as the signs of strong spirituality. Most of the time, true holiness has nothing to do with how tightly a person wears her hair. Holiness begins in the love of God at the center of our hearts, if it's a true work of God.

How much better if these two women had hearts of love and compassion; if what came out of their mouths reflected changed hearts; and if they had said something like, "Oh, that troubled boy went forward last night, praise the Lord. Isn't that wonderful? We really need to pray for him that God has his way in this young man's life." That would have been the language of compassion, not of derisive cynicism.

God saved us to transform us into the likeness of Jesus.[22] When we draw close to God and his presence is made known in our lives, he affects our hearts. Then, out of our transformed hearts flow Christlike actions and speech. God changes everything.

We need a pattern for the Christian life that is based in experiential knowledge of God, not just head knowledge *about* him. The disposition of our hearts will be fundamentally transformed by knowing God. Then, and only then, will our actions be evidence of God's gracious activity in our lives.

STAGE 7 OF REVIVAL

An overwhelming sense of God's presence falls powerfully on the broader community of believers, restoring the people of God to the fear of the Lord and their first love for God.

CHAPTER 15

YOUR MISSION, SHOULD YOU CHOOSE TO ACCEPT IT

I LOVED THE movie *Amazing Grace*, about English politician and activist William Wilberforce, who was powerfully used by God to abolish slavery throughout the British Empire in the early nineteenth century. The one thing that bothered me about the movie, however, was that it ignored the role of the spiritual awakening that swept through Great Britain at that time in history. Without the impact of the revival and the influence of men such as John Wesley and George Whitefield, I do not believe that Wilberforce would ever have had the traction to spearhead abolition throughout the empire. Nineteenth-century historian J. Wesley Bready attributes to John Wesley the "inspiration both of the abolition of the Empire slave trade and of the emancipation of Empire slaves."[1]

Similarly in the United States, the fall of slavery is typically associated with the Civil War—and certainly the war and political climate had much to do with it. Yet abolition in America was also due in large part to the spiritual leadership of men such as evangelist Charles

Finney and theologian Lyman Beecher. The famous prayer revivals begun in New York City under Jeremiah Lanphier soon spread to other large cities like Philadelphia and Chicago. Hundreds of thousands of businesspeople around the country would leave their workplaces at lunchtime for prayer. In this era, called the Second Great Awakening, cities and towns throughout the Northeast were transformed, and all kinds of ministries were launched to help the least, the last, and the lost. In the process, the culture of America was changed for the good.[2]

Which brings us to the final point of this book. Our encounters with the presence of God have a purpose. They are not meant merely to enliven our passion for God. They are not meant simply to energize our worship services. They are not meant to relieve spiritual boredom and are certainly not meant to create a sense of spiritual superiority.

Rather, they are sent from God to transform our lives, make us more like Christ, and lead us to one purpose, the ultimate purpose of God's presence: God's *mission*.

God is on mission, and we are invited to join him.

A Missionary God

It's in our nature to be consumers—of God, of church, and of all things that improve our lot in life. This propensity in us is reflected in Peter's ill-timed suggestion on the Mount of Transfiguration.[3] There, the presence of God was shown to Peter, James, and John in a powerful way. Jesus was transfigured right in front of them to confirm for them who he truly was—the holy Son of God. His face shone like the sun and his clothes were as white as the brightest light. What was Peter's reaction? It was a consumer mind-set. He said, essentially, "Whoa, cool. Let's build three shelters and settle down right here so we can keep on experiencing this!" Why not? Whole religious movements have been established around far less.

The Lord didn't even respond to Peter's recommendation. Rather than allowing his disciples to stay on the mountaintop, enjoying a supernatural manifestation of God's presence, Jesus led them directly down the mountainside and immediately began to discuss with them his impending suffering and death.

It turns out that the experience on the mountaintop was a tipping point in the life and ministry of Jesus and his disciples. Leaving the mountaintop experience behind, there was work to be done. Painful work. Costly work. A broken humanity to be redeemed and reconciled to the Father. In fact, in Luke's account of the Transfiguration, he records that it was the point from which Jesus "stedfastly set his face to go to Jerusalem."[4]

God's intention is never that we become *consumers* of his blessings. We are to be *recipients*, yes; but as we receive, God intends for us to become *distributors* of those blessings in the lives of the people to whom he sends us. He invites us to join him on his mission to be a light to the nations.

Asbury Theological Seminary professor Stephen Seamands writes,

God is therefore in his very essence a missionary God. As theologian Paul Stevens emphasizes, "Mission is God's own going forth. . . . He is Sender, Sent, and Sending." The Father is the first missionary, who goes out of himself in creating the world and sending the Son for our salvation. The Son is the second missionary, who redeems humanity and all creation through his life, death, resurrection, and exaltation. The Holy Spirit is the third missionary, who creates and empowers the church, the fourth missionary, to go into the world. . . .

Mission, then, is not essentially a human activity undertaken by the church and its leaders out of obligation to the Great Commission, gratitude for what God has done for us, and the desperate plight of the world. It is God's own mission in which we are invited to participate.[5]

Let's trace this invitation through Scripture, beginning with God's first mission, recorded in Genesis. God's purpose in creation has always been to have a people who would be partners with him in his work, a witness to the nations. Throughout history, when God has revealed himself to people, it has been to transform their lives and then to give them a job to do.

Adam and Eve on God's Mission

God's initial mission for Adam and Eve was for them, in loving dependence on him, to be fruitful, increase in number, fill the earth, subdue it, and rule over it.[6] The earth was going to be incredible, a testimony to God's amazing love and creative power.

When Adam and Eve rebelled, God had every reason to wipe them off the face of the earth and start fresh. But in his infinite wisdom, he didn't. Instead, he came down to Eden in the cool of the evening and started calling, "Adam, Eve, where are you?" He knew exactly where they were. Adam and Eve had gone into hiding, just like we do when we sin. They'd sewn fig leaves to cover their shame. But God, being rich in mercy, met with them in love, with kindness, justice, and grace.

God didn't ignore their sin. He cast them out of Paradise under a curse, but not until first reassuring Adam and Eve that his ultimate mission was to restore them to himself—and that they'd be part of the plan to redeem all of humankind, even though they were now fallen.

In Genesis 3:15, God hints at the details of his mission to come—the offspring of the union of Adam and Eve will be a male child who will one day crush Satan's head and authority. The seed of the sent Messiah is in God's declaration. Adam and Eve will be included in a lineage eventually bringing forth the Messiah, the Savior of the world. In the meantime, they're to work the ground and populate the earth, and become a people who love and serve God.

The mission—God's reconciliation of humanity to himself—was established in Genesis 3.

Noah on God's Mission

By the sixth chapter of Genesis, humanity had sunk to an all-time low, and God "regretted that he had made man on the earth."[7] Then the presence of God encounters Noah, who, we are told, "walked with God."[8] We're all familiar with the story of Noah and the Flood. But Noah's story is not just about a boat. Hebrews 11:7 and 2 Peter 2:5 reveal Noah's true mission: to be a preacher of righteousness, a man who proclaimed the heart of God to any and all who would listen and be saved.

Noah's experience with the presence of God was not for his personal benefit, so he could write a book or brag to his neighbors that he had encountered God. It was for him to build an ark to save people from the coming judgment of God on the sins of the world.

The fact that not many people responded to Noah's pleas reminds us that big numbers are sometimes not part of God's plan. Though only a handful of people went into the ark, God's mission was still accomplished.

Abram (Abraham) on God's Mission

In Genesis 12, we encounter Abram in Haran. He's part of a pagan family worshiping pagan gods. Nevertheless, Abram had an experience with God. We're not told the details, other than that God spoke to him explicitly and promised him that he would be the father of a great nation, his name would be great, and he would be a blessing to the nations of the world. Abram is told to travel to an unknown destination via an unknown route. Because of his obedience, he became the father of our faith. Though Abram was greatly blessed by his encounter with the presence of God (God even changed Abram's name to Abraham), God's appearance to him was not for his personal gain or aggrandizement. It was so that he would become a blessing to the nations of the world.

In Romans 4:16, Paul notes that this blessing of God's encounter with Abram is a blessing that continues even today. Paul repeats the teaching in Galatians 3:8: "The Scripture, foreseeing that God would justify the Gentiles by faith, preached the gospel beforehand to Abraham, saying, 'In you shall all the nations be blessed.'" In other words, all the nations will be blessed because they will have the opportunity, through faith in Jesus, to become God's people.

God's mission became Abram's mission.

God always begins with the end in mind.

Moses on God's Mission

Moses grew up as a prince in Egypt, living large; but even in his early years, he had an idea of his purpose to deliver the people of Israel from their bondage. In Hebrews 11:24-25, we're told that by faith, Moses turned his back on his heritage in Pharaoh's household for the sake of God's mission. Acts 7:23-25 records Moses' initial mishandling of his mission: "When he was forty years old, it came into his heart to visit his brothers, the children of Israel. And seeing one of them being wronged, he defended the oppressed man and avenged him by striking down the Egyptian. He supposed that his brothers would understand that God was giving them salvation by his hand, but they did not understand."

Why did Moses initially fail at his mission? It was because he tried to fulfill God's mission under his own initiative and power. He knew he was called by God to be a deliverer, but when he tried to do it in his own strength, he failed miserably. After that, he ran with his tail between his legs into the wilderness of Midian, where he was assigned care of his father-in-law's sheep. That's where we pick up the story of Moses some forty years later. By then I'm sure he was convinced he was washed up. He was eighty years old, past his prime. He was living a long way from his heritage in Pharaoh's household, and a long way from the people of God. He didn't even have his own sheep.

At this low point in Moses' life, God came near. In Exodus 3:1-2, Moses encounters a burning bush that isn't consumed by the flames. Remarkable! Spectacular. When he goes to take a closer look, he is amazed to discover the presence of God in the bush. God on God's terms. The burning bush was not meant to make Moses feel better about himself or his depressing circumstances, but rather to arrest his attention and deploy him—this time under God's initiative—to be the deliverer of Israel under the power and authority of God. God chose Moses as his instrument of deliverance. And God chose the time when the deliverance would happen. And it was then that he interrupted Moses with his presence.

Do you see the very practical application for our lives today? The point is not that we go about seeking our own burning bushes. It's that we *draw near to God*. He will reveal himself to us in due season. And when he does, it is important for us to remember that he is a God on a mission. He is always on mission, and the closer we get to him, the more clearly we will see what he's doing in our world and the role he has for us to fill.

When we find out what God is doing, we're invited to join him with confidence. One of the reasons that following Christ is such a marvelous adventure is that he does different things in different lives. His mission is all about redeeming lost souls to himself, but it's not a cookie-cutter mission. We have to continually ask, "What is God doing here? In my life? My family? My church? My neighborhood? My workplace?" Then we can join him on his mission.

The Israelites on God's Mission

Once the Israelites were freed from slavery in Egypt, God led them through a time of testing and refining in the wilderness. God's presence went with them, but not so that the people could experience a thrill or warm fuzzy feelings. It was for guidance and protection and to advance the mission of God among the people of God—to take the Israelites where God wanted to take them by means of a specific route.

At the entrance to the Promised Land, after forty years of wandering in the wilderness and just before Joshua led Israel into their first battle in Jericho, he sent out scouts. The scouts found safety in the house of a prostitute, Rahab, and this unlikely resident of Jericho revealed her understanding of God's mission.

> I know that the LORD has given you the land, and that the fear of you has fallen upon us, and that all the inhabitants of the land melt away before you. For we have heard how the LORD dried up the water of the Red Sea before you when you came out of Egypt, and what you did to the two kings of the Amorites who were beyond the Jordan, to Sihon and Og, whom you devoted to destruction. And as soon as we heard it, our hearts melted, and there was no spirit left in any man because of you, for the LORD your God, he is God in the heavens above and on the earth beneath.
>
> JOSHUA 2:9-11

Rahab's testimony reveals why God wants a people of his presence. It's never to have a self-absorbed, isolated people who think they're better than everybody else because of their encounters with God. Rather it is so that his glory seen in the lives of his people would make him known to the nations. That was his purpose for having a people called the Hebrews. And that is his purpose for the people called his church. Through both, his mission is to reconcile the nations unto himself.

The Judges on God's Mission

After God's people settled in the Promised Land, God frequently sent messengers in his name, sometimes in strange and mysterious ways, to reveal his word to his people and to call Israel back to himself when they strayed. Even when God's people rejected him, God continued with his mission.

I think of God's encounter with Gideon. Clearly the motive was *mission.* Judges 6:14 says, "And the LORD turned to [Gideon] and said, 'Go in this might of yours and save Israel from the hand of Midian; do not I send you?'"

Gideon had a job to do on God's mission. His encounter with the presence of God revealed that mission and emboldened the reluctant warrior to step out in faith.

Jesus on God's Mission

The greatest demonstration of the missional heart of God is when the Father sent his own Son to earth to die for the sins of the world and redeem humankind to himself. As our example for being on mission, Jesus, in his humanity, depended on his encounters with the Father and the power of the indwelling Holy Spirit to fulfill his mission. Jesus told Pharisees, "The Son can do . . . only what he sees the Father doing."[9] In John 8:28, Jesus says that he speaks "just as the Father taught me." This is a bit tricky for us to trace out, given that Jesus is fully divine all the while he has humbled himself and taken on human flesh, yet Scripture shows that the Father, Son, and Holy Spirit are in mutual submission and "always at work" in the mission of God.[10]

Jesus' earthly ministry began at his baptism, when the Holy Spirit descended on him and remained on him in the form of a dove. Soon after, Jesus was sent out into the wilderness by the Holy Spirit, where he withstood temptation. Jesus then came back from the wilderness in the power of the Holy Spirit, ready to begin the next three years of public ministry.

What is the ministry of Christ? It's summed up well in Luke 4:18-19:

> The Spirit of the Lord is upon me,
>   because he has anointed me
>   to proclaim good news to the poor.
> He has sent me to proclaim liberty to the captives
>   and recovering of sight to the blind,
>   to set at liberty those who are oppressed,
> to proclaim the year of the Lord's favor.

The Disciples on God's Mission

Calling disciples was one of the first things Jesus did at the inaugura-
tion of his earthly ministry. There are two instructive Greek words
used for "disciple" in the New Testament. One describes the *location*
for discipleship—tucked in close behind Jesus.[11] The other describes
the *activity* of discipleship—imitating the Master's lifestyle.[12] The
nature of that disciple-Master relationship is the only effective context for our being on God's mission today. While on earth, Jesus'
physical presence was with his disciples to lead them on their mission. He continually communicated his mission to them. He trained
them on the job and then sent them out as the twelve and later as the
seventy-two to do the work of God.

In John 17:18, Jesus prays to the Father, "As you sent me into the
world, so I have sent them into the world." After Jesus is resurrected,
he repeats this charge: "Peace be with you. As the Father has sent me,
even so I am sending you."[13]

Where was Jesus sending his disciples? The destination is revealed
right before Jesus ascends to heaven:

> He presented himself alive to them after his suffering by
> many proofs, appearing to them during forty days and
> speaking about the kingdom of God.
>
> And while staying with them he ordered them not
> to depart from Jerusalem, but to wait for the promise of
> the Father, which, he said, "you heard from me; for John
> baptized with water, but you will be baptized with the Holy
> Spirit not many days from now. . . .
>
> "*You will receive power when the Holy Spirit has come upon
> you, and you will be my witnesses in Jerusalem and in all Judea
> and Samaria, and to the ends of the earth.*"
>
> ACTS 1:3-5, 8 (ITALICS ADDED)

That's the mission of God for us today—to be filled with the power
of the Holy Spirit and deployed on God's mission; we are to be

witnesses locally, regionally, nationally, and to the nations where he may send us. That word *power* is key to the mission. The word in Greek (*dýnamai*) is not, as some may think, a spiritual Fourth of July fireworks display leaving only smoke in the air and spent shells on the ground.[14] It literally means "supernatural capacity, efficiency, and courage." We are made strong in God's presence and power to be God's witnesses—to do exactly what he said his mission was.[15] And the *how*—the power—comes from God's Spirit within us.

Saul (Paul) on God's Mission

In Acts 9, when the light of God's presence overwhelmed Saul on the Damascus road, it wasn't to give him a goose-bump experience, but to arrest his attention, redirect the trajectory of his life, and send him on to be a light to the Gentiles. Shortly after Saul's conversion experience, the Lord sent a local prophet, Ananias, to lay hands on Saul and pray for the restoration of his sight. The Lord said to Ananias, "Go, for he is a chosen instrument of mine to carry my name before the Gentiles and kings and the children of Israel."[16]

Without hesitation, Paul embarked on that mission. "And immediately he proclaimed Jesus in the synagogues, saying, 'He is the Son of God.'"[17] Then he went to Arabia for three years to be trained before launching the first of several missionary journeys to win souls and plant churches.[18]

The Church on God's Mission

The entire trajectory of the New Testament church, from Acts to Revelation, shows the mission of God in action. Early believers ministered as they discerned the leading of the resurrected Jesus. Mission and ministry occurred in places such as Jerusalem, Samaria, Lystra, Ephesus, and Rome. Continually, God reconciles the world to himself through Jesus Christ.

The message has indeed gone out exactly as Jesus prophesied in Acts 1:8. There is no scriptural reason to believe he's doing anything differently today. Every historical revival has produced the immediate result of revived Christians passionately active in their witness. One of the characteristics of historical revivals is dramatic transformation of believers and remarkable conversions of unbelievers, resulting in great social change. Revival prepares and equips the church for mission—it is the mission of God *turbocharged*.

Saved to Be on Mission

If I could leave you with one thought in the final pages of this book, it would be this: The presence of God, though amazing, was never intended to be a place for us to camp. That would defeat the whole purpose of being in God's presence. Rather, God's purpose in revealing his presence to us is so that we might be *changed*; that we might discover what God is doing in the world and join him in doing it—only now in the power of the Holy Spirit. We are to reflect the glory of the Lord in our lives so that God can draw people to himself through us. He is a God on a mission. We are saved to be on mission with him. And what is this mission? It's seen clearly in Philippians 2:15-16:

> That you may be blameless and innocent, children of God without blemish in the midst of a crooked and twisted generation, among whom you shine as lights in the world, holding fast to the word of life, so that in the day of Christ I may be proud that I did not run in vain or labor in vain.

Consider one last example of a Christian on God's mission: Dr. Michael Haglund, the neurosurgeon I mentioned in chapter 4. A few years ago, we were invited by his home church to bring our choir and intercessors for a series of special meetings on the presence of the Lord and to help them launch midweek prayer meetings. While we were there, Dr. Haglund asked me if I wanted to observe him doing brain surgery. I said I'd be honored.

When I arrived at the hospital, he had me join him on rounds, where I met the patient who was to have surgery that morning. The doctor had previously obtained permission from the patient for me to observe the procedure. We moved to the patient's bedside in a group—Dr. Haglund, several of his operating staff, and me. He introduced me and said to the patient, "I'm a Christian, and I'm going to be asking the Lord to help me and heal you in surgery today. Would it be all right if I prayed with you before surgery?" The patient nodded, and we bowed our heads and prayed right there. Dr. Haglund told me later that he asks all his patients if they want prayer, and only once in seven thousand cases has anyone refused.

The doctor led me back to the area where the team scrubbed up. I had in mind that I'd be positioned in a Seinfeld-type balcony, from which I'd observe the procedure (being careful not to drop my Junior Mints), but that was not to be the case. With the help of a nurse, they had me in scrub clothes and masked. I said, "So I'm not going to be in a gallery?"

"No," the surgeon said, "you're going to be right over my shoulder the whole time."

That sort of proximity to surgery made me a little nervous, I must admit. But the doctor had everything under control. We went into the operating room. The anesthesiologist and his team were already there and the patient was already heavily sedated. Also present were several nurses, a few attending surgeons, and some technical staff. All in all, I'd say there were ten people in the room at any one time. Fred Hammond worship music filled the room from speakers in the ceiling. Duke University is a prestigious secular university hospital, keep in mind. I asked Dr. Haglund later if anybody ever complained about the worship music.

"No," he said, "and if they did it wouldn't make any difference. It's my operating room, and I want the presence of the Lord to be in this place most of all."

The next six hours were one of the most amazing experiences I've ever witnessed. Dr. Haglund's specialty is surgically treating epilepsy.

With the patient's brain exposed, the surgeon turned to me and said through his mask and loud enough that I am sure everyone in the room heard him, "Doesn't this make you want to worship? I know what this brain is capable of, its functions, the intricacies of its design, and whenever I open one up and see the beautiful and complex surface of the brain, it just makes me want to worship God for designing such an amazing structure."

The anesthesiologist woke the patient in order to lead him through various motor and language exercises. The surgeon then stimulated the brain with a small electrical current to identify the various functions of the brain and mapped them in order to minimize the risk of damaging those functions during the procedure. The surgery progressed successfully.

In addition to witnessing the marvels of modern medicine, I was most amazed by how the doctor's Christian faith and bold witness were so evident, even at a university research hospital. He's filled with the power of God, and God's mission is the primary motivating factor in his life.

He later told me of a time when a patient was brought into his department with an inoperable spinal cord stroke. Nothing could be done for him. Time was short, and it might be only a matter of hours or days before the patient would pass away. On rounds, Dr. Haglund stopped in to see the man and to clarify for the patient that the staff had adequately prepared him for the probability that he wasn't going to be on earth much longer. Very tactfully, Dr. Haglund asked him if he was ready to meet God. The patient said he didn't believe in God. Leaning in closer, Dr. Haglund whispered, "That's the wrong answer. The thief on the cross had not done any good works, but he believed in Jesus and was saved. I want you to think about this because you could be meeting him soon. I have a surgery scheduled, but as soon as I'm done I'll come back to talk with you more on this."

Dr. Haglund went into surgery, and while he was there, the patient he had spoken to went into cardiac arrest but was revived with CPR and a defibrillator. When Dr. Haglund finished his surgery, he went back to the man's room. The patient was visibly shaken and appeared quite frightened. But the cardiac arrest had not affected his speech or thought processes.

"Have you thought any more about the question I asked you about meeting God?" Dr. Haglund asked.

The patient nodded.

"Would you like me to talk with you more about this God who loves you?"

The patient nodded again.

So the doctor shared with him the plan of salvation—that Jesus had come into this world and died on a cross and rose again, conquering sin, the devil, and death, in order to reconcile us to God. At the conclusion of sharing the plan of salvation, Dr. Haglund asked, "Would you like to receive Jesus as your Savior?"

"Yes," the patient said.

Right then and there, Michael led him to the Lord.

It was now the early hours of the morning, and Michael left to finish his rounds. But the patient had a peace about him that had been missing before. Three days later, the patient passed away.

Dr. Haglund's concern for the mission of God does not stop within the boundaries of his department. A few years ago, he learned that the hospital in Kampala, the capital of Uganda, had a well-trained neurosurgical staff but no equipment. Dr. Haglund prayed, and with the help of the Duke Global Institute and the chancellor of the Duke University Health System, filled a cargo plane with nine tons of medical equipment and supplies to take to Uganda. That one act has turned into an annual neurosurgery trip with between twenty and fifty medical professionals from Duke participating. Today, Dr. Haglund heads up an entire branch of the university's outreach, helping to bring medical equipment and assistance to Uganda. He is on God's mission!

Friends, that's why we are saved. To join God on his mission and bring the presence of God to those he puts in our path.

You might be wondering what God has in store for you. Few of us will be called to go to Uganda to build a neurosurgical wing in a hospital. Few will be called to end this generation's social abominations, like William Wilberforce did in his day. But we are all called to be on God's mission. It may be as simple as taking a plate of cookies to our neighbors in the name of Jesus. It may be volunteering at a homeless shelter, teaching Sunday school to a group of fourth grade boys, leading a teen Mothers of Preschoolers (MOPS) outreach, or becoming the next Billy Graham. God is in control, and he will direct our paths as we submit ourselves to him and invite his presence.

God has been on a mission since the beginning of time. He is always at work to redeem broken and lost people and reconcile them to himself. That's what the presence of God is all about. That's why we seek him and draw close to him. That's why we listen for his voice and take his word into our hearts. Our hearts are transformed, and the desires of our lives are changed in his presence to reflect his heart. But there will be no tabernacles built on the mountaintop to enshrine our experience of God's presence. No sir!

As we draw near to the Lord, we are transformed by our experience of his presence, we wait on him for his timing and his plans, and then we go out boldly with joy to fulfill his mission in the power of his Holy Spirit.

STAGE 8 OF REVIVAL

Believers are remarkably transformed and unbelievers are dramatically converted, resulting in great social change.

ACKNOWLEDGMENTS

THE CONTENTS OF this book represent the fruition of a miracle that began when I was a young boy (and into my teenage years) and I experienced the amazing unfolding of God's revealed presence in my father's life and ministry in South Africa. By the time I left for America at the age of seventeen, I was forever inoculated against what A. W. Tozer called the Christian life lived in a rut of routine and boredom,[1] or what one participant of the Hebrides Island revival referred to as "desperately normal."

As you read this book, you got an idea of the kind of man my father was and the authenticity of his life and his relationship with the Lord. I owe him and my mother a huge debt of gratitude for their spiritual heritage and for imparting to me a lifelong desire to live my life in God's presence.

When I accepted my first senior pastorate in Cedar Rapids, Iowa, I launched with great enthusiasm into all the ministry-success techniques and church-growth programs of that day. But it wasn't long before I had worked myself into fatigue and discouragement. That was when the radio broadcasts of David Mains, on *Chapel of the Air*, reminded me of what I had experienced of God as a child. David introduced me to revival historians such as Leonard Ravenhill, Richard Owen Roberts, and many other authors on the subject, whose books now fill three shelves in my study. Though I have personally met few of these historians, I feel a kinship with them and share a similar hope that God will visit his church once again with seasons of refreshing.

Through the years, few friendships have been as meaningful to me in my pursuit of God's presence as those with pastors Jim Cymbala of the Brooklyn Tabernacle and Michael Durso of Christ Tabernacle in Queens, New York. Whenever I am able to participate in their services or prayer meetings, I find myself enveloped in a tangible sense of God's presence that softens my heart and makes me want to be more like Jesus. The lives of these men and the churches they pastor embody everything I believe to be true about the experience of God's presence.

Over the past thirty-two years, it has been my privilege to pastor two congregations: First Assembly of God, Cedar Rapids, Iowa, and Westgate Chapel, Edmonds, Washington. In both of these churches, God has blessed me with congregations who have joined me, without reservation, in the pursuit of God's presence. When God called us to pray, they stood with me, praying with great faith. When it was time to worship, they worshiped with abandon. It was their lives, their testimonies, and their experiences with God that often motivated me to keep going. And the same is true of the pastoral colleagues that served with me at both churches. There is no way I could have done this without them.

Writing a book on the presence of God has proven to be a daunting task, especially for my first book. How does one adequately and carefully describe the indescribable? I owe a great debt of gratitude to the theological scholars God has brought into my life. Some, such as Henry Knight III and Randy Maddox, I know only from their written works on this subject. Others, such as Steve Land, Jackie and Cheryl Johns, Rob Wall, and Daniel Castelo, have become friends and have been extremely generous with their time and contributions. They have all helped provide the theological framework for this book.

I will forever be indebted to my agent, Ann Spangler, for seeing something of eternal value in the heart of this book and taking on a complete novice, patiently and skillfully coaching me in every step of the writing process. I also owe a debt of gratitude to writer and editor Marcus Brotherton, who helped me get my thoughts into print. He believed in the message from the very beginning and became an amazing collaborator and friend in the process.

Finally, I want to thank my wife, Rita, for being a true partner in the writing of this book, and my daughters, Vanessa and Kathryn, and their husbands, for living out its message with me. There are none in my life, besides my parents, who have as consistently and selflessly pursued the presence of God. The presence of God is more than an experience. It is a life lived, and they have lived it with me every step of the way.

NOTES

CHAPTER 1: UNTAMED LION

1. C. S. Lewis, *The Lion, the Witch, and the Wardrobe* (New York: HarperCollins, 1950), 48.
2. 1 Chronicles 16:11; James 4:8
3. See Matthew 1:23.
4. Exodus 33:18–34:7
5. Hebrews 11:6, NIV
6. 1 Corinthians 2:1-4, NIV
7. Duncan Campbell, "Revival in the Hebrides," from a sermon preached in 1968. A transcript of the full sermon can be found online at http://www.revival-library.org/pensketches/revivals/hebrides.html.
8. See Exodus 3:1-6; 13:21-22; 1 Kings 19:11-12.
9. See Exodus 34:28-29.
10. 2 Corinthians 4:4, NIV
11. 2 Corinthians 3:18, NIV
12. Duncan Campbell, "Revival in the Hebrides."
13. Isaiah 63:1, NRSV

CHAPTER 2: DRIVEN TO WORSHIP

1. Terry Clark, "Hear the Heavens," copyright © 2000 by Clark Brothers Keepers. Lyrics quoted by permission.
2. See 1 Kings 17:8-16.
3. See 1 Kings 17:17-24.
4. See 1 Kings 18:30-39.
5. 1 Kings 19:11, NLT
6. 1 Kings 19:11, NLT
7. 1 Kings 19:12, NLT
8. 1 Kings 19:13, NLT

9. NLT
10. Song of Songs 5:8
11. Romans 10:13
12. NLT
13. See James 4:8.

CHAPTER 3: A CANDLESTICK IN THE DARKNESS
1. This version of the quote is from my favorite depiction of the story, which is the 1998 movie version starring Liam Neeson. In Victor Hugo's original, the bishop says, "Jean Valjean, my brother: you belong no longer to evil, but to good. It is your soul that I am buying for you" (Victor Hugo, *Les Misérables*, trans. Charles E. Wilbour [New York: Fawcett, 1961], 33).
2. For a fuller description of the debate, see Peter Vardy, *An Introduction to Kierkegaard* (Peabody, MA: Hendrickson, 2008), xii, 27–30; Roger E. Olson, *The Story of Christian Theology* (Downers Grove, IL: InterVarsity, 1999); and Howard Hong, *Works of Love* (New York: Harper & Row, 1962), 95.
3. Vardy, *Introduction to Kierkegaard*, 27.
4. 2 Corinthians 3:3, NLT
5. John Wesley, *The Heart of Wesley's Journal* (Grand Rapids: Kregel, 1989), 43.
6. A. Skevington Wood, *The Burning Heart* (Minneapolis: Bethany, 1978), 68 (italics added).
7. Colossians 1:16, NLT
8. Colossians 1:17
9. Hebrews 1:2-3, NLT
10. Romans 1:20
11. See Revelation 2:4.
12. See Revelation 3:14-21.
13. Matthew 26:47, NKJV
14. John 18:3
15. See Ezekiel 1:28; Daniel 10:9; Revelation 1:17.
16. 1 Kings 8:10-11
17. 1 Corinthians 3:16-17
18. *The Original Memoirs of Charles G. Finney*, ed. Garth M. Rosell and Richard A. G. Dupuis (Grand Rapids: Zondervan, 1989), 130.
19. Ibid., 131.
20. Ibid., 132.
21. See James 4:8.
22. Philippians 2:13, NLT
23. See Randy Maddox, *Responsible Grace: John Wesley's Practical Theology* (Nashville: Abingdon, 1994).
24. Ibid., 84.
25. 2 Chronicles 34:27
26. See 2 Chronicles 34:14-18.

27. See 2 Chronicles 34:19-21.
28. See James 4:8.

CHAPTER 4: START EXPECTING

1. Edward Morgan, *The Life and Times of Howell Harris*, reprint edition (Denton, TX: Needs of the Times, 1998), 35.
2. See Galatians 5:22.
3. Romans 14:17
4. See 2 Corinthians 5:18-19.
5. Henry H. Knight III, *The Presence of God in the Christian Life* (Lanham, MD: Scarecrow, 1992), 10.
6. NIV

CHAPTER 5: REMEMBERING THE WAY WE WERE

1. The "owner's manual" for this kind of love is 1 Corinthians 13. See especially verses 4-7.
2. See Luke 8:4-15.
3. Philippians 2:12, NLT
4. Philippians 2:13, NLT
5. See John 6:44.
6. See James 4:8.
7. Even though the apostle Paul did not know Christ before the Ascension, he had a life-changing encounter with the Lord on the road to Damascus and subsequent experiences with the Lord in dreams, visions, and even a personal visit to his prison cell in Jerusalem (see Acts 9:1-6; 10:9-16; 16:9-10; 18:9-10; 22:17-21; 23:11; 2 Corinthians 12:1-4).
8. See Revelation 2:4.
9. Revelation 2:2
10. See Revelation 2:2-3.
11. Revelation 2:4, NASB
12. See Revelation 2:5.
13. Philippians 2:15, NASB
14. Revelation 2:5
15. Mark 10:15
16. 2 Corinthians 13:5, NLT
17. See 1 John 4:8, 16.
18. Stephen Seamands, *Ministry in the Image of God* (Downers Grove, IL: InterVarsity, 2005), 147–148. Sadhu Sundar Singh (1889–c. 1929) was a Sikh who converted to Christianity and became a missionary in India.
19. 1 John 4:19
20. Henry H. Knight III, *The Presence of God in the Christian Life*, (Lanham, MD: Scarecrow, 1992), 11 (italics in the original).

CHAPTER 6: CAN YOU HEAR ME NOW?

1. 1 Timothy 6:16
2. See Exodus 3:5.
3. See 1 John 4:8, 16.
4. See Exodus 24:17; Deuteronomy 4:24; 9:3; Hebrews 12:29.
5. See Hebrews 10:19.
6. Matthew 3:12
7. See Deuteronomy 6:4; Hebrews 13:8.
8. See A. Skevington Wood, *The Burning Heart* (Minneapolis: Bethany, 1978).
9. See Hebrews 13:15.
10. Isaiah 6:5, NASB
11. Ephesians 2:6
12. See Acts 8:9-24.
13. Acts 8:13
14. Acts 8:19
15. Acts 8:20-23, NIV
16. Acts 8:24, NIV
17. Adam Makos with Marcus Brotherton, *Voices of the Pacific* (New York: Berkley, 2013), 161.
18. Ibid., 162–163.

CHAPTER 7: SPEED BUMPS ON THE ROAD TO GOD'S PRESENCE

1. George Barna, *Growing True Disciples* (Colorado Springs: WaterBrook, 2001), 75.
2. Dallas Willard, *The Divine Conspiracy* (San Francisco: Harper, 1998), 36–38 (italics in the original).
3. 2 Corinthians 5:17
4. Theodore H. Runyon, "A New Look At 'Experience,'" *The Drew Gateway*, vol. 51, no. 3 (1987), 49.
5. See John 3:1-7; Romans 5:1.
6. See Colossians 1:27.
7. See 1 John 2:15-17.
8. See Hebrews 11:6.
9. See 1 Peter 5:7.
10. See Colossians 3:2.
11. NIV
12. NIV, italics added
13. See 1 John 1:3.
14. See Romans 8:31.

CHAPTER 8: WHERE REASON KANT, EXPERIENCE CAN

1. NIV
2. Stanley J. Grenz, *A Primer on Postmodernism* (Grand Rapids: Eerdmans, 1996), 2–3.

3. Cheryl Bridges Johns, "A Disenchanted Text: Where Evangelicals Went Wrong with the Bible," in *A New Evangelical Manifesto*, ed. David P. Gushee (St. Louis: Chalice, 2012), 24.

4. Romans 10:2, NLT

5. See 1 Corinthians 14:15.

6. Deuteronomy 6:5

7. Matthew 22:37, NIV

8. Matthew 22:39-40, NIV

9. NIV

10. See Acts 9:1-9.

11. Acts 16:14, italics added

12. John Wesley, "Sermon 127: On Living without God," in *The Works of the Rev. John Wesley*, vol. 7 (New York: J & J Harper, 1826), 313.

13. Isaiah 7:2

14. Isaiah 7:4-5, 7, NIV

15. Isaiah 7:9, NIV

16. See 1 Peter 5:8.

17. Frederick Buechner, *Telling the Truth: The Gospel as Tragedy, Comedy, and Fairy Tale* (San Francisco: Harper & Row, 1977), 92–96.

18. See, for instance, Harriet Brown, "A Brain in the Head, and One in the Gut," *New York Times*, August 25, 2005; http://www.nytimes.com/2005/08/24/health/24iht-snbrain.html?pagewanted=all&_r=0.

19. Grant Soosalu and Marvin Oka, "Neuroscience and the Three Brains of Leadership," *mBraining: The New Field of mBIT*, December 3, 2012, http://www.mbraining.com/mbit-and-leadership.

20. Ibid.

21. NLV

22. See Hebrews 11:6.

CHAPTER 9: WE ARE WHAT WE LOVE

1. See Zechariah 3:2.

2. Stephen Tomkins, *John Wesley: A Biography* (Grand Rapids: Eerdmans, 2003), 61.

3. Ibid., 196.

4. Gregory S. Clapper, *As If the Heart Mattered: A Wesleyan Spirituality* (Nashville: Upper Room, 1997), 21.

5. Randy L. Maddox, "A Change of Affections," in *"Heart Religion" in the Methodist Traditions and Related Movements*, ed. Richard B. Steele (Lanham, MD: Scarecrow Press, 2001), 11.

6. Theodore H. Runyon, "A New Look at Experience," *The Drew Gateway*, vol. 51, no. 3 (1987), 44.

7. See 2 Corinthians 4:4.

8. See Isaiah 6:10; Matthew 13:14-15; John 12:39-40.

9. Runyon, "A New Look at Experience," 46.

10. Maddox, "Change of Affections," 12.
11. See John 3:6.
12. Runyon, "New Look at Experience," 47.
13. Romans 8:16
14. Henry H. Knight III, *The Presence of God in the Christian Life* (Oxford: Scarecrow, 1992), 22.
15. See Romans 8:29.
16. James K. A. Smith, *Desiring the Kingdom: Worship, Worldview, and Cultural Formation* (Grand Rapids: Baker, 2009), 42.
17. Ibid., 41, 47, italics added.
18 See 1 John 4:16.
19. Stephen Seamands, *Ministry in the Image of God: The Trinitarian Shape of Christian Service* (Downers Grove, IL: InterVarsity, 2005), 12.
20. Ibid., italics in the original.
21. See John 3:16.
22. Matthew 22:37, NLT
23. 1 John 4:19
24. See Romans 8:48.
25. See Clapper, *As If the Heart Mattered*, 18.
26. Maddox, "Change of Affections," 11.
27. Iain H. Murray, *Jonathan Edwards: A New Biography* (Edinburgh: Banner of Truth, 1987), 253.
28. Ibid.
29. Genesis 4:1, KJV, italics added
30. Thomas H. Groome, *Christian Religious Education: Sharing Our Story and Vision* (New York: Harper & Row, 1981), 141.
31. Spiros Zodhiates, *The Complete Word Study New Testament: King James Version,* electronic ed. (Chattanooga, TN: AMG, 1991).
32. NKJV
33. Jeremiah 17:5
34. Jeremiah 31:33, italics added
35. See Hebrews 11:6.
36. John 3:8
37. See Ephesians 2:10.
38. Matthew 25:40

CHAPTER 10: THIS PRESENT WEIRDNESS
1. My father began his ministry as a Baptist minister, but after he experienced the presence of God in the church he led, the staid denominational leaders grew disquieted. So Dad switched to the Full Gospel Church of God so as not to be a source of contention.
2. J. I. Packer, *Knowing God* (Downers Grove, IL: InterVarsity, 1973), 6 (italics added).

3. Ibid.
4. See Ezekiel 4.
5. See Acts 9:1-9.
6. Steven Jack Land, *Pentecostal Spirituality* (London: Sheffield Academic, 1997), 190.
7. J. Gwynfor Jones, "Reflections on the Religious Revival in Wales 1904–05," *Journal of the United Reformed Church History Society*, vol. 7, no. 7 (October 2005), 427–445.
8. H. Elvet Lewis, G. Campbell Morgan, and I. V. Neprash, *Glory Filled the Land: A Trilogy on the Welsh Revival* (Wheaton, IL: International Awakening, 1989), 189.
9. James 1:17; 2 Corinthians 11:14
10. See, for instance, Theodore Runyon, *The New Creation: John Wesley's Theology Today* (Nashville: Abingdon, 1998), 160–167.
11. 1 John 4:1
12. Runyon, *The New Creation*, 161.
13. Ibid.
14. Philippians 3:8, NIV
15. Runyon, *The New Creation*, 162.
16. Author's interview with Dr. Richard Owen Roberts, Wheaton, Illinois, November 8, 2007.
17. "Marks of Fanaticism," *The Apostolic Faith*, 1.2 (October 1906), 2, cited in Steven Jack Land, *Pentecostal Spirituality*, 162.
18. Runyon, *The New Creation*, 164.

CHAPTER 11: A HOLY TAILWIND

1. See John 3:4.
2. John 3:5, 8
3. Lycurgus M. Starkey, Jr., *The Work of the Holy Spirit* (New York: Abingdon, 1962), 37.
4. Ibid.
5. Randy L. Maddox, "A Change of Affections," in *"Heart Religion" in the Methodist Traditions and Related Movements*, ed. Richard B. Steele (Lanham, MD: Scarecrow Press, 2001), 18.
6. H. W. F. Gesenius, *Gesenius' Hebrew and Chaldee Lexicon to the Old Testament Scriptures*, trans. Samuel Tregelles (Bellingham, WA: Logos Bible Software, 2003), 760–761.
7. Gordon D. Fee, *Paul's Letter to the Philippians*, The New International Commentary on the New Testament (Grand Rapids: Eerdmans, 1995), 421.
8. John 13:36-37, NIV
9. John 14:5
10. John 14:8, NLT
11. John 14:16-17
12. John 14:20

13. Galatians 2:20
14. Colossians 2:9
15. Steven Jack Land, *Pentecostal Spirituality*, 204.
16. See John 6:63.
17. See John 14:16. The Greek word for "counselor" is *paraklete*, meaning "one called alongside to help—one who provides help, comfort, and counsel." It is also a legal, technical term meaning "advocate, defender, one who appears in another's behalf." Timothy Friberg, Barbara Friberg, and Neva F. Miller, *Analytical Lexicon of the Greek New Testament*, vol. 4 of Baker's Greek New Testament Library (Grand Rapids: Baker, 2000), 296.
18. See John 14:26.
19. See John 16:13.
20. See John 16:8.
21. See John 16:13.
22. See Acts 1:8.
23. See Acts 13:4.
24. See Romans 8:23.
25. See Romans 8:26.
26. See 2 Corinthians 5:17.
27. See 2 Corinthians 1:22; Ephesians 1:13; 4:30.
28. See Galatians 5:22-23.
29. See 1 Thessalonians 1:6.
30. Job 26:14, NIV
31. See Ephesians 4:30.
32. See 1 Thessalonians 5:19.
33. See Acts 7:51.
34. See Acts 5:1-11.
35. See Matthew 12:31.
36. The word *you*—as in "you are God's temple" in 1 Corinthians 3:16—is plural in Greek, referring to the gathering of God's people in Corinth. However, in 1 Corinthians 6:19, Paul warns individual believers against sexual immorality, since they as individuals are also the temple of the Holy Spirit. A temple is both an individual Christian and a community of faith, a local church.
37. See 1 Kings 8:10-11.
38. See Hebrews 9:11, NIV.
39. See Matthew 18:20.

CHAPTER 12: TOGETHER WE ARE

1. Deuteronomy 6:4
2. R. Laird Harris, Gleason L. Archer, Jr., and Bruce K. Waltke, *Theological Wordbook of the Old Testament*, electronic ed. (Chicago: Moody, 1999), 30.
3. Italics added
4. John 5:20

5. John 14:31
6. See Romans 8:9, 11, 14; 1 Corinthians 3:16, 12:3, 10; Philippians 3:3; 1 Peter 4:14; 1 John 4:2.
7. Michael S. Heiser, *Glossary of Morpho-Syntactic Database Terminology* (Logos Bible Software, 2005).
8. Genesis 1:26
9. John 17:20-21, NIV
10. Romans 12:4-5, italics added
11. See John 17:21.
12. Richard B. Hays, *The Moral Vision of the New Testament: A Contemporary Introduction to New Testament Ethics* (San Francisco: Harper, 1996), 196–197.
13. See Hebrews 10:25.
14. 1 Peter 2:4-5
15. 1 Peter 2:10
16. See Exodus 33:3.
17. Exodus 33:15-16, NASB
18. Revelation 5:9
19. 1 Peter 2:5
20. Spiros Zodhiates, *The Complete Word Study Dictionary: New Testament*, electronic ed. (Chattanooga, TN: AMG, 2000).
21. See Romans 12:5.
22. Most scholars agree that 1 Corinthians 5:9 refers to an earlier letter from Paul that has been lost to history.
23. 1 Corinthians 5:4
24. 1 Peter 5:8
25. "More Than Enough," lyrics by Robert Gay, Brooklyn Tabernacle Choir Songs. Used by permission.
26. "Angie" is a pseudonym.

CHAPTER 13: GOD'S POSITIONING SYSTEM

1. Luke 10:41-42
2. Hebrews 12:2, italics added
3. See Revelation 2:5.
4. Richard Foster, *Celebration of Discipline,* twentieth anniversary edition (San Francisco: HarperCollins, 1998), 7 (italics in the original).
5. See, for instance, *The Spirit of the Disciplines* by Dallas Willard, *Working the Angles* by Eugene Peterson, and *Breakthrough Prayer* by Jim Cymbala.
6. See Revelation 2:5.
7. Acts 2:42
8. James A. Swanson, *A Dictionary of Biblical Languages with Semantic Domains: Greek New Testament*, electronic ed. (Oak Harbor, WA: Logos Research Systems, 1997).

9. Spiros Zodhiates, *The Complete Word Study Dictionary: New Testament*, electronic ed. (Chattanooga, TN: AMG, 2000).

10. 2 Peter 1:21

11. See Hebrews 1:1-2.

12. For more information on this reading plan, see www.churchawakening.com.

13. Richard Foster, *Celebration of Discipline*, 7.

14. Philippians 2:3

15. See Galatians 6:2; Hebrews 10:24-25.

16. See 1 Corinthians 11:17-34.

17. See Luke 22:19; 1 Corinthians 11:24.

18. Gerhard Kittel, Gerhard Friedrich, and Geoffrey W. Bromiley, *Theological Dictionary of the New Testament*, vol. 1, electronic ed. (Grand Rapids: Eerdmans, 1964), 348.

19. Eugene Peterson, *Working the Angles: The Shape of Pastoral Integrity* (Grand Rapids: Eerdmans, 1995), 46. The McNamara quotation is from William McNamara, O.C.D., *The Human Adventure: The Art of Contemplative Living* (Garden City, NY: Doubleday/Image, 1976), 89 (italics in the original).

20. See Matthew 25:40.

21. 1 Peter 4:9

22. Hebrews 13:16

23. See Acts 2:46.

24. See John 4:23.

25. See Acts 13:2.

26. See James 4:8.

27. Hebrews 6:19

CHAPTER 14: FORGED IN THE FIRE

1. "It's Not in Vain," by the Brooklyn Tabernacle Choir. Used by permission.

2. J. P. Louw and Eugene Albert Nida, *Greek-English Lexicon of the New Testament: Based on Semantic Domains*, vol. 2, electronic version of the 2nd ed. (New York: United Bible Societies, 1996), 118.

3. James A. Swanson, *A Dictionary of Biblical Languages with Semantic Domains: Greek New Testament*, electronic ed. (Oak Harbor, WA: Logos Research Systems, 1997).

4. Hebrews 2:3

5. David J. Hanson, "Drug Abuse Resistance Education: The Effectiveness of DARE," http://www.alcoholfacts.org/DARE.html.

6. James 1:14

7. 2 Chronicles 12:14, italics added

8. Matthew 12:34

9. Matthew 15:8, italics added

10. Mark 6:52, italics added

11. Luke 21:34, italics added

12. Acts 5:3, italics added
13. Acts 8:21, italics added
14. Romans 2:29, italics added
15. See John 4:23.
16. Henry H. Knight III, *The Presence of God in the Christian Life* (Oxford: Scarecrow, 1992), 129.
17. Randy Maddox, "A Change of Affections," in *"Heart Religion" in the Methodist Traditions and Related Movements*, ed. Richard B. Steele (Lanham, MD: Scarecrow Press, 2001), 21.
18. Steven Jack Land, *Pentecostal Spirituality: A Passion for the Kingdom* (Cleveland, TN: CPT, 2010), 125-126. The phrase "affective transformation in which lives [a]re formed and shaped" is from Henry H. Knight III, "The Relationship of Narrative to the Christian Affections," an unpublished paper, Emory University, 1987.
19. John Wesley, *Explanatory Notes Upon the New Testament* (1754) (Hong Kong: Forgotten Books, 2012), note 20, 416.
20. Isaiah 6:5
21. Psalm 119:32
22. See Romans 8:29.

CHAPTER 15: YOUR MISSION, SHOULD YOU CHOOSE TO ACCEPT IT

1. John Wesley Bready, *England: Before and After Wesley: The Evangelical Revival and Social Reform* (London: Hodder and Stoughton, 1938), 225.
2. Timothy L. Smith, *Revivalism and Social Reform* (New York: Abingdon, 1957), 167.
3. See Matthew 17:1-9.
4. Luke 9:51, KJV
5. Steven Seamands, *Ministry in the Image of God: The Trinitarian Shape of Christian Service* (Downers Grove, IL: InterVarsity, 2005), 161. Seamands quotes R. Paul Stevens, *The Other Six Days* (Grand Rapids: Eerdmans, 1999), 194.
6. See Genesis 1:28.
7. Genesis 6:6
8. Genesis 6:9
9. John 5:19
10. John 5:17, NIV
11. Cleon L. Rogers Jr., and Cleon L. Rogers III, *The New Linguistic and Exegetical Key to the Greek New Testament* (Grand Rapids: Zondervan, 1998), 8.
12. Ibid., 120.
13. John 20:21
14. Gerhard Kittel, Gerhard Friedrich, and Geoffrey W. Bromiley, *Theological Dictionary of the New Testament* (Grand Rapids: Eerdmans, 1964), 186–187.
15. See Luke 4:18-19.
16. Acts 9:15

17. Acts 9:20
18. See Acts 13:2; Galatians 1:17-18.

ACKNOWLEDGMENTS
1. See A. W. Tozer, *Rut, Rot, or Revival* (Harrisburg, PA: Christian Publications, 1993).

ABOUT THE AUTHOR

Alec Rowlands is the senior pastor of the two-thousand-member Westgate Chapel in Edmonds, Washington, a position he has held since 1988. Altogether, he has been in pastoral ministry for more than thirty years.

Born in King William's Town, South Africa, Alec came to the United States as a college student and earned a bachelor's degree from Wittenberg University, master's degrees from Miami University and Assemblies of God Theological Seminary, and a doctorate of ministry from Carey Theological College at the University of British Columbia, Canada.

Alec is the founder and president of Church Awakening, a statewide spiritual renewal network of more than 1,300 pastors from a broad range of denominational backgrounds in the state of Washington. He regularly speaks to churches and universities around the country and internationally.

He and his wife, Rita, live in Edmonds.